GUIDE TO IDAHO PADDLING

Flatwater & Easy Whitewater Trips

Kath and Ron's

Guide to Idaho Paddling

Flatwater and Easy Whitewater Trips

Katherine Daly

Ron Watters

GR The Great Rift Press

KATH AND RON'S
GUIDE TO IDAHO PADDLING
Flatwater & Easy Whitewater Trips

Printed in the United States of America

Published by:
The Great Rift Press
1135 East Bonneville Avenue
Pocatello, Idaho 83201

ISBN: 1-877625-07-8

Library of Congress Catalog Card Number: 99-94741

Warning

The activities described within this book are dangerous. It is the reader's responsibility to ensure that they have sufficient skill and fitness to participate in these activities safely. The authors or publisher does not assume liability or responsibility to any person or entity for injuries, death, loss or damages which are caused, directly or indirectly, by the information contained within this book.

Table of Contents

Preface

WE START THIS BOOK with a mystery . . .

Somewhere out there in Idaho, there's a river. In the morning, when you first slip your boat onto the water, mist is rising from its surface. As you paddle downstream, the only things visible are the dark surface of the water, and sedges and grasses with strings of dew clinging delicately to their sides. It is quiet. Deathly quiet. The kind of quiet almost unknown in this fast-paced world.

Then the sun suddenly breaks through. Within a few minutes, the mist rises and all is bright and blue and green. The river twists and turns through meadows and scattered patches of pines and firs. There are no rapids, just a few riffles. You can relax, let your guard down and gaze, enjoy, breathe deeply, take it all in.

Signs of wildlife are everywhere: elk, moose, deer, beaver. Red-tail hawks soar above. Through the crystal clear water, large trout dart past the boat seeking the safety of shaded pools. It is the perfect river. The perfect place. The perfect anecdote to too many days in the city.

This beautiful river really exists. The description above wasn't made up. Of all of the rivers we ran in Idaho, we both agree that this one was the most beautiful, the most refreshing and most delightful of them all.

Before we say much more about the river—and the mystery—we'd like to introduce ourselves.

WE'RE Kathy Daly and Ron Watters. We're a couple of long-time Idahoans who love rivers and the Gem State's magnificent outdoors. We've been running rivers for a long time, and we hope through this book we can share with you our love for Idaho rivers and some of our knowledge about them.

For years, it's been difficult to get good information on Idaho's easy rivers—the kind that you can float with a family and not worry about rounding a corner and ending up in a big rapid.

That's what this book is all about. It's about laid-back, easy-going trips where you can hang a foot over the edge of the boat and wet a line, or have a fun paddle through playful rapids. We tried to provide good details, decent maps, and an easy-to-use format. Although flat rivers are not all that easy to find in a mountainous state like Idaho, we've searched them out and included runs throughout the state that you can do with the entire family.

For a little fun, we've also included some spirited easy whitewater rivers. They are mostly class II, the novice range on the river difficulty scale. We ran everything in an open, tandem canoe which we found a good way to get the feel of a river's nuances and its difficulties.

We hope that as you get to know Idaho through its magnificent rivers, that you'll also want to help protect these waters and the fish and wildlife which depend upon them. As Idaho grows, the demand for water and riverside lands will also grow. Rivers are no longer something we can take for granted, but something for which we have to work and fight. You can help by joining one of the river conservation groups that we have listed in the text and introduction.

SO WHERE IS THIS PERFECT RIVER, the one that so impressed us with its beauty, the most beautiful river of them all? As we said, it is in this book. We could point to it and say it's on page . . . . but, well, that would be a little too easy.

It's just one of those places you have to find on your own. So go out and spend some time on Idaho's rivers. You'll find it, maybe not right away, but you will find it. We can't say exactly when and where—that's the mystery. But one day, you'll be on a river and suddenly it will come to you: *Yes! This is the one!*

General Information on Paddling Idaho Rivers

WHAT AN EXTRAORDINARY PLACE this Idaho. From the cool-and-damp, cedar and hemlock forests of north Idaho to the dusty sage deserts of south Idaho, it is a diverse state: a state of rolling hills, deserts, jumbled mountain ranges—and, of course, rivers.

Rivers. Lots of rivers. Small rivers. Large rivers. Magnificent rivers. It's the rivers that we are interested in here. They are truly our lens to Idaho, a way, like no other, of seeing this state and appreciating its wild and varied landscape.

Who This Book is For

We have prepared this guidebook to aid in exploring Idaho through its rivers. There are other guidebooks on Idaho's whitewater rivers, but in this book we concentrate on the state's easy rivers: flatwater and mild whitewater in the class I and II range (and a couple of class III stretches). If you're not sure what we mean by class I or II, we've included information, later in this chapter, on the river difficulty scale, but basically class I means flat or nearly flat water and class II means easy rapids for novices.

This book is for anyone interested in rivers. In particular it's for families with children and folks with little experience on rivers. But

it's also for boaters who have been running rivers for a while. We cover a number of rivers here that have never been written about, and you'll find plenty of new places to explore.

How It Was Done

We ran all of the rivers in this book in an open canoe. Running a river in an open canoe, we feel, is the most sensitive way of testing a river's difficulty. If the waves are a little tall or a rapid is a bit technical, you'll know right away in a canoe. Since this book is written for everyone, no matter what their ability, we wanted to try to give you an accurate idea of how difficult each river is. Plus, we wanted to make sure that Idaho paddlers had a book that they could use and trust for reliable information—which brings us to the next topic, the type of craft which may be used on the rivers covered in this book.

The late Pierre Pulling is shown in this mid 1970s photo with his grandson Ted. An Idaho State University biology professor, Pulling is a little known but important figure in the canoeing world. From the 1920s to the 1970s, the colorful and erudite Pulling was an outspoken advocate of the highly efficient, but largely ignored, Native American style of canoeing. Due in part to Pulling's efforts, most flatwater canoeing technique now taught by organized groups is rooted in native style.

Mini-cats ideally suited for fishing are one of the several types of craft which can be used on the rivers covered in this book. Other boats include canoes, kayaks, open kayaks, lake kayaks, drift boats, row boats, rafts, cata-rafts, and inflatable kayaks.

What Kind of Craft Can Be Used

Obviously, since we used an open canoe, everything in the book can be run in a canoe. For many of the rivers, you need nothing special. They can be run in an ordinary, run-of-the-mill lake canoe. Lake canoes have a V-shaped hull or the hull is flat with a keel (a rib that runs down the bottom of the canoe). The V-shape, or rib, helps the canoe go in a straight line which is why it's good on lakes.

For the other half of the rivers in the book, you'll want something a little more maneuverable: a canoe that turns well, a river canoe. Since all of the paddle trips in this book are on rivers, it makes sense that a river canoe will be the most ideal craft to use. A river canoe has a flat, oval or rounded bottom without a keel which allows it to turn easily.

Don't worry. You don't have to go out and buy a new canoe. There are plenty of rivers in this book to keep you busy for years in a lake canoe. However, if you really like running rivers, then some time down the road, you'll want to get a river canoe.

In addition to canoes, the rivers in this book can be run in kayaks, open kayaks, lake kayaks, rafts, inflatable kayaks, row boats, drift boats, catarafts and mini-cats used for fishing. In each river description, we include a list of the craft that can be used on that river. For drift boaters, we'll let you know if ramps are available, and if there are no ramps, how difficult it is to carry the boat in and out of the river. And when a river has lots of slow water, we'll remind inflatable boat users (rafts, catarafts, inflatable kayaks) that it will take some work—a lot of paddling or oaring—to get downriver.

River Right and River Left

Throughout the river running world, the accepted way of indicating right and left on a river is from the perspective of looking downstream. Thus, in the text when we speak of stopping and taking out on the right shore, we mean the right shore of the river as you face downstream. Often river runners will say "river right" or "river left," the term "river" added to emphasize that it's the river's downriver direction that determines right and left.

You'll notice that all of the maps in this book are oriented so that downstream on the river is at the top of the page. As you look at the map, then river right and river left are the same as your right and left as you face the book, making it much easier to follow descriptions in the text.

Surprise! No Crowds

One of the great surprises we found while researching this book is the number of people we saw on these rivers. They were surprisingly few—or nonexistent. Certainly, some of Idaho's easy rivers are used a lot, but the great majority have few people paddling them. Time and time again, we found ourselves on a beautiful stretch of river and were amazed when we saw absolutely no one.

What a contrast that is with the state's popular whitewater rivers. Take for example, the main Payette River, north of Boise. This class III stretch of whitewater is crowded with bumper to bumper boats, and off the river, the parking lot is jammed with vehicles and people. But look at the Payette River below the class III stretch, and it's a completely different story. You'll see only a smattering of boats—if any at all.

We've been running Idaho whitewater rivers for many years. But frankly, some of that scene is getting tiresome: the crowds, inconsiderate people at take-outs (too-many-rats-in-a cage syndrome), and more and more fees and permits. That's why we found Idaho's easy rivers a refreshing change. What people you do see are friendly and welcoming. They are less in it for the adrenaline rush, but rather more for the experience of just getting out and enjoying a day on the river.

Life Jackets

We really recommend that you learn as much as you can about river running and safety, but want to remind you of one of the basics: wear your life jackets. Even in slow moving class I water, wear them. Make sure that the jacket fits snugly and it can't slip over your head.

High Water

All rivers have periods of high water. In Idaho it often comes in the spring or early summer when the snow melts, but it can also occur during periods of extended rain or in the winter during warm spells. During these times, the current is forceful and the river spills over its normal banks flowing through the trees and bushes along the river's bank. Eddies, the stopping places along the river, are few and often are turbulent and more difficult to catch.

Reminders are included throughout the text, but we can't repeat it too much: rivers, even easy class I rivers, are dangerous during high conditions. One of the best pieces of advice that we can give you besides wearing your life jacket, is to stay off rivers when the water is high.

Generally high water in Idaho comes in the spring or early summer, but it varies with climatic conditions and weather patterns. For up-to-date information, the US Geological Survey keeps track of river flows and provides information on the Internet (see more details on page 22). But regular river reports are also available in Idaho newspapers. When the reports show high water, wait a few weeks and let the river come down.

Supporting Local Businesses

When you run rivers, be sure to patronize businesses near the river. Buy gas, groceries, and stop in the small gift shops and bookstores. Make a point to tell them that you're boating nearby. By supporting small local business, it helps develop a grass roots support from the business community, which is vital when it comes to protecting rivers, and protecting our access to those rivers.

We also encourage you to support other small Idaho businesses: river supply companies, sporting good stores, bookstores, small clothing and equipment manufacturers and guides and outfitters. They help keep the state's economy healthy and vibrant and are one more reason for our elected leaders to pay attention to the needs of river users.

Paddling & Private Lands

Many of the rivers in this book go across private land. Fortunately, Idaho has enlightened laws dealing with river access. We have included a special appendix with the latest information from Idaho's Attorney General detailing what is permissible under the law and what is not. Briefly put, however, Idaho rivers which pass through private property can be paddled as long as you put in at public access sites, and you stay below the high water mark for picnicking, fishing and camping. Be sure to check out the appendix. You'll find some very useful information.

Public Land Fees

Over the last few years, public land agencies have instituted fees for an ever increasing list of resources and facilities: rivers, hiking areas, boat ramps, launching sites, trailheads, picnic areas, primitive camping areas, and the list goes on and on. We think that the fee program has gone way too far. Already, our national forests in Idaho are starting to seem like so many stops on an eastern tollway: as you move from one national forest to another, or from one river to another river, there's one more fee, one more toll to pay.

Our wallets are becoming filled with permits, passes and licenses. Each time you go to another river, you have to rifle through your glove compartment to make sure you have the correct parking permit displayed.

Fortunately, this is not yet a problem on many of the rivers covered in this book, but it will be if this nonsense continues. It certainly has become a major problem elsewhere on our public lands in Idaho.

It's easy to criticize public land agencies, but the blame really lies with our elected officials. They are the ones who approved the fee program in the first place. And they are the ones who continue to provide only meager budgets to agencies for recreation. The expense of providing parking and outhouses at river access points is far less than building roads. Yet our elected officials always seem to have plenty of money to build roads.

Federal and state government provide millions of dollars of corporate welfare, but somehow can't provide a parking lot and outhouse for free. We think something is terribly wrong with that, and we encourage you to write your congressmen and senators and tell them it's time to provide adequate funds for recreation and do away with the fee program.

River Conservation

Rivers need your help. We need to keep dams off of them and in some cases, remove existing dams. One of the most important priorities for the rivers described in this book is protecting the riparian zone, the band of trees and green marsh lands near streams. This is not easy since many of the rivers in this book flow through private land. Private lands are being subdivided and the prime building spots, of course, are along the river. Without adequate setback laws (ample distance from building sites to the river), we'll lose this important scenic buffer area which is so vitally important for wildlife and quality fish habitat.

Idaho needs better laws dealing with water diversions. Water users make their money and their livelihoods off of a public resource, yet many diversions that we've come across are atrocities: trash laying around, concrete slabs thrown into the stream, and dangerous rebar sticking out of the river. Water users should provide warning signs at diversions and a public access portage trail—and they should clean up their mess. It's only common courtesy and respect for a precious and valuable resource which we all own.

We are also concerned about public access to rivers. We have lost, and will continue to lose, access sites as more private lands are developed. Many access points at bridges are tenuous. Fancy paved parking areas aren't needed, but we do need adequate places to park vehicles and, at least, a decent trail to the river for launching boats.

These things just don't happen. We, as boaters, need to work for them. Some things can be done individually or in small groups, such as talking with the county commissioners to provide better parking at bridges, or showing up at zoning hearings and asking for reasonable set backs, or working with farmers to string fences high enough over a river that a boat can get under.

Unfortunately many of us don't have the time to lobby for river protection and better access, but we can join an organization which will help do that for us. We feel strongly that anyone who runs rivers or partakes in Idaho's outdoors has an obligation to support one or more conservation organizations working for the protection of our outdoor resources.

The main state group working for river protection is Idaho Rivers United, PO Box 633, Boise, Idaho 83701. Website: `http://www.desktop.org/iru`. Jot them a letter or contact them via their website—and join them.

In addition to Idaho Rivers United, other small grassroots organizations work to protect specific rivers. Sign up as a member, give them support, and send them money. Then you can feel good about having played a part in protecting our magnificent outdoors.

River Difficulty

This book is about easy rivers, and thus we tried to be as conservative as possible when rating rivers. Rivers are rated on the International Scale of River Difficulty. The scale goes from class I to class VI, where I is easy water and class VI is extremely difficult and dangerous. The rivers covered in this book are mostly class I and II with some class III. The American Whitewater Affiliation defines each of those classes in the following terms:

Class I *Easy.* Fast moving water with riffles and small waves. Few obstructions and easily missed with little training. Risk to swimming is slight; self rescue is easy.

(This is the classification that we feel needs to be expanded. Many rivers in Idaho are commonly classified class I, but no matter how you look at them, they simply don't meet the "little training" or "risk to swimming is slight" tests.)

Class II *Novice.* Straightforward rapids with wide, clear channels which are evident without scouting. Occasional maneuvering may be required, but rocks and medium sized waves are easily missed by trained paddlers. Swimmers are seldom injured and group assistance, while helpful, is seldom needed.

Class III *Intermediate.* Rapids with moderate, irregular waves which may be difficult to avoid and which can swamp an open canoe. Complex maneuvers in fast current and good boat control in tight passages or around ledges are often required; large waves or strainers may be present but are easily avoided. Strong eddies and powerful current effects can be found, particularly on large volume rivers. Scouting is advisable for inexperienced parties. Injuries while swimming are rare; self-rescue is usually easy but group assistance may be required to avoid long swims.

The Expanded Class I Scale

Class I water? It's easy. Any beginner can run it, right? We say no. As we have spent more and more time on so-called class I water, we have come to learn that it covers a lot of ground. Let's take a look at two stretches of water in Idaho: Big Springs in the Island Park area and the Boise River below the city of Boise. Both are rated class I.

Big Springs flows through open meadows with barely a discernible current. It's definitely easy, one can do it with little training, and it is a good trip for families.

But the Boise River is another story. As the Boise goes around the south side of the several-mile-long Eagle Island, it is swift and flows through a narrow, twisting river channel with lots of overhanging trees. Eddies are small and hard to catch and you can come around a corner and suddenly be faced with a tree all the way across the river.

Is this stretch of the Boise River easy? No. Can you do this stretch with little training? Once again, the answer is no. In fact, it takes good boating skills and a fair amount of experience. Moreover, we feel that something like the Boise takes more finesse, knowledge and training than many class II rivers. Yet no one would ever rate the Boise River (other than the short rapids created by its diversions) as class II.

If you are a beginner, or if you are going out with your family or friends, the class I rating fails to tell you what you are really getting into.

To help provide a better gauge of the difficulty of this type of water, we use an expanded class I system in this book. Instead of using something completely new which might be confusing, we utilize the international scale but expand it slightly. For those who are comfortable with the international scale, it's there, but those who want a finer way of distinguishing between rivers, it's included as well. For instance, we rate the Boise River around Eagle Island as the following: class I+ (1.5).

Here's a closer look at the expanded class I scale:

Class I (1.0) *Flat, lake-like water.* No current or very slow moving current. One can easily paddle upstream and downstream. This the safest water for families and children. Since the water is slow moving, downriver trips against strong winds, may be taxing.

This water is suitable for flat water canoes (with V-shaped bottoms) and lake and sea kayaks as well as all other river craft. Inflatable boaters, however, may find this water sluggish,

Class I (1.1) *Flat water with some current.* One can paddle upstream, but it takes more effort. Since it has current, it may have some minor eddies. This is also safe water for family trips. Suitable for flat water canoes, lake kayaks and other river craft. (Easy class I water.)

Class I (1.2) *Flat water with current, minor riffles and some eddies.* Paddling upstream is possible in some places, but in other places it may be very difficult or not possible at all. These rivers may have some overhanging trees and brush. Unless experienced and competent, families with small children probably should not run them. This water can be run in lake canoes and kayaks, but boats designed for rivers are more suitable. (Moderately easy class I.)

Class I+ (1.3) *Moving water with mini-rapids.* Small, mini-rapids may occur in swift areas of the river—or where the river slides down gravel bars. The river may have some swift corners with overhanging trees on the outside of bends. Rocks and boulders may be present which need to be avoided, but the current is gentle and not strong enough to cause a boat to get wrapped or broached.

Basic maneuvering skills are needed, including the ability to move to the right or left and avoid the outside of bends, and the ability to miss an occasional rock. Boaters should know the basics of an eddy turn and how to use an eddy to stop, as well as understanding the preliminaries of reading water. River canoes and kayaks are preferable to lake boats. (This is the beginning of class I+ water.)

Class I+ (1.4) *Swift water with mini-rapids, small waves and obstructions.* The river may bend sharply and the current on the outside of bends is more forceful. Such rivers may have narrow channels with long stretches of overhanging trees and brush in which a boat can get hung up and flipped over.

Canoeists and kayakers should have a good understanding of how to lean boats while in the current, or while turning in and out of eddies, or if accidentally pushed up against an obstruction. Boaters should be very comfortable maneuvering the boat through rocks and have the ability to catch small eddies. A sureness of technique is needed to stop quickly if fences, trees or diversions are encountered.

The best craft are river canoes, kayaks and other river boats. Note that some inflatable kayaks may be too sluggish to handle the type of maneuvering needed for this type of river. (This is difficult class I water, well into the class I+ range.)

Class I+ (1.5) *Rapid water with small rapids, waves and obstructions.* The river may be very narrow and have many sharp turns and long stretches of overhanging trees and brush. In higher flows, trees, log jams and other strainers are dangerous.

Some waves may be present which, if run sideways, can swamp a canoe. Improper leans in a canoe or kayak can cause a capsize. Boaters must have the ability to read the water, anticipate future moves and react quickly. A well-practiced, reliable eddy turn is a must.

Water Levels

When possible, we provide information on the best flow levels to run the river. You can find out the latest flow information from the U.S. Geological Survey's (USGS) web site on the Internet at the following (very long) address:

```
http://wwwidaho.wr.usgs.gov/rt-cgi/gen_tbl_pg
```

In the "Basic Stats" box included with each river description, you'll find the name of the gauge that is used by the USGS. For instance, for the Eagle Island segment of the Boise River, you'll see under Basic Stats that the Glenwood gauge is used for water flow information. When you look at the list of Idaho Rivers at the USGS web

site, pick the Boise River-Glenwood gauge to get the appropriate information.

If you don't have access to the Internet, you can also obtain flow information from the newspaper. Many of Idaho's largest newspapers publish weekly river flow information, usually in the outdoor section.

For those rivers on which flow data is not available over the Internet, we provide a phone number to the appropriate entity that can provide it. In some cases, flow information is difficult to get, and we make some suggestions on the best season to run it.

No matter what level, or what people say about river levels, always use your best judgment. If something looks too high, wait and come back a week or two later when it has gone down and you feel more comfortable about running it.

Maps

The maps included in this book were scanned from original United States Geological Survey (USGS) maps, and although they've been simplified greatly, we tried to retain their accuracy and keep them to scale. Nothing, of course, is better than having the original USGS topographic maps along with you, but in the absence of those, at least the maps in the book will help in getting you down the river.

Map booklets which include the appropriate sections of USGS topographic maps are available (see below). In addition, as a convenience, we have included a list of topographic maps in the appendix that are needed for each river. The maps can be ordered from the USGS or picked up at outdoor stores.

Orientation of Maps

All the maps in this book have been oriented so that downstream is at the top of the map. This is the same way you would orient a map when sitting in a boat. As we have mentioned before, by positioning it this way, you can look at the map, and river right, and river left, appear as they should as one runs the river.

The only time that this system may be a bit confusing is when a river runs in a southerly direction. In that case, south is at the top of the map, just the reverse of what you normally expect. Once you get used to this system, however, it is more practical than the haphazard methods of orienting maps used in other guidebooks and far more convenient from a river running standpoint.

River Map Booklets

Having good maps along makes all the difference. You can keep track of landmarks and your location on the river, decide in advance on places to stop, and identify nearby high points. With good maps you can learn much about the surrounding land and develop a more intimate understanding of the river.

The best maps to carry with you are 7.5 minute USGS topographic maps, but they are big and unwieldy to use while on a river. Far more convenient are map booklets made specifically for floating rivers which you flip through as you work your way downstream.

We have prepared map booklets of each of the rivers described in this book. Each booklet fits into a standard waterproof map carrier and includes the appropriate detailed topographic maps of the river. To enable the maps to be used with a GPS device, we have retained the coordinate systems along the map edges. In addition, we have added river mileages, take-out and put-in points and useful landmarks close to the river. The booklets are available at outdoor stores or directly from us at the Great Rift Press at 1-800-585-6857.

Mileages

River mileages shown on the maps and used in the text were determined by doing careful measurements of the river on 7.5 minute USGS topographic maps. The measurements are intended to be realistic and include the twists and turns of the stream.

In most cases when river mileage was available on a USGS map, we used it. But in some cases, particularly on the upper stretches of rivers, such as the upper Salmon in the Sawtooth Valley, we found the mileages so far off that we recalculated it and used what we feel is a more accurate accounting of stream distances.

Overall Design of this Book

Realizing that people use guidebooks differently depending on circumstances and needs, this book utilizes several different methods of conveying material. One method, used by all guidebooks, of course, is through written descriptions. Each new river segment is introduced along with a very quick rundown on where it is located, how difficult it is, and what its outstanding features are. Following the introduction is a more detailed description of the river.

The second method of imparting information is through summary charts which are boxed off from the text. There are two types of charts. One is the "Basic Stats" chart which includes a brief rundown of the river, and the other is the "Mileage Chart," a convenient listing of river distances.

The Basic Stats chart is a quick guide to each river and includes difficulty, best water levels, length of trip and whether any portaging is involved. You'll find Basic Stats helpful when paging through the book at home to make quick comparisons between rivers.

The Mileage Chart, on the other hand, is useful while you're on the river. It includes river mileages to landmarks, rapids and take-out locations which we hope will assist in keeping track of your location.

Lastly, we use icons and symbols which encapsulate information in a visual manner. The icons (which are listed below) show the type of road access to put-in and take-out points. They also provide a feel for what the river landscape is like and whether the trip involves camping or portaging, among other information.

Icons and Symbols Used in this Book

Road Condition Icons

The following icons identify the condition of access roads to take-out or put-in points along the river.

Paved Roads
Passable in all vehicles.

Gravel or Dirt Roads
Passable in most vehicles. Those in low clearance vehicles may need to use caution in some areas.

Rough Roads
Passable only in high clearance or four-wheel drive vehicles.

River Landscape Icons

Landscapes icons give you a quick idea of the type of terrain surrounding the river.

Valley Landscape
Mostly open or marsh land.

Valley Landscape
Scattered patches of deciduous trees along river.

Valley Landscape
Many deciduous trees along river.

River landscape icons continued . . .

Valley Landscape
Scattered patches of conifer trees along the river.

Valley Landscape
Many *conifer* trees along the river.

Canyon Landscape
Open or sparse trees.

Canyon Landscape
Sparse or thick conifer forest surrounding the canyon.

Hilly Area or Canyon with Moderate Slopes.
Open or sparsely forested.

Other Icons

Portage
This river has one or more portages.

Ramp
A concrete or dirt ramp is available for drift or row boats.

Overnight Trip
Camping along the river.

Difficulty Icons

Difficulty Icons are found at the beginning of each section of river described in the book. The wavy lines in the middle of the icon indicate the river's difficulty. The more wavy and numerous the lines, the more difficult the river. Here are some examples:

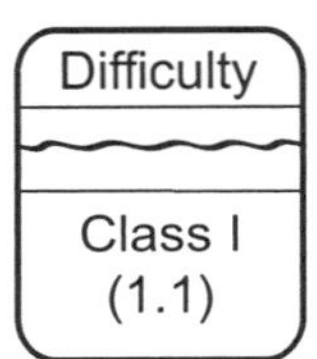

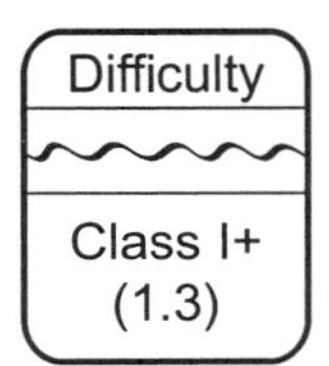

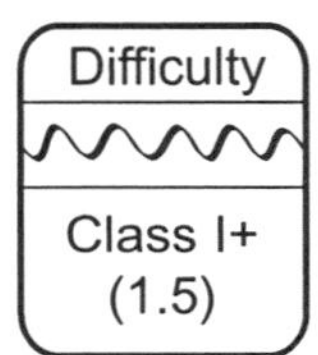

Map Symbols

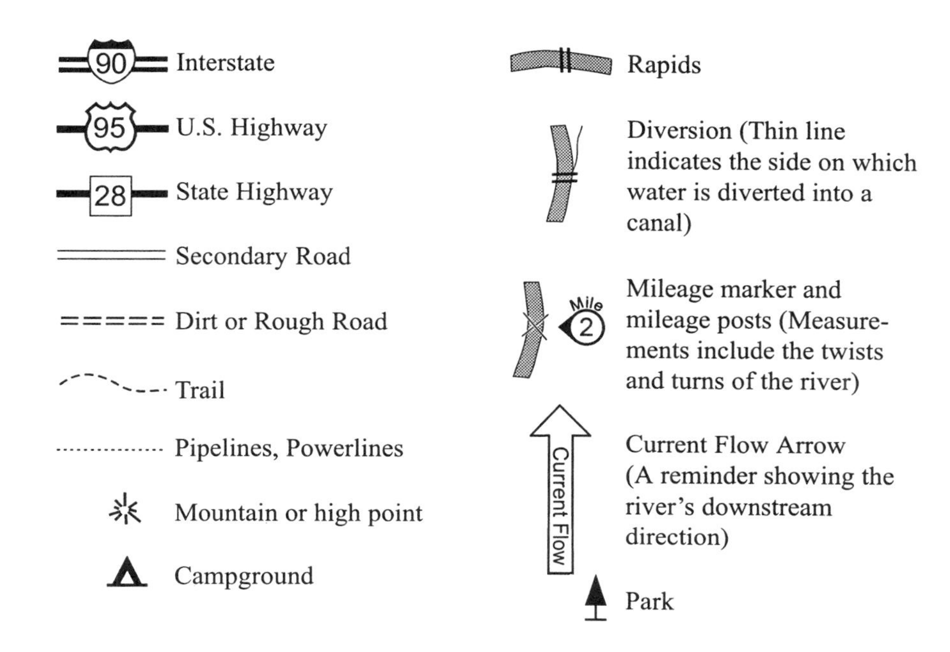

Overview Maps

The maps on the next three pages show an overview of the paddling rivers included in this book and their locations within the state. Information on specific rivers and more detailed maps are found on the pages indicated.

You may notice from the page numbers on the overview maps that the rivers have been arranged so that those in the same geographical area are grouped close to one another in the book. Rivers are ordered starting with those in the southeastern part of the state and then working in an approximate direction to the north and west. Thus, southeast Idaho rivers are listed first. Central Idaho rivers occupy the middle of the book and north Idaho rivers are last. Different segments of the same river within a regional area are ordered with the uppermost sections first, followed by the downstream segments.

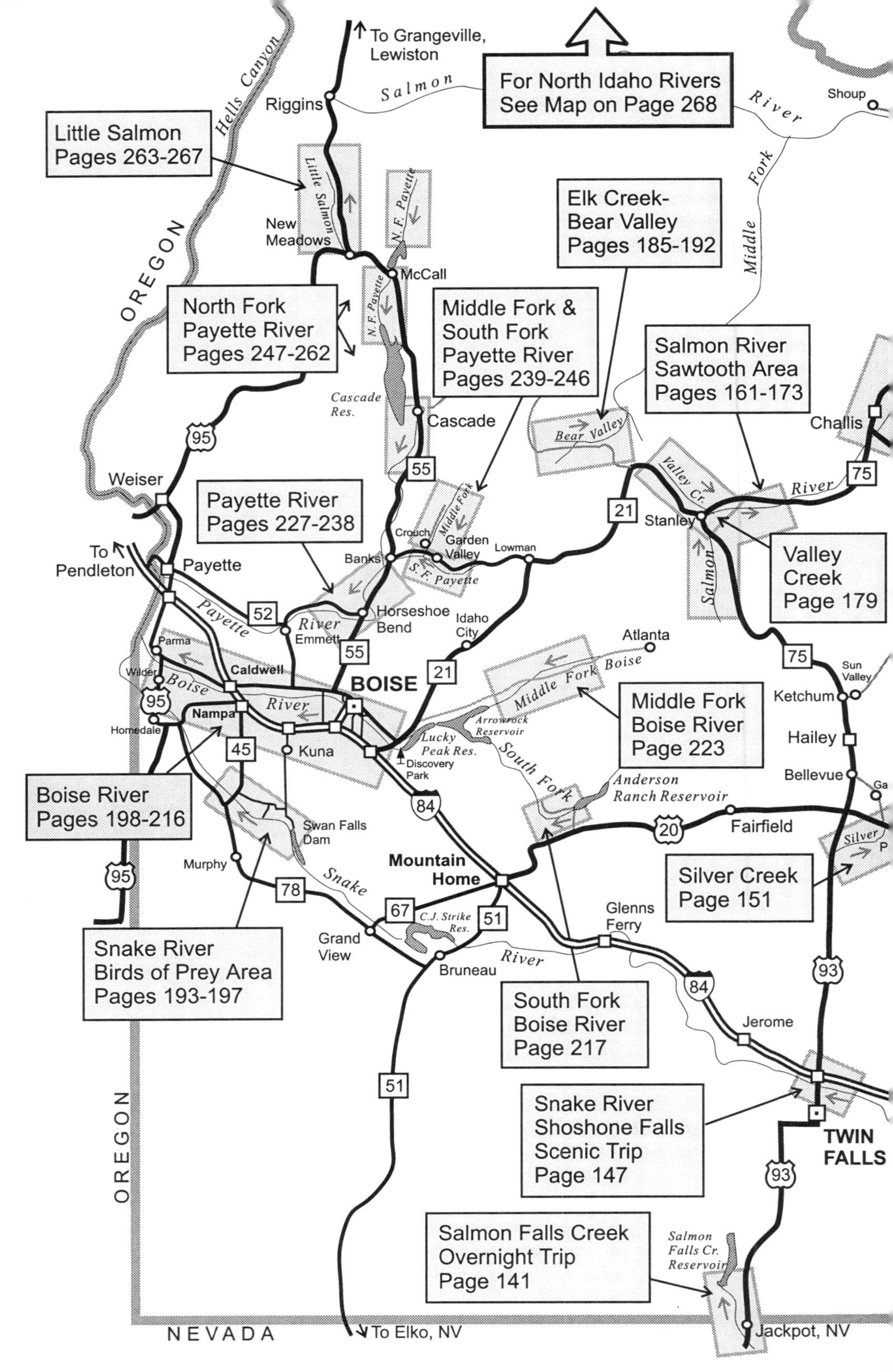

To Grangeville, Lewiston
For North Idaho Rivers See Map on Page 268
Salmon River
Shoup
Hells Canyon
Riggins
Little Salmon Pages 263-267
Little Salmon
N. F. Payette
New Meadows
McCall
OREGON
North Fork Payette River Pages 247-262
Elk Creek- Bear Valley Pages 185-192
Middle Fork
Middle Fork & South Fork Payette River Pages 239-246
Cascade Res.
Cascade
Salmon River Sawtooth Area Pages 161-173
Bear Valley
Challis
95
Weiser
55
Valley Cr.
River
75
21
Stanley
Payette River Pages 227-238
Crouch
Middle Fork
Garden Valley
Lowman
To Pendleton
Banks
S. F. Payette
Salmon
Valley Creek Page 179
Payette
52
Horseshoe Bend
Idaho City
Payette River
Emmett
Atlanta
Parma
55
75
Sun Valley
Caldwell
Middle Fork Boise
21
Wilder
Boise River
BOISE
Ketchum
95
Middle Fork Boise River Page 223
Nampa
Homedale
Arrowrock Reservoir
Hailey
Kuna
Lucky Peak Res.
45
Discovery Park
South Fork
Bellevue
Boise River Pages 198-216
84
Anderson Ranch Reservoir
Ga
Swan Falls Dam
20
Fairfield
Silver
Murphy
Mountain Home
Snake
Silver Creek Page 151
95
78
67
C.J. Strike Res.
51
Glenns Ferry
Grand View
Snake River Birds of Prey Area Pages 193-197
River
Bruneau
84
93
South Fork Boise River Page 217
Jerome
51
Snake River Shoshone Falls Scenic Trip Page 147
TWIN FALLS
OREGON
93
Salmon Falls Creek Overnight Trip Page 141
Salmon Falls Cr. Reservoir
NEVADA
To Elko, NV
Jackpot, NV

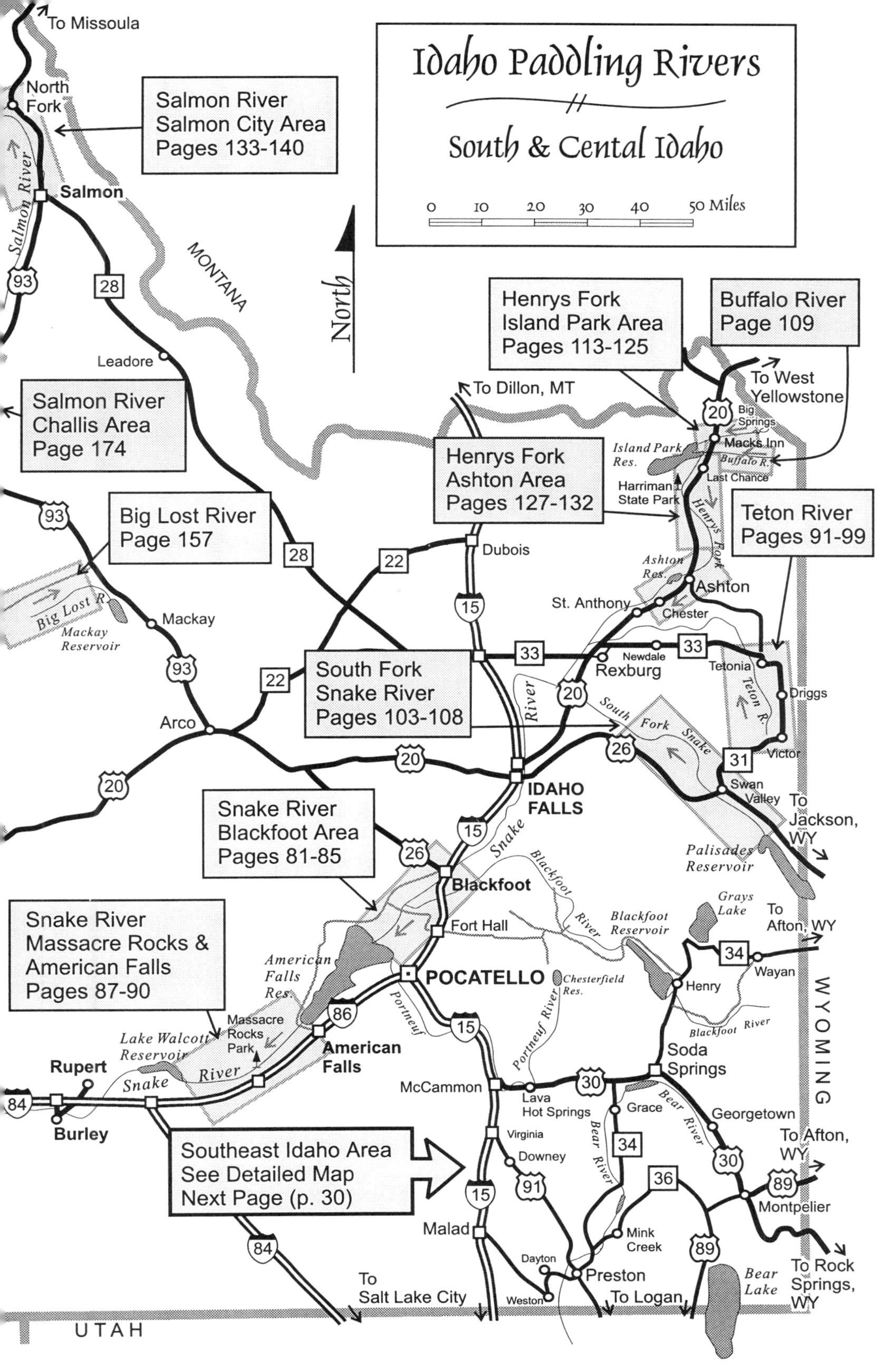

Idaho Paddling Rivers
South & Cental Idaho
0 10 20 30 40 50 Miles
North
To Missoula
North Fork
Salmon River Salmon City Area Pages 133-140
Salmon River
Salmon
93
28
MONTANA
Leadore
Salmon River Challis Area Page 174
Henrys Fork Island Park Area Pages 113-125
Buffalo River Page 109
To West Yellowstone
20
Big Springs
Macks Inn
Buffalo R.
Island Park Res.
Last Chance
Harriman State Park
To Dillon, MT
Henrys Fork Ashton Area Pages 127-132
Henrys Fork
Teton River Pages 91-99
93
Big Lost River Page 157
28
22
Dubois
Ashton Res.
Ashton
Big Lost R.
Mackay Reservoir
Mackay
15
St. Anthony
Chester
33
33
Newdale
Rexburg
Tetonia
93
22
South Fork Snake River Pages 103-108
River
20
South Fork Snake
Teton R.
Driggs
Arco
26
31
Victor
20
20
IDAHO FALLS
Swan Valley
To Jackson, WY
Snake River Blackfoot Area Pages 81-85
15
Snake
26
Blackfoot
Blackfoot River
Palisades Reservoir
Snake River Massacre Rocks & American Falls Pages 87-90
Fort Hall
Blackfoot Reservoir
Grays Lake
To Afton, WY
34
Wayan
American Falls Res.
POCATELLO
Chesterfield Res.
Henry
86
Portneuf
Portneuf River
Massacre Rocks Park
15
Blackfoot River
Lake Walcott Reservoir
American Falls
Soda Springs
Rupert
River
Snake
McCammon
30
Lava Hot Springs
Bear River
84
Burley
Grace
Georgetown
Virginia
34
Bear River
Southeast Idaho Area See Detailed Map Next Page (p. 30)
Downey
30
To Afton, WY
15
91
36
89
Montpelier
Malad
Mink Creek
84
89
Dayton
To Salt Lake City
Preston
To Logan
Bear Lake
To Rock Springs, WY
Weston
UTAH
WYOMING

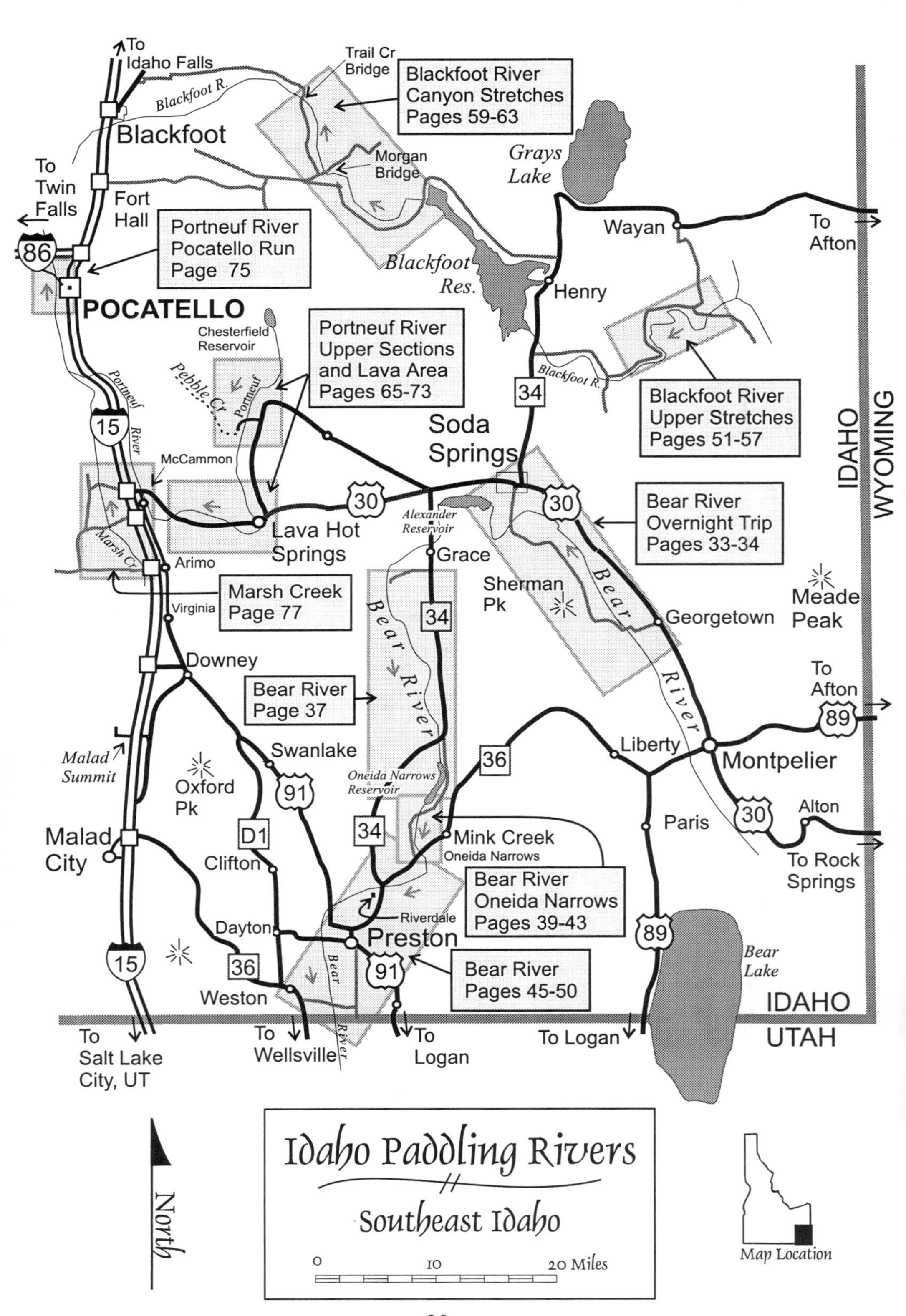
To Idaho Falls
Trail Cr Bridge
Blackfoot River Canyon Stretches Pages 59-63
Blackfoot R.
Blackfoot
Morgan Bridge
Grays Lake
To Twin Falls
Fort Hall
Portneuf River Pocatello Run Page 75
86
Wayan
To Afton
Blackfoot Res.
Henry
POCATELLO
Chesterfield Reservoir
Portneuf River Upper Sections and Lava Area Pages 65-73
Pebble Cr
Portneuf
Blackfoot R.
34
Blackfoot River Upper Stretches Pages 51-57
Portneuf River
15
Soda Springs
IDAHO
WYOMING
McCammon
30
30
Bear River Overnight Trip Pages 33-34
Alexander Reservoir
Lava Hot Springs
Grace
Marsh Cr
Arimo
Marsh Creek Page 77
Sherman Pk
Virginia
34
Bear River
Georgetown
Meade Peak
Downey
To Afton
Bear River Page 37
Bear River
89
Liberty
Montpelier
Malad Summit
Swanlake
36
Oxford Pk
91
Oneida Narrows Reservoir
Paris
30
Alton
Malad City
D1
34
Mink Creek
Oneida Narrows
To Rock Springs
Clifton
Bear River Oneida Narrows Pages 39-43
Riverdale
Dayton
Preston
89
Bear Lake
15
36
91
Bear River Pages 45-50
Weston
Bear River
IDAHO
UTAH
To Salt Lake City, UT
To Wellsville
To Logan
To Logan
North
Idaho Paddling Rivers
Southeast Idaho
0
10
20 Miles
Map Location

Idaho Rivers

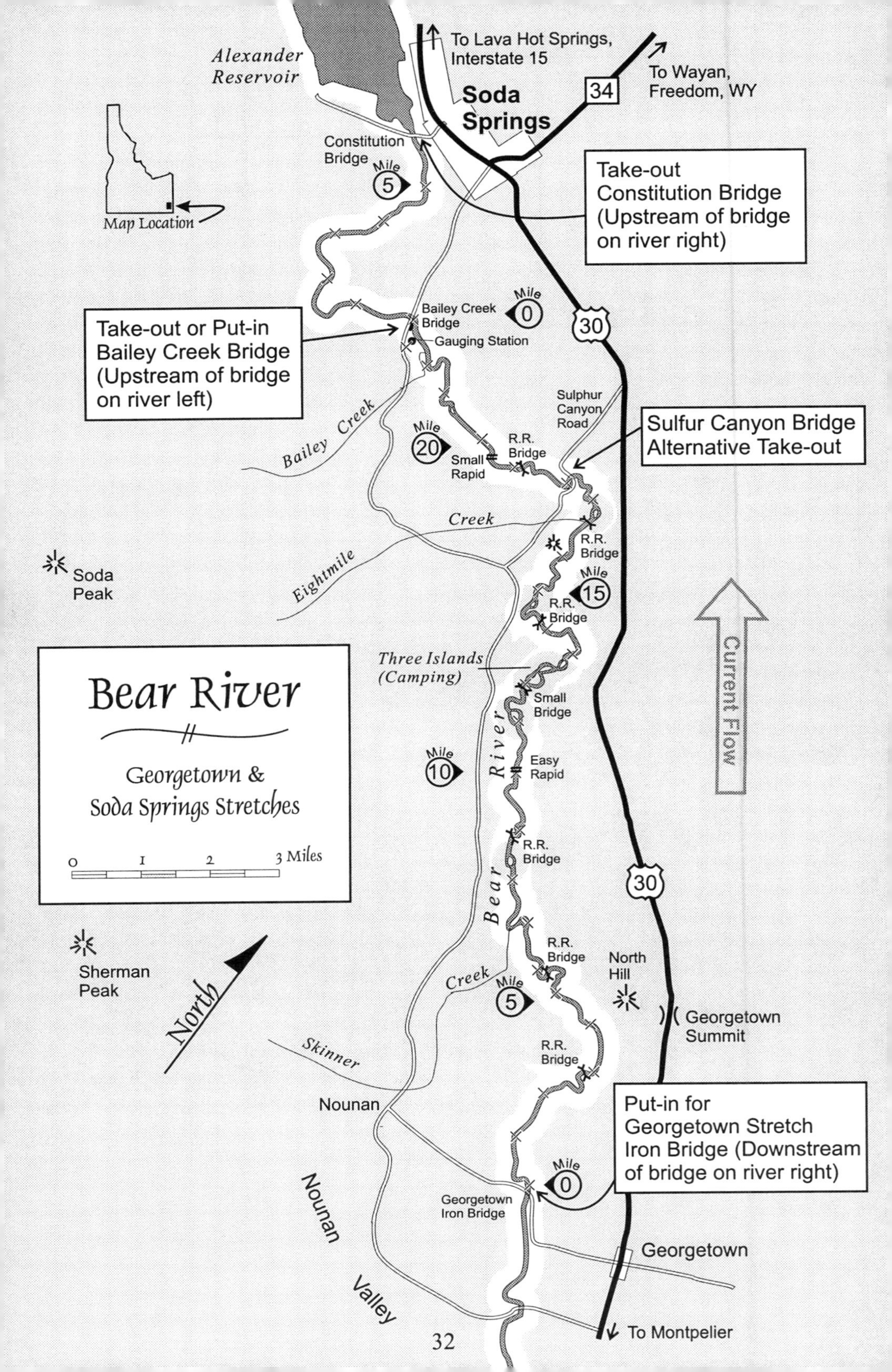
Bear River
Georgetown & Soda Springs Stretches
0
1
2
3 Miles
Alexander Reservoir
To Lava Hot Springs, Interstate 15
34
To Wayan, Freedom, WY
Soda Springs
Map Location
Constitution Bridge
Mile 5
Take-out Constitution Bridge (Upstream of bridge on river right)
Bailey Creek Bridge
Mile 0
Gauging Station
30
Take-out or Put-in Bailey Creek Bridge (Upstream of bridge on river left)
Bailey Creek
Sulphur Canyon Road
Sulfur Canyon Bridge Alternative Take-out
Mile 20
Small Rapid
R.R. Bridge
Creek
Eightmile
R.R. Bridge
Soda Peak
Mile 15
R.R. Bridge
Current Flow
Three Islands (Camping)
Small Bridge
Mile 10
River
Easy Rapid
R.R. Bridge
Bear
30
Sherman Peak
North
R.R. Bridge
North Hill
Creek
Mile 5
Georgetown Summit
Skinner
R.R. Bridge
Nounan
Put-in for Georgetown Stretch Iron Bridge (Downstream of bridge on river right)
Mile 0
Georgetown Iron Bridge
Nounan Valley
Georgetown
To Montpelier

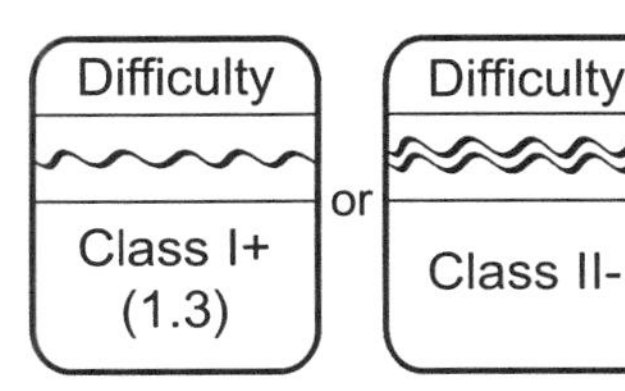

Bear River

Georgetown Stretch and Soda Springs Whitewater Practice Run

THE BEAR RIVER is an outstanding paddling river and is particularly well suited for canoeing. Over the next few pages, we have included a number of different segments that can be run. The part of the Bear described here is an overnight trip, starting near Georgetown, north of Montpelier and ending just outside of Soda Springs. It is also possible to do shorter runs on this segment, but an overnight trip is the best way of getting to know the river intimately.

This is a great stretch for families and scout groups. For the last several years, Ron has been doing this trip as a finale to his beginning canoe workshop. It's rated class I+ (1.3) and has a couple of short, mini-rapids, but in normal summer flows, the water is never very forceful, and in most places, it's shallow enough that you can wade to the shore if someone spills.

The Bear is not a wilderness river. It flows through pasture and farm land, and the Union Pacific rail line parallels the river along most of this stretch. Trains do come by, but the occasional train doesn't seem to distract from the river experience. Moreover, it's doubtful that you'll see another boat on the river. Amazingly, in all the years that we've run the Bear, we've never come across another paddler. If you want to get away from the crowds, this is one place to go.

Also included in this section is a 5-mile stretch of the Bear from Bailey Bridge to Soda Springs. It's a fun class II- stretch, great for practicing whitewater skills with eddies, easily-avoided boulders and small rapids.

Basic Stats (Georgetown Stretch)

Difficulty: Class I+ (1.3).

Levels/Season: The Bear is runnable most of the summer. Good flows range from 500 to 1,700 cfs at the Bailey Creek gauge. Flow information is not available on the Internet but can be obtained by calling the Soda Point Dam at (208) 547-3697.

Distance/Time: 23 miles for overnight trip (8-10 hours). A shorter 18-mile trip or 5-mile trip can be taken by using the alternative put-in and take-outs.

Getting to the Take-out. Bailey Creek Bridge. Note that the water is swift at Bailey Creek Bridge and some beginning paddlers may have trouble stopping in the eddy on the left just above the bridge. If you are paddling with a beginning group, it's best to take-out at Sulfur Canyon Bridge, 5 miles upstream.

The road to Bailey Creek Bridge is reached from the junction of US 30 and Idaho 34 in Soda Springs. If you are heading south on US 30 towards Georgetown and Montpelier, take a right. The Bailey Creek Bridge is 2.6 miles from the junction. Park in the large pull-off on the left. (The river take-out is upstream of the bridge on river left).

Alternative Take-out. Sulfur Canyon Bridge. To get to the bridge, drive from Soda Springs towards Montpelier on US 30. About 3 miles out of Soda Springs, watch for a sign indicating Sulfur Canyon. Take a right and drive 2 miles until reaching the bridge.

Getting to the Put-in. Georgetown Iron Bridge. Drive to Georgetown which is 18 miles southeast of Soda Springs on US 30. Look for the LDS church on the left side of the highway in the center of Georgetown. Just opposite the church, turn to the right (west), drive 2.2 miles to the iron bridge over the Bear River. The put-in is on the downstream side of the bridge on river right.

The Trip. The river on this stretch flows through open pasture land with hawthorns clustered in patches along portions of the river. You'll notice that the Bear carries a lot of sediment. This is actually how the Bear has always looked. Trappers described its waters as "thick." During the first part of the trip, you'll have some views of Sherman Peak, the prominent point off to the left (west) side of the river. Pelicans, ducks and geese are common throughout the trip.

One low bridge is located 5.7 miles from the start. Pull off on the left and take a look before continuing. In low water, a canoe can barely slip under the left side of the bridge. The left bank just above the bridge is grassy, and if the bridge looks too low for your comfort, unload the boat and drag it around on the left shore.

Camping. The best place to camp is at the midway point just downstream from the grain elevator at Manson. The grain elevator is visible in the distance to the left of the river. After spotting the elevator and going through some more twists and turns, you'll pass under a small bridge with plenty of head room (12 miles from the start). The first of three islands comes about .2 mile after the bridge. We've found adequate camping on the right side of the first and third islands.

Shuttle. 23 miles, mostly paved, some dirt. An onerous bike shuttle can be done on Highway 30, a heavily traveled truck route. A more pleasant shuttle route follows the back road which parallels the Bear River on its west side. Give yourself lots of time for this shuttle. This is a long, long ride with a lot of up and down, but it is far less stressful than riding on Highway 30.

Craft. Canoes, kayaks. Small inflatables, in windy conditions, may get bogged down on the slow portions of the river. Drift boats can also do the trip, but no ramps are available and the low bridge mentioned above would have to be portaged.

Mileage Chart
Georgetown Stretch

Mile	Description
0	Put-in. Georgetown Iron Bridge (downstream of the bridge on river right).
2.9	Railroad bridge.
5.7	Very low bridge. Scout on left.
5.8	Railroad bridge.
7.3	Mouth of Skinner Creek (left).
8.8	Railroad bridge.
10	Small rapid (class I+).
12	Small bridge near Manson, plenty of headroom.
12.2	First of three islands (camping on right side of islands).
14.2	Railroad bridge.
16	Cliff on left side of river for .5 mile.
16.6	Mouth of Eightmile Creek (left) and railroad bridge.
17.8	Sulfur Canyon Bridge.
18.9	Last railroad bridge.
19.6	Small rapid with a couple of rolling waves (class I+).
22.9	Gauging station (left).
23	Take-out. Bailey Creek Bridge (upstream of bridge on left).

Soda Springs Whitewater Practice Run
(Bailey Creek Bridge to Constitution Bridge)

Basic Stats (Soda Springs Whitewater Practice Run)

Difficulty: Class II-. A good place to practice eddy turns, paddling around boulders and picking your way down rapids.

Levels/Season: Same as Georgetown stretch on previous page.

Distance/Time: 5 miles / 2 hours.

Getting to the Take-out. Constitution Bridge. On the west edge of Soda Springs, look for the sign along Highway 30 pointing the way to the hospital. Drive a couple of blocks to the hospital. Just beyond the hospital is Constitution Bridge. The take-out is upstream of the bridge on river right. Plenty of parking.

Getting to the Put-in. Bailey Creek Bridge. See the directions to the take-out for the Georgetown Stretch on the previous page.

The Trip. This is a perfect whitewater practice stretch that can be run a couple of times in an afternoon. It is particularly nice for beginning kayakers and open canoeists that want to start learning about whitewater. The rapids consist of some swift portions of river and easy rock dodging. Everything can be seen from the seat of your boat and scouting is not necessary.

Shuttle. 5 miles, all paved. Bike shuttle on secondary paved roads and along Highway 30 through Soda Springs.

Craft. Canoes, kayaks, inflatables, drift boats (no ramps).

The Georgetown stretch of the Bear River is a wonderful paddle trip for families—and, if desired, you can also spend a night on the river. This is the view from the first of the three islands near Manson, one of the camping spots along the way.

Difficulty
Class I (1.0)

Bear River

Oneida Narrows Reservoir Paddle and Gentile Valley Stretch

A DELIGHTFUL CANOE TRIP can be made from end to end across Oneida Narrows Reservoir south of Soda Springs. This beautiful, slender reservoir is surrounded by conifers, an congenial change to the predominately sage-covered hills of southeast Idaho. For a memorable trip, try this sometime early in the morning when water is glass-like, and the air is fresh and still.

Basic Stats

Difficulty: Class I (1.0). Flat, backwaters of Oneida Reservoir.

Season: Spring through fall.

Distance/Time: 4.5 miles / 3 hours.

Getting to the Take-out. Oneida Narrows Reservoir Boat Ramp. Oneida Narrows can be reached from Preston or Soda Springs. (See next section on page 39 for a description of approaching the reservoir from Preston). If coming in from Soda Springs, just west of Soda, take Idaho 34 to the south through Grace and Thatcher. About 4.5 miles past Thatcher and just before the bridge over the Bear River, turn left on Oneida Narrows Road (a sign at the corner indicates Maple Grove, a hot springs and Oneida Reservoir). Follow this winding dirt road to the south for about 7 miles to the concrete boat ramp and small park at Oneida dam.

Getting to the Put-in. Backwaters of Oneida Narrows. The put-in for this trip is on the Oneida Narrows road about 2 miles south (towards Oneida Dam) of its intersection with Idaho 34. Watch for a short dirt road that turns off the Oneida Narrows road and goes a short distance to the water's edge of the reservoir. There's no ramp here, but it is a reasonable place to launch a canoe or kayak.

The Trip. The best time to do this trip is early in the morning before the wind gets started. On calm and quiet mornings, you can make the paddle from one end to the other in a couple of hours. It's unlikely that the reservoir will have any motorized traffic then, but as the day warms up, so do the motorboats.

Even though the reservoir is narrow throughout, it's still best to keep near one shore while paddling. If the wind comes up or if anyone in your party has problems, you can get them to shore quickly.

Shuttle. 7 miles, narrow dirt road. The bike shuttle is on a winding mountain road, an agreeable mountain bike ride on weekdays, but it can be disagreeable when it's busy on weekends.

Craft. Canoes and kayaks.

The Gentile Valley Stretch of the Bear. The Bear River can also be run through the Gentile Valley, the rolling, green valley above Oneida Narrows Reservoir. Unfortunately, the river is often low here. But if you don't mind the river's slow pace and dragging your boat now and then, it can be run during most of the summer. It is rated a class I (1.3) in low water with some mini-rapids here and there. The first access point is below Grace Power Plant to the southwest of Grace. (You may have of heard of a class V whitewater stretch located in this area. It's through Black Canyon located just upstream from the Grace Power Plant.)

Other access points below Grace Power Plant include the Niter Bridge to the west of Niter, the bridge near the Thatcher Church south of Niter, and the Thatcher Bridge. The take-out is the backwaters of Oneida Narrows Reservoir, described on the previous page.

If you start from just below Grace Power Plant, it's a 24-mile trip to the reservoir. Because of the typical low water conditions found on this stretch, those doing the full 24 miles should plan to camp one night along the river.

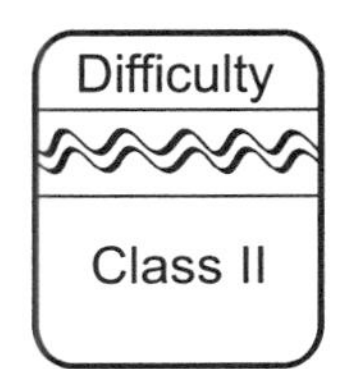

Bear River

Oneida Narrows Whitewater Stretch

THE ONEIDA NARROWS is the Bear River's most popular whitewater canoe and kayak stretch. Located just below Oneida Dam, northeast of Preston, it's also one of the most scenic parts of the river, running through a narrow canyon with slopes of juniper and deciduous trees. The river naturally carries a substantial load of silt, but not on this stretch. When it comes out of the reservoir, it's clear and cold. Because of the water quality, this segment is well-known for its fine trout fishing.

Basic Stats

Difficulty: Class II (to the cattleguard take-out). Has some moderately long stretches of class II. The lower half of the run to the Highway 36 bridge has two class III- diversions to run.

Levels: Water levels are dependent on releases from the dam. We suggest staying under 1800 cfs at which level the current is getting to be forceful. Flow information is not available on the Internet, but can be obtained by calling Pacific Power and Light at 1-800-547-1501.

Distance/Time: 4 miles to the cattleguard take-out / 1.5 to 2 hours. 5.9 miles to the Highway 36 bridge.

Getting to the Take-out. Highway 36 bridge. From Preston, drive toward Montpelier on Idaho 36. About 5 miles out of Preston, Idaho 34 and 36 separate. Stay on Idaho 36. At 3 miles from the Idaho 34 & 36 junction, the Oneida Narrows Road comes in from the left, and .5 mile farther, you'll come to the Highway 36 bridge over the Bear River. The take-out is on the upstream or downstream side of the bridge on river left.

Alternative Take-out. Midway Cattleguard. Some boaters may want to take out at the cattleguard to avoid the two class III- diversions located on the second half of this run. The cattleguard take-out is located on the Oneida Narrows Road, 6 miles upriver (north) from the road's intersection with Highway 36. Or if you are coming in from the other direction, it's

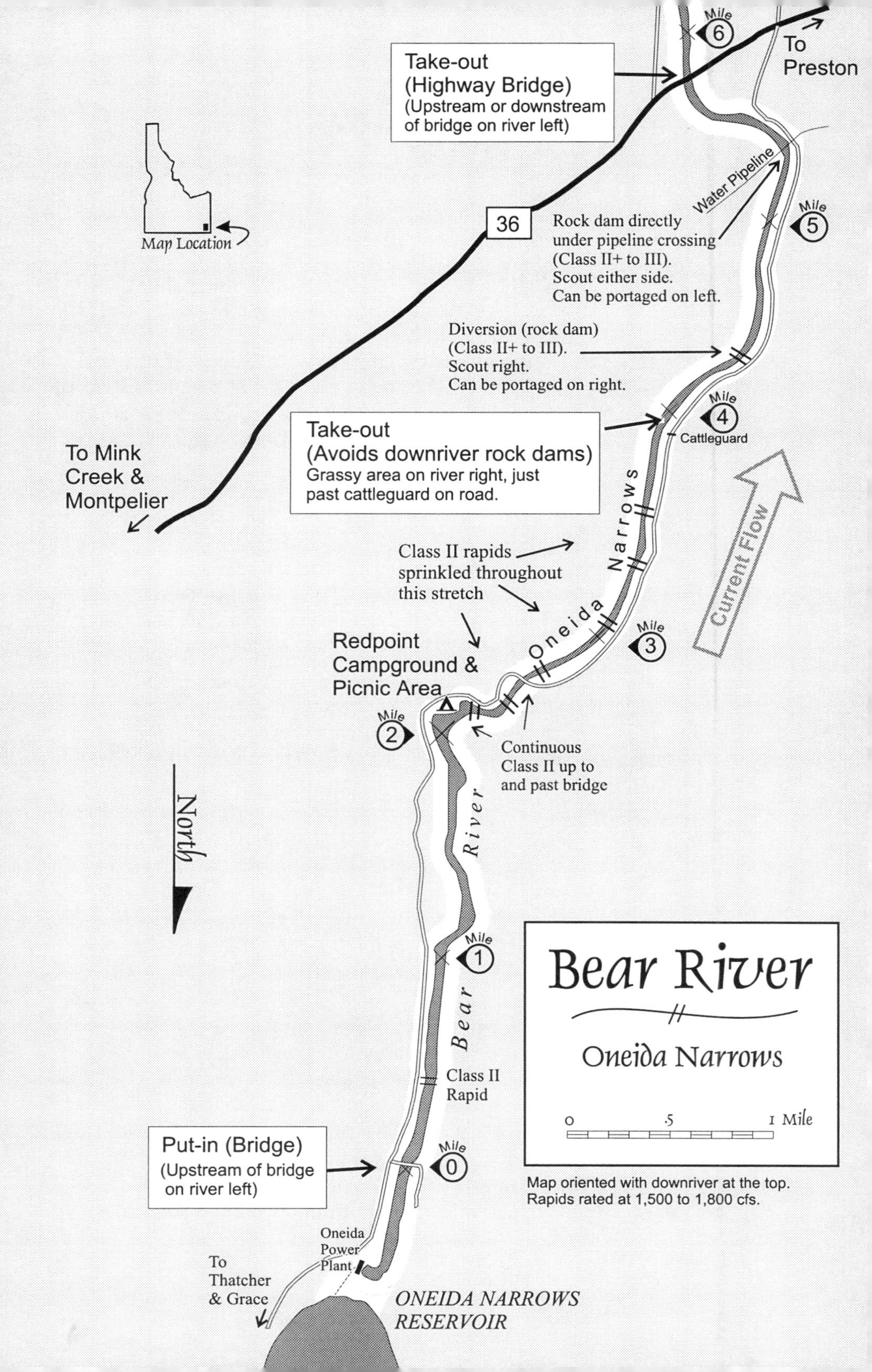

Bear River
Oneida Narrows
0
.5
1 Mile
Map oriented with downriver at the top.
Rapids rated at 1,500 to 1,800 cfs.
Take-out
(Highway Bridge)
(Upstream or downstream of bridge on river left)
To Preston
Mile 6
Map Location
36
Water Pipeline
Rock dam directly under pipeline crossing (Class II+ to III).
Scout either side.
Can be portaged on left.
Mile 5
Diversion (rock dam)
(Class II+ to III).
Scout right.
Can be portaged on right.
Mile 4
Cattleguard
Take-out
(Avoids downriver rock dams)
Grassy area on river right, just past cattleguard on road.
To Mink Creek & Montpelier
Oneida Narrows
Current Flow
Class II rapids sprinkled throughout this stretch
Mile 3
Redpoint Campground & Picnic Area
Mile 2
Continuous Class II up to and past bridge
North
Bear River
Mile 1
Class II Rapid
Put-in (Bridge)
(Upstream of bridge on river left)
Mile 0
Oneida Power Plant
To Thatcher & Grace
ONEIDA NARROWS RESERVOIR

located 4.3 miles south of the put-in at the upper bridge. The take-out is a grassy area along the river, just downstream from the cattleguard.

Getting to the Put-in. Upper bridge (below dam). The upper bridge is located near the base of Oneida Dam. It's about .2 mile below the Oneida Station power plant or 6 miles north of Highway 36 on Oneida Narrows Road. The put-in is on river left, upstream of the bridge.

The Trip. Canoeists will want to have some previous whitewater experience before undertaking this trip, but once ready for it, this is an outstanding open canoe run. It's also a great stretch for kayakers and paddlers in inflatable boats. Drift boaters can run it, but since no ramps are available, it entails some work carrying boats in and out.

Oneida Narrows has two nice features. One is that you can scout all the rapids and rock dams from the road which closely follows the river. And second is that the natural progression of the river gives you a chance to get warmed up.

Starting from the upper bridge, the river begins with some class I water with one class II rapid a half mile down. At the two-mile point, beginning at Redpoint Campground on river left, the river rocks and rolls with a fairly long, continuous class II stretch. From there expect a couple more class II rapids before the midway cattleguard take-out.

If you continue beyond the cattleguard, you'll need to scout two rocky diversion dams, both class III-. The first one is at the 4.4-mile point (scout right) and the second is at the 5.4-mile point just below a pipeline crossing. To scout the second, pull off on the right or left and climb out on the pipeline. From the pipeline diversion, it's a short distance to the take-out at the Highway 36 bridge.

Shuttle. 6.5 miles, mostly dirt. Bike shuttle: the road is a narrow dirt road which can be fairly well traveled on weekends.

Craft. Canoes, kayaks, inflatables. Drift boats can get down it, but no ramps. Launching drift boats involves a considerable effort.

Mileage Chart (Rapids were rated at a flow of 1,600 cfs)	
0	Put-in. Upper bridge (upstream or downstream of the bridge on river left).
.4	Class II rapids just before island.
2	Right hand bend.
2.1	Red Point Campground (left). Continuous stretch of class II water begins.
2.7	Bridge.
4	Cattleguard take-out.
4.4	Rock Dam (class III-). Scout on right. Can be portaged on right.
5.2	Powerline crossing.
5.4	Pipeline crossing. Rock Dam (class III-) just below pipeline. May be scouted by pulling off on either side and climbing out on the pipeline. May be portaged on left.
5.9	Take-out. Highway 36 bridge (upstream or downstream of the bridge on river left).

The Oneida Narrows stretch begins in this open valley just below Oneida Dam. Lively class II rapids are found in the narrows proper where the river is constricted by the steep-faced mountains in the background of the photograph.

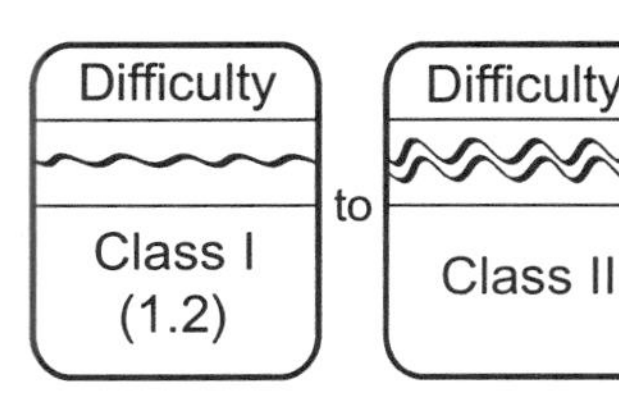

Bear River

Four Stretches in the Preston Area

THE FOUR SEGMENTS described here take the Bear River from the mouth of Oneida Narrows to the Utah border. The first segment, Mink Creek, starts at the end of the Oneida Narrows run and is mostly class II-, a tad easier than the Narrows.

It's a pretty stretch, starting among shaded, tree-lined banks in a small canyon. Osprey inhabit this and the next stretch and you'll likely see them. It does have one diversion dam near the end that must be portaged on river right.

The second segment, starting near the Highway 34 and 36 junction, northeast of Preston, flows southwest initially through a cottonwood thicket and then through open pasture and farmland. The river starts with class I+ (1.4) water with one runnable diversion early on, but quickly turns into a slow moving class I stretch. Along this stretch we saw some of the largest bulrushes and cattails in all of Idaho. By August, they tower over you in the marsh lands on either side of the river.

The third segment from the US 91 bridge to the Dayton Bridge, is probably the least desirable. A long row of car bodies near the beginning have been used to stabilize the river bank. It is, however, a fairly easy trip (class I, 1.2) with no diversions and it has two hot springs which will be of interest.

The fourth segment, Hidden Valley of the Bear, is our favorite stretch (class I, 1.2). It begins at the Dayton-Preston Bridge and ends at the Weston Bridge, a distance of 7.4 miles.

Here the river is isolated from surrounding agricultural land by tree cover, including some huge, ancient cottonwoods midway down. The highway is out of earshot and it's quiet and unaffected. One diversion dam is found on this stretch, and in low water you may want to carry your boat around on the left, but in higher flows (above 1,500 cfs at Oneida), it barely forms a ripple.

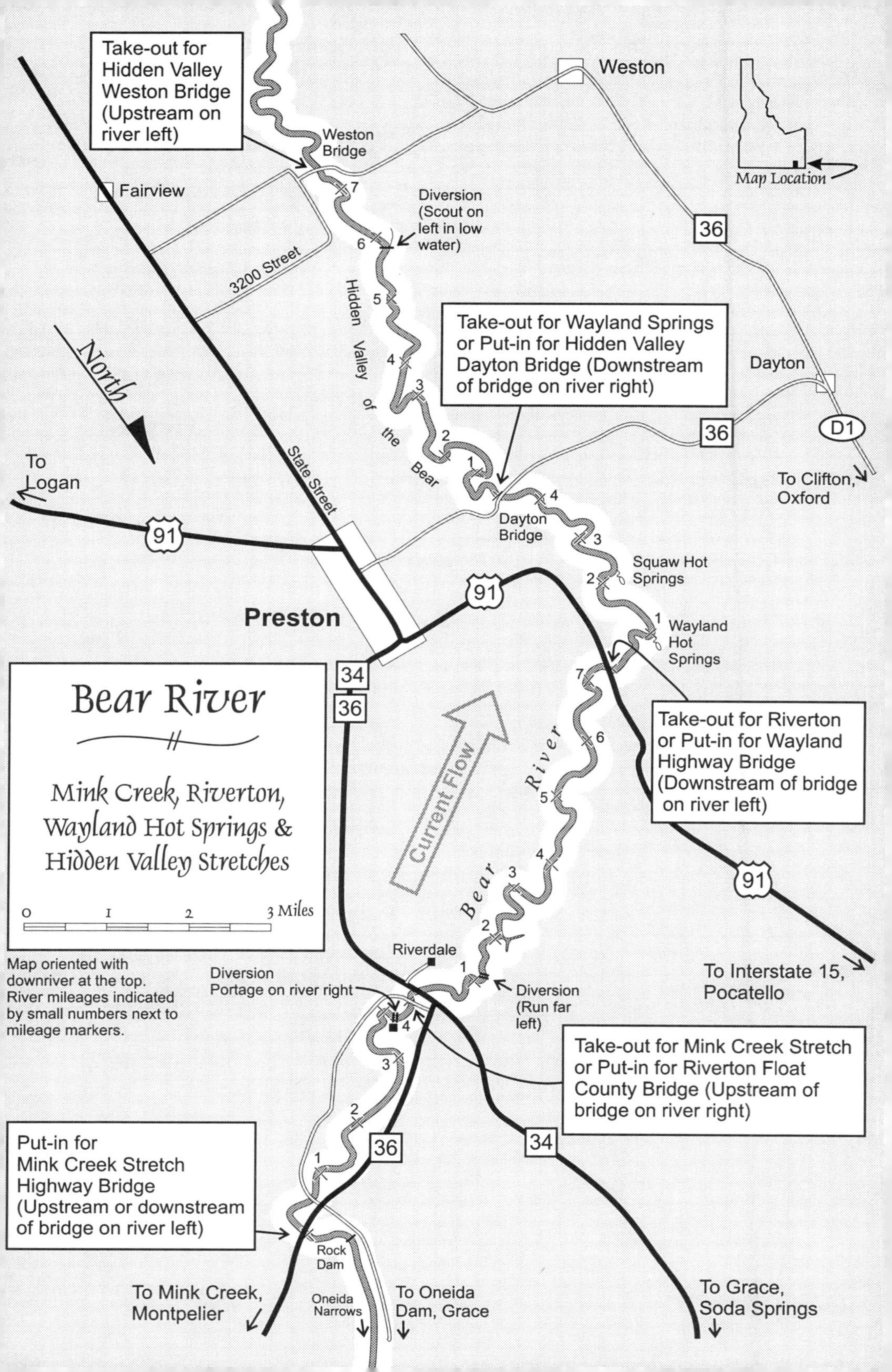
Take-out for Hidden Valley
Weston Bridge
(Upstream on river left)
Weston
Weston Bridge
Fairview
Diversion (Scout on left in low water)
3200 Street
Hidden Valley of the Bear
North
Take-out for Wayland Springs or Put-in for Hidden Valley
Dayton Bridge (Downstream of bridge on river right)
Dayton
36
D1
To Clifton, Oxford
To Logan
91
State Street
Dayton Bridge
Squaw Hot Springs
Wayland Hot Springs
Preston
34
36
Take-out for Riverton or Put-in for Wayland
Highway Bridge
(Downstream of bridge on river left)
Map Location
Bear River
Mink Creek, Riverton, Wayland Hot Springs & Hidden Valley Stretches
0 1 2 3 Miles
Current Flow
Bear River
Map oriented with downriver at the top. River mileages indicated by small numbers next to mileage markers.
Riverdale
Diversion
Portage on river right
Diversion (Run far left)
To Interstate 15, Pocatello
Take-out for Mink Creek Stretch or Put-in for Riverton Float
County Bridge (Upstream of bridge on river right)
Put-in for Mink Creek Stretch
Highway Bridge
(Upstream or downstream of bridge on river left)
Rock Dam
To Mink Creek, Montpelier
Oneida Narrows
To Oneida Dam, Grace
To Grace, Soda Springs

Mink Creek Stretch
(From Highway 36 Bridge at end of Oneida Narrows to Riverdale)

Basic Stats (Mink Creek Stretch)

Difficulty: Class II (mostly class II- rapids. The class II rating takes into account the portage around the diversion).

Season: Spring through fall.

Distance/Time: 4.5 miles / 2-3 hours.

Portage: One portage around the right side of a diversion near the end.

Getting to the Take-out. County Road Bridge near Riverdale. From Preston take Idaho 34/36 toward Montpelier. About 4 miles out of Preston, you'll reach the junction of Idaho 36. Take a right on Idaho 36 and drive about 200 feet and then take another right on a secondary road which heads south to a bridge over the Bear River. Just before the bridge, turn left into a parking area. The take-out (no ramp) is along the grassy banks of the river next to the parking area.

Getting to the Put-in. Highway 36 bridge. From Preston, drive toward Montpelier on Idaho 36. About 5 miles out of Preston, Idaho 34 and 36 separate. Stay on Idaho 36. At 3 miles from the Idaho 34 & 36 junction, the Oneida Narrows Road comes in from the left, and .5 mile farther, you'll come to the Highway 36 bridge over the Bear. The put-in is either upstream or downstream of the bridge on river left.

The Trip. Mink Creek Stretch. The whitewater along this stretch is benign: rapids here and there, some rocks, eddies and even small surfing waves. The main obstruction that you need to watch for is a diversion, 4.1 miles from the start and only .4 mile before the take-out. It's easy to recognize. The river makes two bends next to a hillside on the left.

On the second bend, you'll see a house on the right with a lawn which comes to the edge of the river. When you see the house, paddle over to the far right shore. The diversion is located just downstream from the house. The water is slow above the diversion, but, nevertheless, you want to make sure that you have positioned yourself on the right. Stop a couple of yards above the diversion, and drag your boat 20 feet to the base of the diversion. Once finished with the portage, it's a short and easy paddle to the end.

Shuttle. 9 miles, all paved. Bike shuttlers use caution. Highway 36 doesn't have much of a shoulder and is moderately busy.

Craft. Canoes, kayaks, inflatables. No ramps for drift boats.

Osprey fledgling in the nest along the Mink Creek stretch of the Bear River.

Riverdale Stretch
(Riverdale to Highway 91 Bridge north of Preston)

Basic Stats (Riverdale Stretch)

Difficulty: Class I+ (1.4). One diversion early in the trip is easily run on the left.

Season: Spring through fall.

Distance/Time: 7.3 miles / 3-4 hours.

Getting to the Take-out. Highway 91 bridge. From Preston, drive north on US 91. The bridge over the Bear is located about 3 miles north of Preston. The take-out is on river left, downstream of the bridge. Parking for two vehicles.

Getting to the Put-in. County Road Bridge near Riverdale. See directions above for the Mink Creek Stretch take-out (page 45).

The Trip. Riverdale Stretch (Riverdale to Highway 91 Bridge north of Preston). The one obstacle on this stretch is a diversion 1.1 miles from the start. You'll pass a couple of car bodies on a right-hand bend at the one-mile point. Stay close to the left shore at this point. When the concrete head gate of the diversion becomes visible on the right, pull off and stop on the left.

Scout the diversion from the left shore. At 1600 cfs we found the right and middle of the river occupied by a good-sized roller which looked like it could swamp our open canoe. We opted for the easy run down the left side.

From here, you'll encounter some class I+ (1.3) water, but the river quickly settles down to slow moving class I. Take some time on the first couple of miles through the cottonwood riparian zone. This is good bird habitat and you may see hawks and osprey.

Shuttle. 14 miles, all paved. Bike shuttle: reasonably wide shoulders, but the highways are heavily traveled.

Craft. Canoe and kayaks. Inflatables will find this stretch dreadfully slow. Drift boats can run it, but no ramps.

Wayland Hot Springs Stretch
(Highway 91 Bridge to Dayton-Preston Bridge)

Basic Stats (Wayland Hot Springs Stretch)

Difficulty: Class I (1.2). No diversions.

Season: Spring through fall.

Distance/Time: 4.4 miles / 2-3 hours.

Getting to the Take-out. Dayton-Preston Bridge. The Dayton-Preston Bridge is located 2 miles east of Preston on Idaho 36. The turn off to the launching site is 200 feet west of the bridge. Follow the dirt road to the river. The take-out is on river right, downstream of the bridge. No ramp but plenty of parking.

Getting to the Put-in. US 91 bridge. See directions for the Riverdale Stretch take-out (page 46).

The Trip. Wayland Hot Springs Stretch (Highway 91 Bridge to Dayton-Preston Bridge). This is the only stretch of the Bear River in Idaho below the Oneida Reservoir completely free of diversions, and it's a good beginner's run. Although not particularly scenic, this part of the river is interesting from a geological standpoint because of its two large hot springs. The first is Wayland Hot Springs, 1 mile from the start on the right. So much hot water pours into the river that it looks like a steaming tributary entering the river. Be careful, don't plunge your hands into it. Wayland's waters are scalding.

The second, Squaw Springs, is located on the right, 2.3 miles from the start near a run-down house. You can actually paddle up this one a short distance and have a look at the multicolored soil and rocks surrounding the springs.

Below the springs, the river meanders easily to the take-out at the Dayton-Preston Bridge.

The multicolored rocks and mineral deposits surrounding Squaw Hot Springs are reminiscent of geothermal features in Yellowstone.

Shuttle. 6 miles, all paved. Bike shuttle: Highway 91 has a good shoulder, less so for Highway 36. Both are busy highways.

Craft. Canoes, kayaks. Slow for inflatables. Drift boats can run it, but no ramps.

Hidden Valley of the Bear (Dayton-Preston Bridge to the Weston Bridge)

Basic Stats (Hidden Valley of the Bear)
Difficulty: Class I (1.2). Possible portage of a diversion in very low water.
Season: Spring through fall.
Distance/Time: 7.4 miles / 2-4 hours.

Getting to the Take-out. Weston Bridge. As you are driving south through Preston on US 91, take a right on State Street and head toward Fairview. Check your odometer in Preston. Drive 3.3 miles to 3200 Street and take a right (west). Follow this road as it bends around to the south 2.8 miles to 3900S and take another right. Drive a short distance to the bridge. The take-out is on river left, upstream of the bridge.

Unfortunately, for such a fine stretch of water, the parking is not very good. You'll have to park a distance away from the bridge in order to get your vehicle all the way off the road. The take-out also involves carrying your boat up a 15-foot embankment to the road.

Getting to the Put-in. Dayton-Preston Bridge, see directions for the take-out at Wayland Hot Springs (page 47).

The Trip. Hidden Valley of the Bear (Dayton-Preston Bridge to the Weston Bridge). This pretty stretch of river flows through a secluded valley on the Bear River that is not noticeable when you drive through the area. It's all easy water (class I, 1.2) and it's a wonderful stretch for R&R and just enjoying some fresh air.

At the 5.8-mile point (1.6 miles before the end), you'll come to a diversion. The diversion is obvious. A floating raft mounted on 55-gallon drums is tied to the left bank. Pull out above the raft and take a look. In water flows of about 1600 cfs at Oneida Dam, the diversion was hardly noticeable and we floated over it easily. If it's quite shallow, you may need to portage around it on the left.

The ending point is the Weston Bridge. (Note that if you float below Weston Bridge, be sure to carefully scout the very rocky and nasty looking diversion about 1.5 miles downstream from the bridge.) The Bear River below here, as it flows through Utah, has several excellent paddling trips which you might want to try. The book, *Boating the Bear*, published by the Bridgerland Audubon Society (Box 3501, Logan, UT 84323) is a great source of information on the Utah segments and provides additional information on the Bear in Idaho and Wyoming.

Shuttle. 9 miles, all paved. Bike shuttle: use caution, busy rural roads.

Craft. Canoe, kayaks. In windy conditions, this stretch would be slow going for inflatables.

Difficulty

Class I
(1.1)

Blackfoot River

Blackfoot Special Management Area

THANKS TO THE Idaho Fish and Game Department, the Blackfoot River Special Management Area is one of Southeast Idaho's most scenic trips. Located to the north and east of Soda Springs, the river flows through the Stocking Ranch which the department is managing to help preserve and protect the river. They've done a wonderful job. The banks are reverting back to natural vegetation and the fly fishing . . . well, shall we say, it's pretty darn good.

So is the paddling. It's an easy stretch of river with two options: one is a fun, little stretch with some mini-rapids (class I+, 1.3)—and the other is a laid-back trip (class I, 1.1) for families. It's a very small river, and canoes, kayaks and very small inflatables are the way to float it.

The river flows through meadows and grass lands and the wide-open view across the valley is splendid. It really gives you the feel of going back in time and seeing Southeast Idaho when the river was the domain of the Blackfoot Indians.

Basic Stats

Difficulty: The first half of the trip is class I+ (1.3). The second half is class I (1.1).

Season: July and early August. Avoid it during high water.

Distance/Time: 5.3 miles (first half is 2.8 miles and the second half is 2.5 miles) / 3.5-4.5 hours for the full trip.

Getting to the Take-out. Fishing access near Mill Canyon. Start at Soda Springs and drive 12 miles north on Idaho 34 until coming to Blackfoot River Road (marked with a sign). Turn right. At 9.2 miles from the highway, the road Y's. Take the left branch, staying on Blackfoot River Road. Drive another 3.2 miles from the "Y" and you'll pass the entrance road to Mill Canyon Campground on the left. Drive another .3 mile past the campground entrance, and you'll see a short dirt road which leads to the river. This is the take-out. There's no ramp here but it's an easy place to pull boats out.

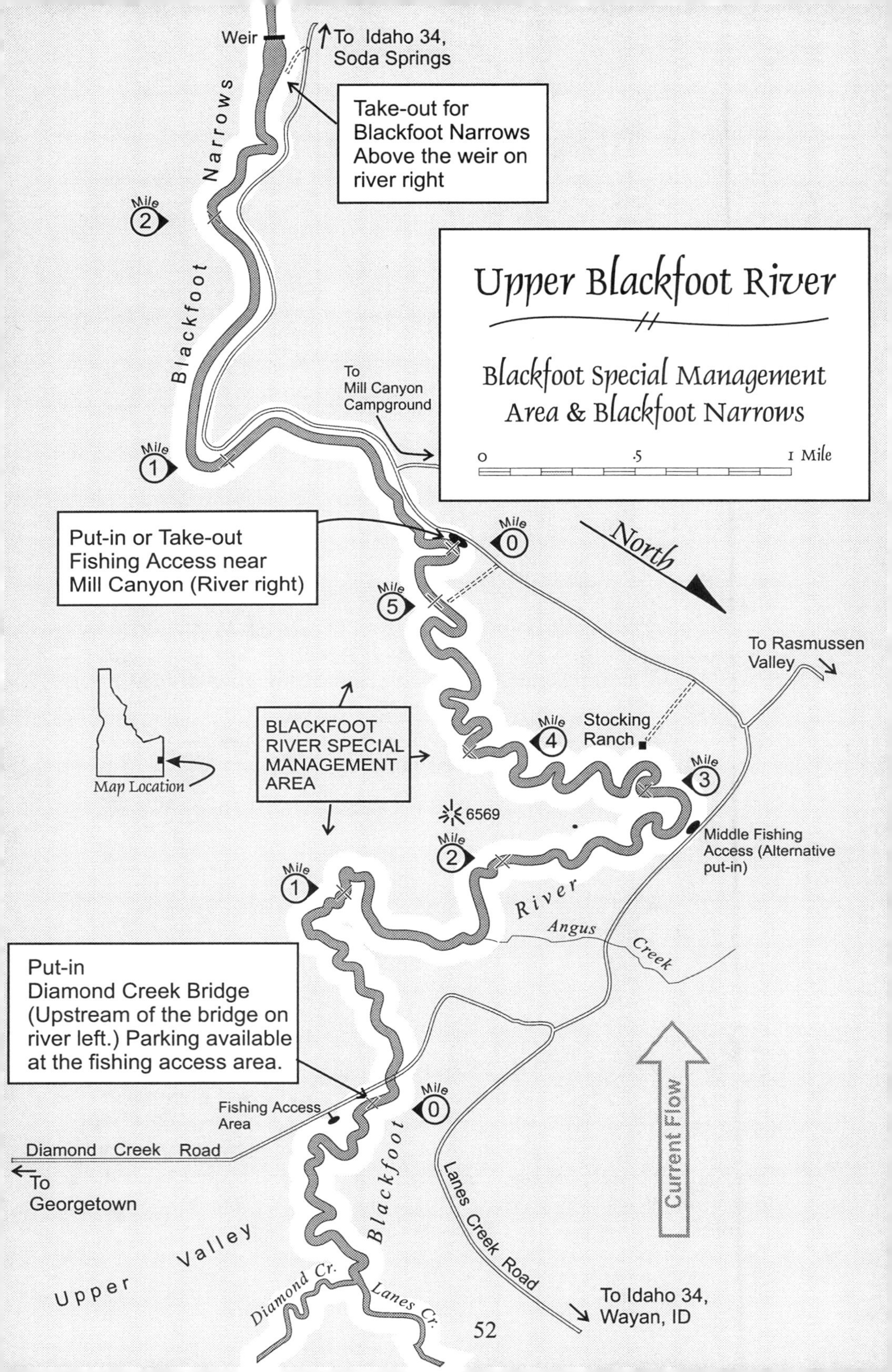
Upper Blackfoot River
Blackfoot Special Management Area & Blackfoot Narrows
0
.5
1 Mile
Weir
To Idaho 34, Soda Springs
Take-out for Blackfoot Narrows Above the weir on river right
Blackfoot Narrows
Mile 2
Mile 1
To Mill Canyon Campground
Put-in or Take-out Fishing Access near Mill Canyon (River right)
Mile 0
North
Mile 5
To Rasmussen Valley
Stocking Ranch
Mile 4
Mile 3
BLACKFOOT RIVER SPECIAL MANAGEMENT AREA
Map Location
6569
Middle Fishing Access (Alternative put-in)
Mile 2
Mile 1
River
Angus Creek
Put-in
Diamond Creek Bridge
(Upstream of the bridge on river left.) Parking available at the fishing access area.
Fishing Access Area
Mile 0
Diamond Creek Road
To Georgetown
Blackfoot
Current Flow
Lanes Creek Road
Upper Valley
Diamond Cr.
Lanes Cr.
To Idaho 34, Wayan, ID

Getting to the Put-in. Diamond Creek Bridge. From the take-out, continue driving to the north and then east on the main gravel road. You'll come to a "Y" in the road. Take the right branch, leading towards Diamond Creek. Just slightly over 3 miles from the take-out, you'll come to a bridge over the river. The easiest place to put in is 100 feet past the bridge where the road comes very close to the river. You can unload your boat here and lift it over the wood fence. After unloading, park your car in the fishing access parking lot down the road a couple hundred feet.

Alternative Put-in: Middle Fishing Access. If you want a very easy and short float (class I, 1.1) which is suitable for families, you may want to run the second half of this segment. To do so the put-in is at the Middle Fishing Access parking area, located 1.5 miles from the take-out. One warning. This put-in involves some work. You'll have to carry your boat about 300 feet down a hill to the river.

The Trip. From the Diamond Creek Bridge, the river winds away from the road and it is peaceful and relaxed. At first, the calm is only occasionally broken by mini-rapids. Some of the rapids have boulders above the surface of the water and you'll need to weave you're way through them. But the current is not forceful and as long as you have basic maneuvering techniques, you'll be fine.

If you want to avoid all swift water, put-in at the mid point. It does, however, require a 300-foot carry down a hill to the river's edge. You will encounter gentle current flowing past several boulders at a fishing access point, .4 mile above the take-out. But the water is slow enough that you can walk your boat along either side of the river if you feel uncomfortable.

Be sure you've memorized the take-out location. It is quite brushy in the area and it is possible to float by and miss it. You won't go too far, however, since the river and road come very close together not far below.

Shuttle. 3.2 miles, all gravel. Bike shuttle is on rural gravel roads. Beware that people traveling these roads tend to drive fast and kick up a lot of dust. You might want goggles (no kidding!).

Craft. Canoes and kayaks are the most ideal, but mini-cats and small inflatables can also float it. It's a bit shallow for drift boats.

Cutthroat trout: a magnificent fish and a pure joy to catch. This beauty was caught and released on the upper Blackfoot River in the Idaho Fish and Game's Special Management Area.

Mileage Chart

0	Put-in. Just above Diamond Creek Bridge on river left.
1.7	Mouth of Angus Creek (right).
2.8	Alternative put-in. Middle Fishing Access (right).
3.2	Stocking Ranch Buildings (right).
4.9	Fishing access, boulders in river.
5.3	Take-out. Fishing access (right).

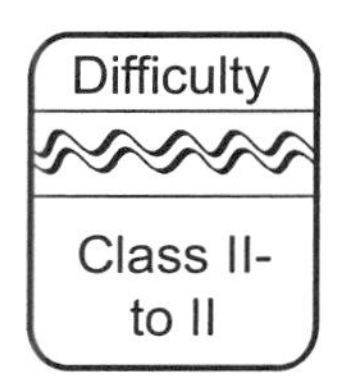

Blackfoot River

Blackfoot Narrows
(Map on page 52)

THE BLACKFOOT RIVER FLOWS from open marsh and grass lands near its source into the Blackfoot Narrows, an unpretentiously small canyon with tree covered slopes. This run is a very short and shallow class II run in low water conditions.

Canoeists, kayakers and boaters in small inflatables who are looking for an easy whitewater stretch will enjoy this. By mid summer, it's shallow enough that you can get out of your boat and wade most parts of the river. This section goes by fast and you may want to run it a couple of times or add a few miles to it by floating the upper part of the river through the Special Management Area.

Basic Stats

Difficulty: Class II- to II (in low water).

Season: Mid summer to early August. Not recommended during high water in late spring and early summer.

Distance/Time: 2.4 miles / 1 hour.

Tucked away in a scenic corner of Southeast Idaho, the Blackfoot Narrows is a fun and unpretentious class II run.

Getting to the Take-out. The Upper Blackfoot Weir. Start at Soda Springs and drive 12 miles north on Idaho 34 until coming to Blackfoot River Road (marked with a sign). Turn right. At 9.2 miles from the highway, the road Y's. Take the left branch, staying on Blackfoot River Road. About 1 mile past the "Y" you'll come to the Caribou National Forest Boundary, and .1 mile beyond the boundary, turn to the right on a dirt road which leads down to a small reservoir that forms behind a weir used to divert water for irrigation purposes.

Getting to the Put-in. Fishing access near Mill Canyon. From the take-out continue driving to the east on the Blackfoot River Road. The river is close to the road and you can scout it as you drive. At 2.3 miles from the take-out, a short dirt road leads off to the right to the river. This is the put-in. (It's the same as the take-out for the previous stretch through the Blackfoot Special Management Area).

The Trip. This stretch can easily be scouted since the road is right next to it. The rapids which are sprinkled from one end to the other have some rock dodging and some eddies to catch. It's boney, and you may have to get out and drag your boat in a spot or two. The end is signaled by the small reservoir that forms behind the Upper Blackfoot Weir. The take-out is on river right.

Shuttle. 2.3 miles. Gravel road. Easy bike shuttle but be prepared for plumes of dust as vehicles speed by.

Craft. Canoes, kayaks, small inflatables.

On the way to the Blackfoot Narrows, the kind of country that can get into the blood: wheat fields blending into mountains.

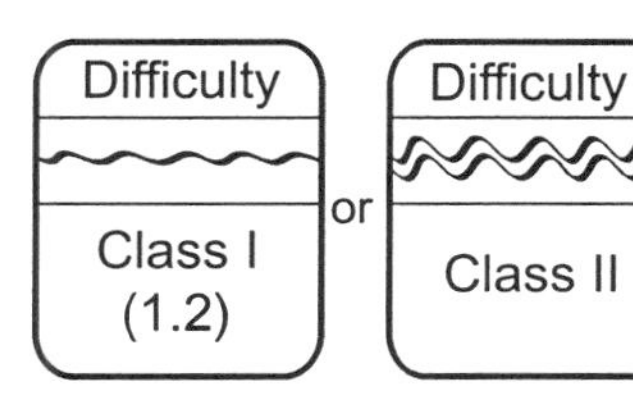

Blackfoot River

Blackfoot River Canyon
(Below Blackfoot Dam)

THE BLACKFOOT RIVER CANYON below Blackfoot Dam is one of those hidden Idaho treasures. Even the vibrant river running community from eastern Idaho doesn't visit it very often—and it's right in their backyard. But what a special and diverse place it is to explore.

Of the three river segments described here, the easiest is a class I (1.2) stretch which starts at Corral Creek and ends at Sagehen Campground. The rest of the segments are in the class II range. (A fourth class III section is also briefly described). All are runnable in open canoes—or kayaks, inflatables and drift boats. The BLM has several primitive campgrounds along the river which, in addition to providing places to picnic and camp, serve as put-in or take-out locations for a variety of trip options.

This is a desert canyon and trees are rare, but surprisingly, there are a few patches of conifers on some of the cooler north facing slopes. The river has some good fishing, but it's also an extraordinary place to watch for birds, particularly birds of prey. In fact, we saw so many hawks, eagles (and a falcon) that this may well be southeast Idaho's birds of prey stretch.

How to Get to the Blackfoot Canyon Area. The roads across the high, hilly country on the way to Blackfoot Canyon can get confusing and more than one way of getting there exists. The one described here is probably the shortest way of reaching it from Interstate 15. Keep an eye on your odometer. Desert roads crisscross this area, and often directional signs are missing.

To get started, take the Fort Hall Exit (exit #80) off Interstate 15. Instead of going to Fort Hall, go the opposite direction towards the east. Check your odometer at the exit. Initially this secondary road heading out across the Fort Hall Reservation is paved, but eventually, it turns to dirt. At 14.5 miles from I-15 you'll cross a railroad track. Take a right here. (If the sign on this road is still here, it will say "Blackfoot Reservoir").

At 16.1 miles from I-15, you'll come to a "Y." Take the left branch. (Again, if the sign's still there, it will indicate Blackfoot Reservoir). Check your odometer. At 8.8 miles past the "Y", you'll reach the Portneuf River Crossroads. The crossroads is located just after crossing a small stream which is the headwaters of the Portneuf River.

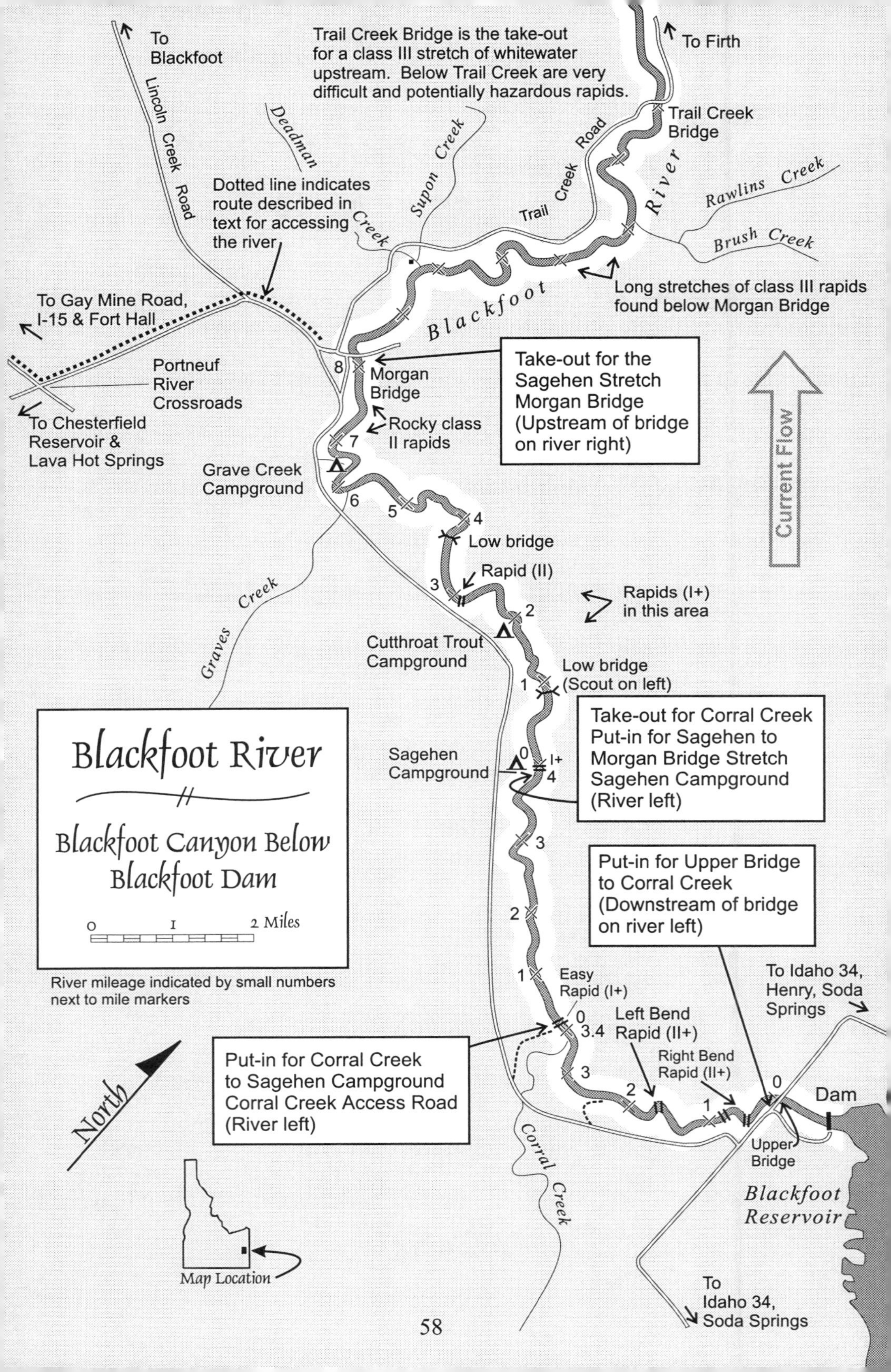

Blackfoot River
Blackfoot Canyon Below Blackfoot Dam
0 1 2 Miles
River mileage indicated by small numbers next to mile markers
North
Map Location
To Blackfoot
Lincoln Creek Road
Deadman Creek
Supon Creek
Trail Creek Bridge is the take-out for a class III stretch of whitewater upstream. Below Trail Creek are very difficult and potentially hazardous rapids.
To Firth
Trail Creek Bridge
Trail Creek Road
Rawlins Creek
Brush Creek
Blackfoot River
Dotted line indicates route described in text for accessing the river
Long stretches of class III rapids found below Morgan Bridge
To Gay Mine Road, I-15 & Fort Hall
Portneuf River Crossroads
To Chesterfield Reservoir & Lava Hot Springs
Morgan Bridge
Take-out for the Sagehen Stretch Morgan Bridge (Upstream of bridge on river right)
Current Flow
Rocky class II rapids
Grave Creek Campground
Low bridge
Rapid (II)
Rapids (I+) in this area
Graves Creek
Cutthroat Trout Campground
Low bridge (Scout on left)
Take-out for Corral Creek Put-in for Sagehen to Morgan Bridge Stretch Sagehen Campground (River left)
Sagehen Campground
I+
Put-in for Upper Bridge to Corral Creek (Downstream of bridge on river left)
Easy Rapid (I+)
To Idaho 34, Henry, Soda Springs
Left Bend Rapid (II+)
Right Bend Rapid (II+)
Dam
Put-in for Corral Creek to Sagehen Campground Corral Creek Access Road (River left)
Upper Bridge
Corral Creek
Blackfoot Reservoir
To Idaho 34, Soda Springs

Take a left at the crossroads. At 2.2 miles from the crossroads you'll reach another road junction. Take a right here.

Drive one more mile and you'll reach another "Y". The left branch of the "Y" goes to Morgan Bridge on the Blackfoot River, while the right goes towards the Blackfoot Reservoir. Along the branch of the road heading to the reservoir are the BLM campgrounds of Grave Creek, Cutthroat Trout and Sagehen, all of which provide access to the river trips described on the next few pages.

Blackfoot Dam (Upper Bridge) to Corral Creek

Basic Stats (Dam to Corral Creek)

Difficulty: Class II+ in low water, perhaps III- in higher water. (Rated at 700 cfs).

Levels/Season: Best flows are in the low to medium range, below 900 cfs. Currently, flow information is not available on the Internet, but can be obtained by calling the Blackfoot Water Users at 208-238-0586. Depending on the year, the river is runnable from spring to late summer.

Distance/Time: 3.4 miles / 1 hour in medium water. Note: most boaters will probably want to extend this run down to Sagehen Campground (7.4 miles) or Morgan Bridge (15.6 miles).

Getting to the Take-out. Corral Creek. Note that Corral Creek is four-wheel drive access. Boaters with a two-wheel vehicle will want to take out at Sagehen Campground (described on the next page). To get to the general vicinity, see "How to Get to the Blackfoot Canyon Area" on page 57.

As you drive towards Blackfoot Reservoir, you'll pass by the turn-offs to Grave Creek, Cutthroat Trout and Sagehen Campgrounds. Check your odometer at Sagehen. At 4 miles past Sagehen, a road turns off to the left and leads towards the river. Turn here and drive 1 mile to the river. The last .2 mile is very steep and requires a four-wheel drive.

Getting to the Put-in. Upper Bridge below Blackfoot Dam. From Corral Creek continue towards the reservoir for 3 miles until coming to a "T" in the road. Take a left and drive a short distance down to a bridge over the river. The put-in is on the downstream side of the bridge on river left.

The Trip. Dam to Corral Creek. When compared to the other two segments of the river downstream from here, this section of the river is the most difficult, though rafters and kayakers with moderate experience won't find it too bad. Canoeists, however, should have put in an apprenticeship on easier whitewater before tackling this one.

It has two class II+ rapids in medium flows. The first is the longest, and it starts on a right bend, .6 mile from the start. The second is found about a mile farther and is a little shorter. Both can be scouted, if desired.

The rest of the river to Corral Creek, which is the first major drainage coming in from the left, is class I+ (1.4). The take-out is just below the mouth of Corral Creek on the left. This is a nice, lively stretch of water if your time is limited. Many paddlers, however, will want to put in a few more miles before calling it a day, and several other take-out places are available downstream.

Shuttle. 5 miles, all dirt. Easy bike shuttle.

Craft. Canoes, kayaks, inflatables, drift boats.

Mileage Chart
Dam to Corral Creek

Mile	Description
0	Put-in. Upper Bridge (.6 mile below the Blackfoot Reservoir Dam). Launch boats downstream of bridge on river left.
.6	Right bend and rapid: class II+ (or III- in moderately high water).
1.8	Left bend and rapid (class II+).
2.5	Four-wheel drive road accesses river on the left shore.
3.4	Mouth of Corral Creek (left).
3.45	Take-out. Corral Creek Road (left).

Corral Creek to Sagehen Campground

Basic Stats (Corral Creek to Sagehen)

Difficulty: Class I (1.2).

Levels: Same as the Dam to Corral Creek Stretch.

Distance/Time: 4 miles / 1-2 hours in medium water.

Getting to the Take-out. Sagehen Campground. To get to the general vicinity, see "How to Get to the Blackfoot Canyon Area" on page 57. Sagehen is one of the campgrounds located between Morgan Bridge and the Blackfoot Reservoir. It's about 5 miles to the west of Graves Creek Campground.

Getting to the Put-in. Corral Creek. For a description on how to reach Corral Creek, see the directions to the take-out for the Dam to Corral segment on page 59. Note that a four-wheel drive is needed on the last .2 mile of Corral Creek access. If need be, boaters without four-wheel drive vehicles could walk their boats down the last steep portion of the road. A small class I+ rapid is located on the river near the road access, but those who want to avoid the rapid can put in just below the swift water.

The Trip. Corral Creek to Sagehen Campground. This is the easiest segment of river in the Blackfoot Canyon, and it's a great stretch for wildlife. On our trip, we saw nesting bald eagles and an array of hawks. The ending point at Sagehen Campground is signaled by a picnic table on the left. A small class I+ (1.3) rapid is found at Sagehen, but it can be avoided by taking out just above it.

Shuttle. 6 miles, all dirt. Easy bike shuttle.

Craft. Canoes, kayaks, inflatables, drift boats.

Mileage Chart
Corral Creek to Sagehen Campground

Mile	
0	Put-in. Corral Creek. River left.
1.2	Primitive roads reach the river on the right and left.
2.9	Right-hand bend and cliff on river left.
4	Take-out. Sagehen Campground (left).

Sagehen Campground to Morgan Bridge

Basic Stats (Sagehen to Morgan Bridge)

Difficulty: Class II. Mostly class I and I+, interspersed with class II. The last part has some rocky class II leading into Morgan Bridge.

Levels: Same comments as the Dam to Corral Stretch.

Distance/Time: 8.2 miles / 4-5 hours.

Getting to the Take-out. Morgan Bridge. To get to Morgan Bridge, follow the directions in "How to Get to the Blackfoot Canyon Area," found on page 57. The Morgan bridge take-out is upstream of the bridge on river right.

Getting to the Put-in. Sagehen Campground. See directions to the take-out for the Corral Creek to Sagehen Campground segment on page 61.

The Trip. Sagehen Campground to Morgan Bridge. At the start of the trip, the river has one class I+ (1.3) rapid, and then it plods along. At .8 mile from the start, you'll come to a low bridge over the river. We were able to float our canoe under it at 700 cfs, but you may want to stop on the left and take a look. Drift boaters should definitely scout it first.

Beyond the bridge for the next mile, the river livens up with some class I+ (1.3 to 1.4) leading up to Cutthroat Campground (2.1 miles from the start). More lively water (class I+ and a little II- to II) is found below Cutthroat. It's all readable from the river and doesn't require scouting. Another bridge is encountered at the 3.9-mile point. At the medium level of 700 cfs we were able to pass under in our canoe, but you may wish to take a quick look.

The most spirited stretch of the entire segment is found below Graves Creek (6.5 miles from the start). The river is very rocky and takes some maneuvering skills to get through without nicking any rocks. The take-out is just above Morgan Bridge. At certain levels, a nice surfing wave forms under the bridge.

Note that the segment of river below Morgan Bridge gets into some long and involved class III water. Be sure that you are well prepared before tackling it.

Shuttle. 9 miles, all dirt. Bike shuttle is possible, but give yourself plenty of time.

Craft. Canoes, kayaks, inflatables, drift boats. Drift boats may need to be portaged at the two low bridges.

Mileage Chart
Sagehen Campground to Morgan Bridge

0	Put-in. Sagehen Campground (river left).
.9	Low bridge. Scout on left.
2.1	Cutthroat Trout Campground (left).
3	Right bend. Class I+ and II rapids.
3.5	Short class II drop. Surfing found here.
3.9	Low bridge.
5.9	Mouth of Grave Creek (left).
6.5	Grave Creek Campground (left). Rocky class II water found below campground.
8.2	Take-out. Morgan Bridge. Upstream of bridge on river right. Note: This is the last take-out before a serious class III stretch below.

Blackfoot River Canyon below the Blackfoot dam.

Blackfoot Canyon Below Morgan Bridge. The beautiful 7-mile canyon on the Blackfoot River between Morgan Bridge and Trail Creek Bridge contains a challenging and invigorating stretch of whitewater, but it's not something to take lightly. Many people have gotten in over their heads on this stretch.

The most difficult part of it is a 2-mile stretch of solid class III rapids which really gets going when the river collides against a large boulder, known as House Rock. There are plenty more large pinball boulders below. If a boater broaches or flips here, they're in for a long, long rocky swim. This stretch can be run in an open canoe, but the canoe should be of a whitewater design and outfitted with large air bags.

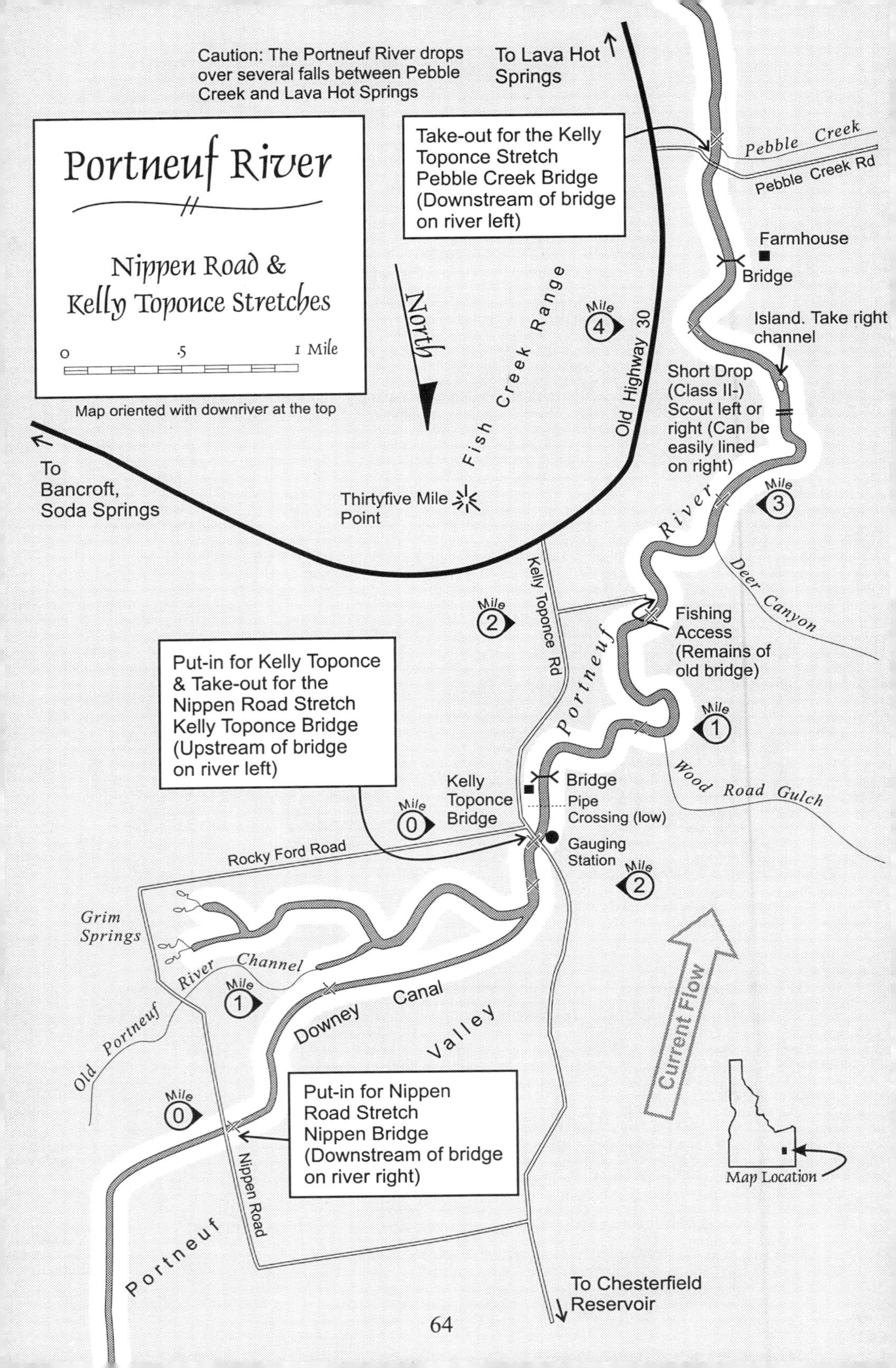
Portneuf River
Nippen Road & Kelly Toponce Stretches
0 .5 1 Mile
Map oriented with downriver at the top
Caution: The Portneuf River drops over several falls between Pebble Creek and Lava Hot Springs
To Lava Hot Springs
Take-out for the Kelly Toponce Stretch Pebble Creek Bridge (Downstream of bridge on river left)
Pebble Creek
Pebble Creek Rd
Farmhouse
Bridge
North
Fish Creek Range
Old Highway 30
Mile 4
Island. Take right channel
Short Drop (Class II-) Scout left or right (Can be easily lined on right)
Mile 3
To Bancroft, Soda Springs
Thirtyfive Mile Point
River
Deer Canyon
Kelly Toponce Rd
Mile 2
Fishing Access (Remains of old bridge)
Portneuf
Mile 1
Put-in for Kelly Toponce & Take-out for the Nippen Road Stretch Kelly Toponce Bridge (Upstream of bridge on river left)
Wood Road Gulch
Kelly Toponce Bridge
Bridge
Pipe Crossing (low)
Mile 0
Gauging Station
Rocky Ford Road
Mile 2
Grim Springs
River Channel
Mile 1
Downey Canal
Valley
Current Flow
Old Portneuf
Mile 0
Put-in for Nippen Road Stretch Nippen Bridge (Downstream of bridge on river right)
Nippen Road
Map Location
Portneuf
To Chesterfield Reservoir

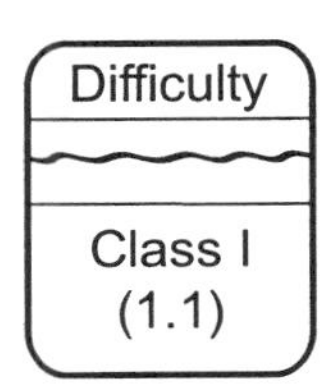

Portneuf River

Upper Portneuf
(Nippen Road and Kelly Toponce Stretches)

THE PORTNEUF RIVER below Chesterfield Reservoir, north of Lava Hot Springs, flows through a high agricultural valley with the peaks of the Portneuf Range on one side and the rolling sage-covered Chesterfield hills on the other. The river here almost disappears when much of its water is diverted into the Downey Canal. It reappears, however, with renewed vigor with the help of large springs close to the Kelly Toponce bridge.

Two runs on the upper Portneuf are described here. The first (from Nippen Road to Kelly Toponce Bridge) actually starts in the Downey Canal. Although running a canal doesn't sound all that enticing, it is, nevertheless, one of the easiest runs (class I, 1.1) available on the entire Portneuf River. It's also a reasonably good stretch of water to fish and you can make an interesting side trip, paddling up the old Portneuf river channel into the huge Grim Springs which replenishes the river with cool, clear water.

The second run, below Kelly Toponce Bridge, is one of our favorites on the Portneuf. At this point, the river is running free in its own channel. Most of this segment is class I+ (1.3-1.4) with one very short rapid (class II-) which can be easily portaged. The water quality is good—and it's a wonderful stretch for fly fishing.

There's a reason for the good fishing. The Idaho Fish and Game Department along with property owners, other agencies and scores of volunteers known as the Friends of the Portneuf have worked together to improve the riparian habitat of the river. They've done a terrific job and our hats are off to them.

Nippen Road to Kelly Toponce Bridge

Basic Stats (Nippen Road to Kelly Toponce Bridge)

Difficulty: Class I (1.1). Flat, straight and easy-going.

Season: Summer. Since flow information is not easily obtained for this part of the Portneuf, take a look at the river from the put-in and take-out bridges. If there's enough water to float a boat at both bridges, then you'll be able to get down the river. If the water appears to be high and swift at one of the bridges, then wait a couple of weeks before running it.

Distance/Time: 2.2 miles / 1-2 hours.

Getting to the Take-out. Kelly Toponce Bridge. From Lava Hot Springs, start driving on US 30 toward Soda Springs (east). On the east edge of Lava, look for a sign indicating Old Highway 30 and Bancroft. Turn left and follow the old highway for about 11 miles from Lava until coming to Kelly Toponce Road. Turn left and drive 1.5 miles to the bridge. The take-out is upstream of the bridge on river left.

Getting to the Put-in. From Kelly Toponce Bridge (described above) take the Rocky Ford Road which leads east from the bridge. Stay on the main road as it bends around to the north. At 2.9 miles from the Kelly Toponce Bridge, you'll reach a bridge over the Downey Canal. This is the Nippen Road put-in.

Note that a no trespassing sign may be posted at the Nippen Road bridge. The owners who live in the house adjacent to the bridge (on river right) do not mind boaters launching there, but as a courtesy, you should stop at the house and ask permission.

The Trip. Nippen Road to Kelly Toponce Bridge. The water moves slowly on this stretch. It's all very straight and you don't have to worry about coming around any blind corners. We didn't encounter any fences, but did come upon one bridge. The bridge consists of two large culverts. The culvert on river left is high enough to float a canoe or small raft under.

Near the end of the trip, the old stream bed of the Portneuf enters. You may wish to take a side trip up the original river channel toward Grim Springs which provides a considerable amount of water to the river. The take-out is just before the bridge on the left.

Shuttle. 2.9 miles. Easy bike shuttle on paved rural roads.

Craft. Canoes, kayaks and small inflatables.

Kelly Toponce Bridge to Pebble Bridge

Basic Stats (Kelly Toponce to Pebble)

Difficulty: Class I+ (1.3 to 1.4) with one very short class II- rapid. Some swift water, bends, and occasional rocks. The class II- rapid is very short (about 30 feet long) and shallow. It can be lined or portaged if desired.

Season: Summer & fall. Same comments as Nippen Road Stretch.

Distance/Time: 4.9 miles / 2-3 hours.

Obstacles: We encountered two fences, but both had been strung high enough that we were able to float under.

Getting to the Take-out. Pebble Creek Bridge. From Lava Hot Springs, take Old Highway 30 towards Bancroft. Pebble Creek Road is marked with a sign, 9 miles from Lava. Turn left and drive a short distance until reaching the bridge over the Portneuf. The take-out is on the downstream side of the bridge on river left. You'll have to hump your boat over a small retaining wall and up a short hill, about 60 feet in all.

Getting to the Put-in. Kelly Toponce Bridge. See directions to the take-out for the Nippen Road to Kelly Toponce Bridge on the previous page.

The Trip. Kelly Toponce Bridge to Pebble Bridge. Shortly after getting underway, you'll approach a farm house and some out buildings on the left. Just before the out buildings, a pipe crosses the river. Small craft such as canoes, kayaks and small inflatables will be able to float under. A short distance from the pipe, next to the farm house is a bridge which also is high enough to pass under. We encountered two fences—located in areas where the current was slow—farther down the river which were strung high enough not to impede boats.

The rustic, wooden fence which you'll see along the river for a good portion of the trip is there because of the efforts of volunteers, private land owners and a variety of agencies who worked together to improve the health of the upper Portneuf. Cattle are kept out of the river except in a few access points for watering. As a result bank erosion has slowed, streamside vegetation is returning and the fishing has improved.

At 3.5 miles from the start, you'll come to a very short rapid (class II-). In normal water flows, it's fairly shallow and you could almost walk down it. We found it a quick and easy run in our canoe. Since it is a shallow rapid, you should scout it first. The easiest side to scout is on the left, but it can be scouted and lined or portaged, if desired, on the right.

Near the end, you'll pass under another bridge which accesses a farm house. The bridge is high enough to float under. Just before the bridge, a tree overhangs a good part of the river, but the current is slow and it is an easy paddle around the far side of it.

The scenery visible from the river includes the Portneuf Range to your right (west). The flat-topped mountain in the distance to the southwest is Haystack Mountain, a part of the Portneuf Range. Dominating the other (east) side of the river is the rocky-topped Thirtyfive Mile Point.

Shuttle. 4 miles, all paved. Easy bike shuttle on paved secondary roads.

Craft. Canoes, kayaks and small inflatables. Drift boats are not recommended because of the low pipe across the river, fences and poor take-out.

Mileage Chart
Kelly Toponce to Pebble

0	Put-in. Kelly Toponce Bridge (upstream of the bridge on river left).
.1	Pipeline crossing.
.2	Farmhouse and bridge.
1.3	Fence crosses river.
2.2	Concrete abutments of an old bridge. Fishing access point.
3.5	Class II- rapid. (Can be lined or portaged on right.)
3.6	Island. Take right channel. Left channel has a fence.
4.3	Farmhouse bridge.
4.9	Take-out. Pebble Creek Bridge (downstream of bridge on river left).

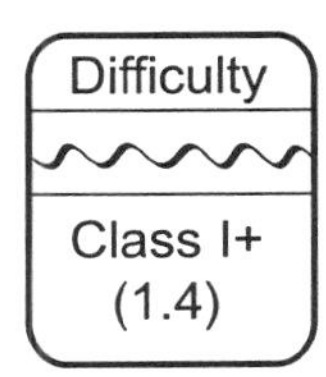

Portneuf River

Lower Lava Run
and Topaz Stretch

THE LOWER LAVA RUN, the first of two river segments starting at Lava Hot Springs, is 2 miles of peppy class I+ (1.4) water and is one of Southeast Idaho's best practice stretches. Starting in the town of Lava Hot Springs, it's the perfect run if you want to dabble in a little whitewater, but don't want to get in too deep.

Beginning canoeists and kayakers will particularly enjoy it. In fact, the Idaho State University Outdoor Program has used it for years as the main river outing for their beginning kayaking class. You can practice turning in and out of eddies and maneuver through small rapids.

The second stretch, the Topaz segment, begins where the first one ends, and is more advanced. It consists of a series of small ledge drops rated class II+. Wait until you're comfortable with your canoeing or kayaking skills before running this stretch. All the ledge drops can be easily scouted—and they should be. The drops are shallow and it is difficult to tell where the best run is from your boat unless you get out and look from the shore.

Lower Lava Run (From Lava Hot Springs to US 30 Bridge)

Basic Stats (Lower Lava Run)

Difficulty: Class I+ (1.4) small rapids. Good stretch to learn basic whitewater techniques in a canoe or kayak.

Levels/Season: Runnable most of the year except high water. Average flows (measured at the Topaz gauge) are between 100-300 cfs which are good levels to run the river. High water usually comes in mid May. We suggest staying off the river above 500 cfs.

Distance/Time: 2 miles / 1 hour.

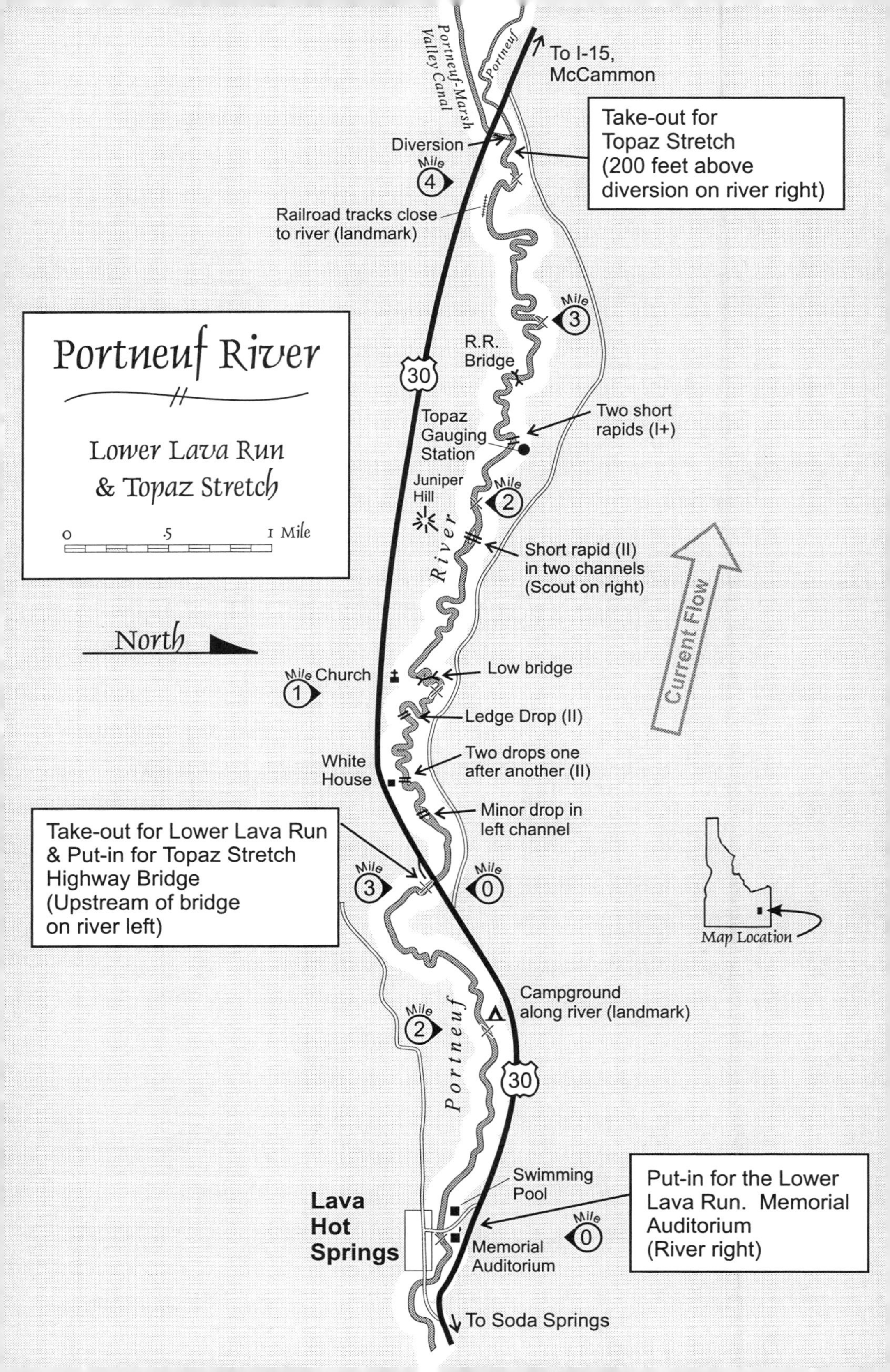
Portneuf River
Lower Lava Run & Topaz Stretch
0 .5 1 Mile
North
Current Flow
Map Location
To I-15, McCammon
Portneuf
Portneuf-Marsh Valley Canal
Take-out for Topaz Stretch (200 feet above diversion on river right)
Diversion
Mile 4
Railroad tracks close to river (landmark)
Mile 3
R.R. Bridge
30
Topaz Gauging Station
Two short rapids (I+)
Juniper Hill
Mile 2
River
Short rapid (II) in two channels (Scout on right)
Mile 1
Church
Low bridge
Ledge Drop (II)
White House
Two drops one after another (II)
Minor drop in left channel
Take-out for Lower Lava Run & Put-in for Topaz Stretch Highway Bridge (Upstream of bridge on river left)
Mile 3
Mile 0
Campground along river (landmark)
Mile 2
Portneuf
30
Swimming Pool
Lava Hot Springs
Put-in for the Lower Lava Run. Memorial Auditorium (River right)
Mile 0
Memorial Auditorium
To Soda Springs

Getting to the Take-out. First Highway Bridge west of Lava. The first highway bridge is on US 30, 1.7 miles west of the turn-off to Lava near the big swimming pool. This is a primitive take-out. If you are driving from Lava toward Interstate 15, park on the other side of the bridge on the left. A small road goes towards the river by the bridge. You can't get turned around on this road, so it's best to park just off the highway.

The take-out is upstream of the bridge on river left. The bank, at the take-out, is rocky and steep. Plus, there's a fence that you'll have to hoist your boat over, but fortunately, some kind soul has constructed a ladder over the fence to make getting in and out a little easier.

Getting to the Put-in. Community Memorial Auditorium and park. Enter at Lava's west entrance by the big swimming pool which is easily seen from the highway. Park in the auditorium parking lot and carry your boat down to the river. Put in anywhere on the grassy stretch alongside the river. This is the end of a popular inner tube run and if it's a typical summer day you'll see lots of people pulling their inner tubes out of the water here.

The Trip. Lower Lava Run. At the beginning of the run, the river's banks are overhung with trees and brush. While moving down the river, you'll want to stay to the inside of bends and avoid the stronger current on the outside where boaters usually run into problems and get tangled up with brush. If you want to avoid much of this part of the river, follow the path along the north side of the river, carrying your boat downriver to the second bridge. Brush is still encountered here, but there's less of it and the river soon leaves the canopy of trees and breaks into the open.

Once on the outskirts of Lava, the river is a delight: here and there are boulders to paddle around, small rapids to run and places to practice eddy turns. The water quality is surprisingly good, and even though the highway is close, it isn't noticeable until reaching the bridge at the end. When you're finished boating, be sure to stop and have a soak at Lava's world famous hot springs.

Shuttle. 2 miles, paved. Easy bike shuttle, but use caution, the highway is very busy.

Craft. Canoes, kayaks, small inflatables.

Topaz Stretch (First Highway Bridge to Second Highway Bridge)

Basic Stats (Topaz Stretch)

Difficulty: Class II+ (rated at 220 cfs). The rapids are a series of short ledge drops.

Levels/Season: Same comments as the Lower Lava Run.

Distance/Time: 4.3 miles / 2.5 to 3 hours.

Getting to the Take-out. Second highway bridge west of Lava. The second bridge is located 5.5 miles west of Lava on US 30 or 6.2 miles east of the junction of I-15 and US 30. If you are driving from Lava toward Interstate 15, turn to the right (north) on a paved road on the far (west) side of the bridge. Immediately after you turn off, a dirt road on the right goes to a place to park under the highway bridge. The actual take-out, however, is upstream.

Be sure to check things out carefully before you do the shuttle. To get to the take-out, walk down the paved secondary road (away from the highway) a couple hundred yards to where the river comes close to the road. This is the take-out. There's no pull-off or ramp here. It's just some tall grass along the river bank. Scout the river below the take-out so you understand what happens here.

You'll find that just below the take-out, most of the Portneuf is diverted off into a large canal (Portneuf-Marsh Valley Canal). The old river channel actually goes over a waterfall which is hidden in the trees and brush and not visible from the road. The water just above the diversion is slow moving and there's no problem stopping a boat, but you want to make sure you've memorized the take-out and don't end up going beyond it.

Getting to the Put-in. First highway bridge west of Lava. See directions for the take-out on the Lower Lava Run on the previous page.

The Trip. Topaz Stretch (first to second highway bridge). This stretch is representative of the Portneuf River: slow water interrupted by quick drops over a resistant lava bed. The key to this stretch is to scout. Each time you approach a drop, pull off to the side and take a look at it. Most of the drops are very shallow with right and wrong ways of running them. The location of each drop is indicated on the mileage chart on the next page.

The river on this stretch flows through open pasture. Some brush grows alongside, but the banks are otherwise grassy. By the way, Topaz, the name of this stretch, comes from the name of a Mormon settlement along the river which had a post office from 1911 to 1912.

Shuttle. 5 miles on the secondary road to the north of the river. The paved secondary road which parallels the river on its north side is the best route for bike shuttling.

Craft. Canoes and kayaks. It can be run in a small inflatable, but the ledge drops are scratchy and you'll want an inflatable floor in your boat.

Mileage Chart
Topaz Stretch

0	Put-in. First highway bridge west of Lava (upstream of bridge on river left).
.4	Minor drop on left channel. Can be avoided by taking right channel.
.6	Two ledge drops one after another just past a two-story white house on the hill on river left. Scout on left.
.9	Ledge drop, just above a white church with a steeple. Scout on left.
1	Low bridge. We were able to float under it, but use caution, a cable was strung across the river underneath the bridge.
1.9	Short rapid in two channels. River is pinched between a juniper-covered hill on the left and open hillside on right. Scout on right.
2.4	Topaz Gauging Station.
2.4	Just past gauging station: two short rapids. (These are the last rapids).
2.7	Railroad bridge.
3.8	Railroad tracks are close to the river on river left.
4.3	Take-out. River right. Paved secondary road is close to right shore. *Note: Do not paddle beyond this point. A diversion dam and falls are below the take-out.*

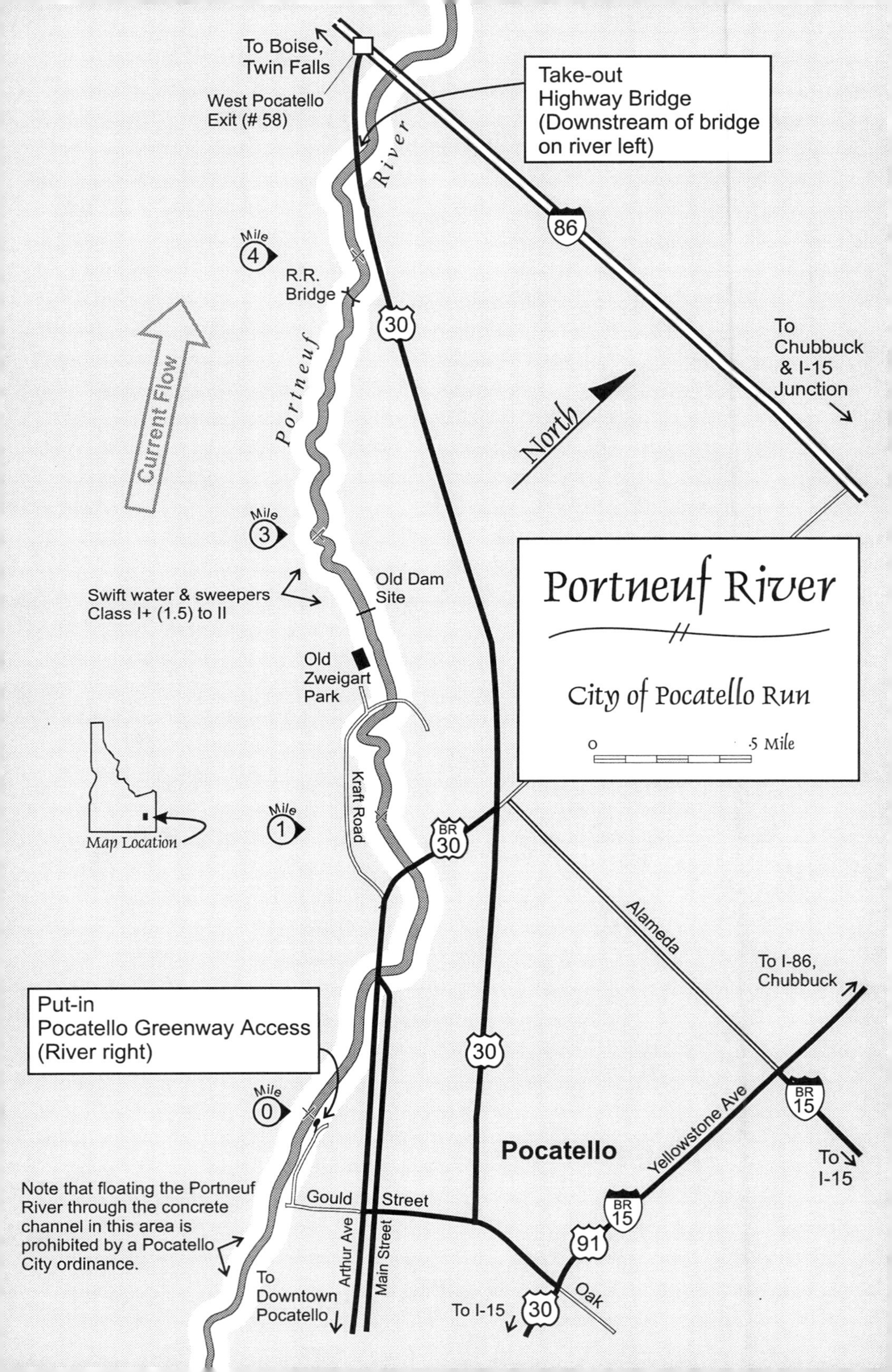

To Boise,
Twin Falls
West Pocatello
Exit (# 58)
Take-out
Highway Bridge
(Downstream of bridge
on river left)
River
86
Mile
4
R.R.
Bridge
30
To
Chubbuck
& I-15
Junction
Current Flow
Portneuf
North
Mile
3
Swift water & sweepers
Class I+ (1.5) to II
Old Dam
Site
Portneuf River
City of Pocatello Run
0
.5 Mile
Old
Zweigart
Park
Kraft Road
Map Location
Mile
1
BR
30
Alameda
To I-86,
Chubbuck
Put-in
Pocatello Greenway Access
(River right)
30
BR
15
Mile
0
Pocatello
To
I-15
Yellowstone Ave
Note that floating the Portneuf
River through the concrete
channel in this area is
prohibited by a Pocatello
City ordinance.
Gould
Street
BR
15
91
Arthur Ave
Main Street
Oak
To
Downtown
Pocatello
To I-15
30

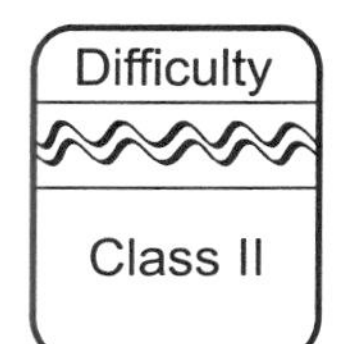

Portneuf River

City of Pocatello Run

IT USED TO BE that you simply couldn't run the Portneuf River below the town of Pocatello. But that's all changed. A dedicated group of volunteers from the Portneuf Greenway has worked over the past few years to bring new life to the river. They cut away downed trees, saw to the removal of an old dam and hauled away truckloads of trash which had accumulated for years.

Now it's a gem of a run: a shaded, hobbit-like waterway with trees arching across the river. Unfortunately, it's not a beginner's stretch. Because of fast-paced current and considerable overhanging trees and brush, it is a class II stretch. Nevertheless, when you are comfortable with your boating skills, this is a short, spirited run which offers an entirely different perspective of the Pocatello valley.

Basic Stats

Difficulty: Class II. The first half of this run to the old Zweigart Park is a class I+ (1.4) with lots of overhanging brush and trees. The rapids begin after old Zweigart Park.

Levels/Season: Generally the river has a peak in early or mid May. Wait until June when the water has dropped below 700 cfs on the Pocatello gauge before running it.

Distance/Time: 3.3 Miles / 1.5 to 2 hours.

Getting to the Take-out. Highway 30 bridge. The bridge can be approached by taking the Highway 30 exit (Exit #58) off Interstate 86 and following the highway toward Pocatello. The bridge over the Portneuf is located approximately one mile from the interstate exit. The take-out is on the downstream side of the bridge on river left.

Getting to the Put-in. From the take-out, continue following US 30 toward Pocatello. Stay on the branch of US 30 which goes toward city center (US 30 Business Route) . Watch for Gould Street and take a right. Follow Gould to the west a few blocks. Take a right at the last possible paved road leading off to the right before Gould ends. Follow this road one block past some apartments and take a short dirt road leading off to the left to a Greenway parking area along the river. The put-in is down a short hill to the river, about 50 feet from the parking area.

The Trip. The character of the river is obvious at the put-in: narrow and crowded by unruly, tree-lined banks. Every so often while floating the river, you'll get a glimpse of the city just beyond the boundaries of the river, but they are few and infrequent. Past the old Zweigart Park, a short stretch of grass on river left, the river begins to pick up.

The main action starts at the remains of an old dam just downstream of old Zweigart Park and continues for about a half mile with the river racing through trees growing right out of the river. The rapids, themselves, aren't that difficult but with trees and brush and a long stretch of fast water, class II is an appropriate rating for this segment. Broaching against a tree is a real possibility, particularly in higher flows and you really want to be sure of your ability to maneuver in tight places before tackling this stretch.

Shuttle. 4 miles, paved. For the shuttle, follow Gould Street back (east) a few blocks to its intersection with Main. Take a left on Main which turns into US 30 (Business Route). US 30 crosses the Portneuf three times. The take-out is at the third bridge. The bike shuttle follows the same route. Expect busy city streets.

Craft. Small craft, canoes, kayaks, inflatables. Drift boats also can do this run, but there are no ramps and boats have to be carried in and out of the river.

Mileage Chart

0	Put-in. Greenway Access near Gould Street. River right.
.5	Bridge.
.8	Bridge.
1.4	Bridge.
1.5	Old Zweigart Park & Packing Plant (left).
1.6	Remains of old dam. Class II water for next .4 miles.
2.9	Railroad bridge.
3.3	Take-out. Highway 30 bridge (downstream of bridge on river left).

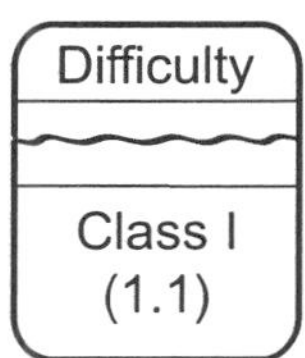

Marsh Creek

Marsh Creek Conservation Area Float
Other Marsh Creek Segments

MARSH CREEK FLOWS through a pastoral valley south of Pocatello. It is a small stream with just enough water to float in a canoe or kayak. Several short stretches can be run, but the one of most interest is along a conservation area between Robin and Goodenough Roads. It's an easy run (class I, 1.1) and an absolutely splendid bird watching trip. Of all the rivers we paddled for this book, we saw more different species of birds on this trip than any other in Idaho.

Basic Stats

Difficulty: Class I (1.1).

Season: Early to mid summer. Also see notes on water level at the end of this section.

Distance/Time: 2.3 miles / 1.5 to 2 hours.

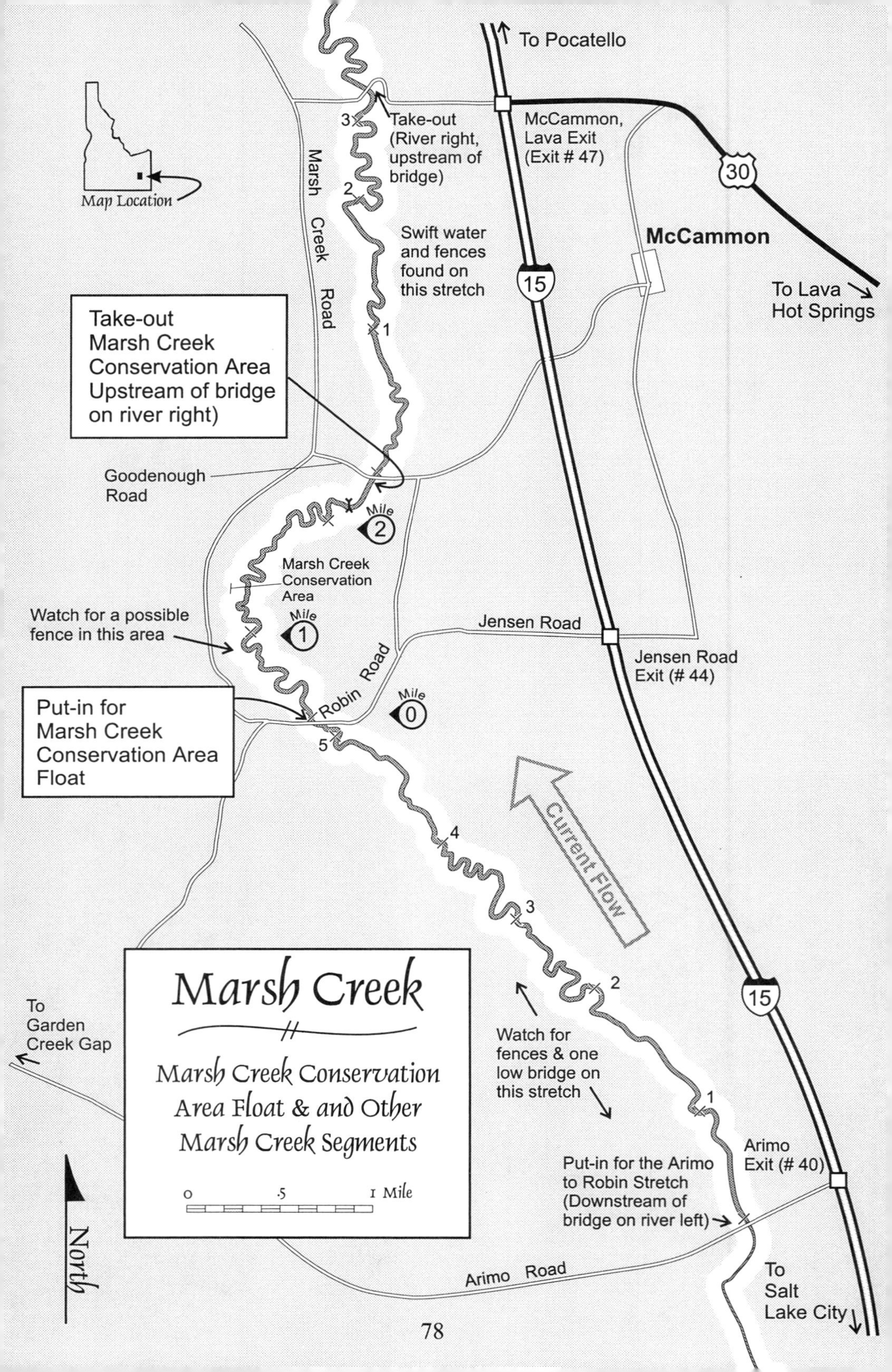

To Pocatello
McCammon, Lava Exit (Exit # 47)
30
McCammon
To Lava Hot Springs
15
Take-out (River right, upstream of bridge)
Marsh Creek Road
Swift water and fences found on this stretch
Map Location
Take-out Marsh Creek Conservation Area Upstream of bridge on river right)
Goodenough Road
Mile 2
Marsh Creek Conservation Area
Mile 1
Watch for a possible fence in this area
Jensen Road
Jensen Road Exit (# 44)
Robin Road
Mile 0
Put-in for Marsh Creek Conservation Area Float
Current Flow
Marsh Creek
Marsh Creek Conservation Area Float & and Other Marsh Creek Segments
0 .5 1 Mile
To Garden Creek Gap
Watch for fences & one low bridge on this stretch
Arimo Exit (# 40)
Put-in for the Arimo to Robin Stretch (Downstream of bridge on river left)
Arimo Road
To Salt Lake City
North

Getting to the Take-out. Goodenough Road Bridge. Take the McCammon and Lava Hot Springs Exit (Exit # 47) off of Interstate 15 and head to the west, the opposite direction from Lava Hot Springs. About a mile from the Interstate the road comes to a "T" at Marsh Creek Road. Take a left and drive 2 miles to Goodenough Road. Take a left on Goodenough Road and drive a short distance to the bridge. The take-out is on river right, upstream of the bridge.

This isn't the most luxurious of take-outs. You'll have to carry your boat about 50 feet up a hill to the road. Moreover, there isn't much of a place to pull-off the road, but park out of the way the best you can. This is a good float trip for a bike shuttle and spotting a bike makes the take-out easier.

Getting to the Put-in. Robin Road Bridge. From the take-out, drive back out to Marsh Creek Road and take a left. Go about 1.5 miles until coming to the junction with Robin Road. Take a left here and drive a short distance to the bridge. Park in the small pull-off by the bridge.

The Trip. The water on this stretch is slow and suitable for canoeists and kayakers of all abilities. Of all the segments on Marsh Creek, this one has the least obstructions in terms of fences and bridges. Along one side of the river is a conservation area, and, as we've mentioned, it is an exceptional area for birds. We encountered one fence about one third of the way down, but it was high enough that we were able to float under it. Near the end of the float is a bridge which is also high enough to float under in normal water levels, but if the water is high, you'll want to stop and check it first.

Goodenough Bridge marks the end of this trip. You *can't* float under this bridge and must take out above it. About 20 feet upstream from the bridge on the right, a clear spring enters the river. Paddle your boat into the spring. It may be a bit overgrown and weedy, but you should be able to get the nose of your boat part way into it, then drag your boat a few feet up the spring. At the end of the spring, carry or drag your boat up a faint (probably overgrown) trail that climbs up to the road. Watch out for thistles!

Shuttle. 2.5 miles, all paved. Easy bike shuttle on paved secondary road.

Craft. Canoes and kayaks including lake kayaks. Paddlers in inflatable boats will find the water very sluggish.

Water Level Information. It is difficult to obtain water flow information on Marsh Creek, but you can eye-ball the flow. If you take the Arimo Exit

(Exit 40) off Interstate 15 and drive to the west within .3 mile you'll come to Marsh Creek passing under the road in a culvert. Look on the downstream side of the culvert.

As you look at the culvert from the river, you'll see a seam of metal on its right side. If the water is 5" to 9" below the seam you'll have a good flow of water. It will be slow and easy going, but will have enough depth to float a boat. If it's above the seam, the river will be high and swift, and if lower than 1 foot below the seam, the river will be getting shallow.

Other Segments of Marsh Creek. You can run from the Arimo Road Bridge to the Robin Bridge, a 5-mile stretch of river. The water is slow and easy, but at least one fence and one low bridge must be portaged.

You can also float between Goodenough Road Bridge and the bridge to the west of Exit 47 on Interstate 15. This 3.2-mile stretch (class I+, 1.4) has swift turns and small rapids and fences. It is also shallow in spots, more so than the two previous stretches.

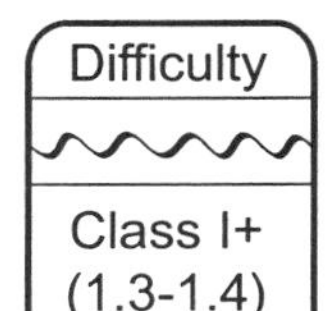

Snake River

Blackfoot to American Falls Reservoir

THE SNAKE RIVER from the town of Blackfoot downstream flows through a broad and flat fertile plain. Although, meandering its way through a major agricultural area, this segment of the Snake is a very attractive portion of the river. Surrounded by a wide riparian zone of cottonwoods and willows, the river is screened from most nearby development. It's a haven for deer, beaver, weasel, coyote and other small mammals. Moreover, you are very likely to see bald eagles which nest along the river.

Even though this stretch is rated class I+, the Snake is a big and commanding river that deserves respect. During much of the summer, strong currents flow through the brush- and tree-lined shores. We recommend that you wait and run the river in late summer or fall when water levels have dropped to below 5,000 cfs. The river is entirely different in low water: slow, friendly and much safer.

Blackfoot to Tilden Bridge Stretch

Basic Stats (Blackfoot to Tilden Bridge)

Difficulty: Class I+ (1.3-1.4) in low water.

Levels/Season: Late summer and fall. Best and safest flows are in the low range (below 5,000 cfs at the Blackfoot gauge).

Distance/Time: 12 miles / 5-6 hours.

Getting to the Take-out. Tilden Bridge. From Interstate 15, take the Fort Hall Exit (Exit # 80) and drive into Fort Hall until reaching US 91. Take a right on US 91 and follow it to the north 6 miles from Fort Hall until coming to Ferry Butte Road. Take a left on Ferry Butte and continue about 4 miles until crossing the Snake River. The take-out is a concrete ramp downstream of the bridge on river right.

Getting to the Put-in. 500 West Street. Take the Arco and US 26 exit (Exit # 91) off Interstate 15 in Blackfoot. Drive towards Arco (east) on US 26. Cross over the Snake River and take the first left on the road heading toward Rockford and Aberdeen. As you drive towards Rockford, look for 500 West, about 1.5 miles from US 26. Turn

Snake River
Blackfoot to American Falls
0 1 2 3 Miles
American Falls Reservoir
Map Location
To Aberdeen, American Falls
Take-out McTucker Boat Access (River right)
Fish Ponds
Mile 24
Mile 26
Mile 22
Mile 20
Mile 18
Mile 16
Mile 14
Mile 12
Mile 10
Mile 8
Mile 6
Mile 4
Mile 2
Mile 0
Fort Hall Bottoms
Snake River
Current Flow
Springfield
Pingree
Jackson Trout Farm (Alternative put-in or take-out)
Take-out or Put-in Tilden Bridge (Downstream of bridge on river right)
North
To Pocatello
Fort Hall
FORT HALL INDIAN RESERVATION
Ferry Butte
Tilden Bridge
91
15
Riverton
Ferry Butte Road
Blackfoot River
Rockford
Alternative Put-in Riverton Boat Access (Riverton Slough)
Riverside
Put-in 500 West Access
Snake River
500 West Put-in
North Channel
500 West
Two Small Diversions
Large Diversion
Blackfoot Boat Ramp
Enlarged Area
26
To Arco
Blackfoot
To Idaho Falls
Alternative Put-in Blackfoot Boat Ramp

left on 500 West and drive .6 mile until it makes a sharp right hand bend. The put-in is on the outside of this bend.

Park off to the side of the road and launch boats in the small channel just off the road. This is not actually the main river but rather the north channel of the river which joins the main river .3 mile downstream.

Alternative Put-in. Boat ramp in Blackfoot. Just upstream from the US 26 bridge is a boat ramp on river left. This is a more convenient place to put-in if you have a drift boat. Be careful, however, just below this put-in is a diversion which should be scouted before running. A clever and fun way of avoiding the diversion is to run the North Channel which leads off to river right just above the diversion. North Channel has two smaller diversions on it, but both create only minor rapids which are easily run.

Alternative Put-in. Riverton Boat Access. The Riverton to Tilden Bridge segment (6 miles) is a very common float trip that cuts the Blackfoot stretch in half. Riverton Road is located 3 miles from US 91 on Ferry Butte Road (see description above). Turn to the right on Riverton Road and drive 2.3 miles to a dirt road that leads off to the left into a parking area and boat ramp.

The Trip. Blackfoot to Tilden Bridge. When the water is low, this is a very lovely part of the Snake River. It has a few waves and riffles and some sweepers, but, overall, it is a fairly easy trip with good fishing, nice riverside scenery and good bird watching. You'll see a couple of homes along the river on the latter half of the trip, but it otherwise is surprisingly isolated. Tilden Bridge, the take-out, can't be missed. It is the only bridge on the stretch.

Shuttle. 13 miles, all paved. An easy, enjoyable 4-mile bike shuttle can be done for the shorter Riverton to Tilden Bridge segment, all on paved secondary roads.

Craft. Canoes, kayaks, inflatables, drift boats.

Tilden Bridge to American Falls Reservoir (McTucker Boat Access)

Basic Stats (Tilden Bridge to McTucker Boat Access)

Difficulty: Class I+ (1.3 -1.4) in low water.

Levels/Season: Same comments as the Blackfoot to Tilden Stretch.

Distance/Time: 14 miles / 5-7 hours. This can be a windy stretch in the afternoon. Start early and give yourself plenty of time.

Getting to the Take-out. McTucker Boat Access. Start at Tilden Bridge. To get to Tilden Bridge, see directions to the take-out for the Blackfoot to Tilden Bridge Stretch on the previous page. From the bridge, drive to the west towards Pingree. Stay on Ferry Butte Road which makes a couple of jogs and eventually comes to the Idaho 39 highway. Take a left and head towards Springfield and Aberdeen.

In a little more than 2 miles on the highway you'll pass a railroad crossing. Check your odometer and drive .2 mile watching for a road which goes off to the left. Turn left and stay on the main road. It makes a jog to the west and back to the south. When the road gets close to the river a left branch goes to a series of ponds called the Fish and Game ponds. You want to branch off to the right before the ponds, following a dirt road which leads to the southeast through an extraordinary thicket of willows to the McTucker boat ramp.

Getting to the Put-in. Tilden Bridge. See directions to the take-out for the Blackfoot to Tilden Bridge Stretch on the previous page.

The Trip. Tilden Bridge to McTucker Boat Access. This is much like the preceding stretch of river. The shore is lined with cottonwoods and willows interspersed with occasional clear springs. The left side of the river is the boundary of the Fort Hall Indian Reservation and part of what is called the Fort Hall Bottoms, a particularly remote and undisturbed part of the reservation, full of marshes, clear-water springs and creeks.

As you get close to the McTucker boat ramp, the river separates into several channels. If you get into the wrong channel, it is possible to miss the take-out and end up in American Falls Reservoir. Thus, when paddling the lower reaches of the river, always take the right channel.

On the left bank of the river, 2 miles above McTucker take-out is the Fort Hall Historic Monument at the site of the original trading post built by Nathaniel Wyeth in 1834. The original fort, which is long gone, was a square stockade surrounded by a 10-foot high wall and was an important stop along the Oregon Trail.

Shuttle. 15 miles, paved and dirt. Bike shuttle on paved secondary roads.

Craft. Canoes, kayaks, inflatables, and drift boats.

Mileage Chart
Both Stretches: Blackfoot to American Falls Reservoir

Mile	Description
0	Put-in. 500 West on North Channel. River right. Note that the Blackfoot Boat Ramp is 2.4 miles upstream from this point and is a better put-in for drift boats.
6	Riverton Put-in (in Riverton slough). Riverton slough enters on river left.
11.4	Mouth of Blackfoot River (left).
11.7	Tilden Bridge and Tilden Boat Ramp (Boat ramp is downstream of bridge on right).
13	Jackson Trout Farm boat and fishing access (right).
24	Fort Hall Historic Monument (left).
26	Take-out. McTucker boat ramp (right).

Idaho State Historical Society

The Snake River country in 1849 near the end of the fur trade era. Above: sketch of the original Fort Hall (probably by William Tappan). Below: lithograph of America Falls.

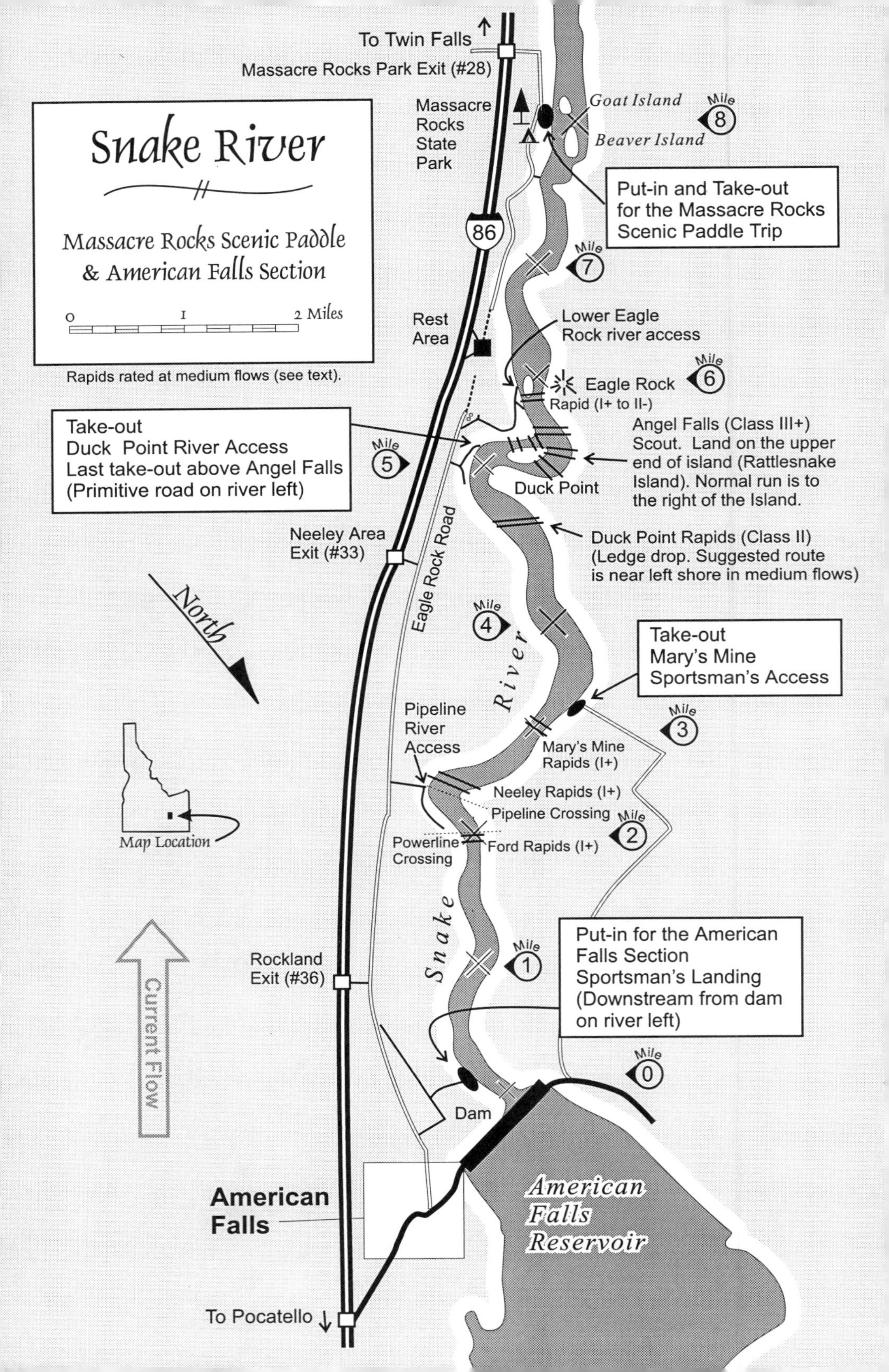
Snake River
Massacre Rocks Scenic Paddle
& American Falls Section
0
1
2 Miles
Rapids rated at medium flows (see text).
To Twin Falls
Massacre Rocks Park Exit (#28)
Massacre
Rocks
State
Park
Goat Island
Beaver Island
Mile 8
Put-in and Take-out
for the Massacre Rocks
Scenic Paddle Trip
86
Mile 7
Rest
Area
Lower Eagle
Rock river access
Mile 6
Eagle Rock
Rapid (I+ to II-)
Take-out
Duck Point River Access
Last take-out above Angel Falls
(Primitive road on river left)
Mile 5
Angel Falls (Class III+)
Scout. Land on the upper
end of island (Rattlesnake
Island). Normal run is to
the right of the Island.
Duck Point
Duck Point Rapids (Class II)
(Ledge drop. Suggested route
is near left shore in medium flows)
Neeley Area
Exit (#33)
Eagle Rock Road
North
Mile 4
River
Take-out
Mary's Mine
Sportsman's Access
Mile 3
Mary's Mine
Rapids (I+)
Pipeline
River
Access
Neeley Rapids (I+)
Pipeline Crossing
Mile 2
Map Location
Powerline
Crossing
Ford Rapids (I+)
Snake
Current Flow
Rockland
Exit (#36)
Mile 1
Put-in for the American
Falls Section
Sportsman's Landing
(Downstream from dam
on river left)
Mile 0
Dam
American
Falls
American
Falls
Reservoir
To Pocatello

Difficulty

Class I
(1.0)

Snake River

Massacre Rocks Scenic Paddle and American Falls Section

FINDING A FLAT WATER STRETCH on the Snake on which you feel comfortable taking a family isn't easy. Fortunately there's a solution: the calm water through Massacre Rocks State Park. The water is slow enough that you can start at the park and paddle upstream. Moreover, hard-shelled boats such as canoes and kayaks are the best way of seeing the park and its bird life and distinctive cliffs of stark basalt rising up from the river.

For those looking for some whitewater, it can be found in the segment of river above Massacre Rocks and below American Falls dam. Much of the upper part of the American Falls stretch is flat water, interrupted with some class I+. Lower on this stretch, however, are Duck Point Rapids (class II) and Angel Falls, a long class III to III+ rapid around Rattlesnake Island. One or both can be avoided, if desired, by taking out at alternative access points.

Massacre Rocks Scenic Paddle

Basic Stats (Massacre Rocks Scenic Paddle)

Difficulty: Class I (1.0). Flat lake-like water.

Season: All year.

Distance/Time: 3 mile round trip. It's an up and back trip, you can make it as short or long as you desire.

Getting to the Put-in and Take-out. Massacre Rocks State Park. Massacre Rocks is well marked with signs on Interstate 86 about 10 miles east of American Falls. The best place to launch non-motorized craft is the road which goes past the visitor's center and down to a parking area near the river. A small fee is charged for the use of the park.

The Trip. Massacre Rocks Scenic Paddle. Carry your boat down to the river and paddle upstream (upstream is to the right as you look at the river). You can paddle upstream about 1.5 miles (3 mile round trip) before you start running into swifter current.

One of the most notable birds that you are likely to spot on this stretch is the white pelican. They pass overhead in gathered flocks, gliding and turning with such coordination that the flock will be dark one moment and then explode in a flash of white against the sky. The pelicans that you see here have made an incredible trip: each day they come all the way from the Great Salt Lake to feed on the plentiful fish in the river, and later in the day, they make the same trip back.

Craft. Canoes and kayaks including lake kayaks.

American Falls Section
(American Falls Dam to Massacre Rocks)

Basic Stats (American Falls to Massacre Rocks)

Difficulty: Class III to III+ for the full run through Angel Falls. A shorter class I+ stretch can be run if you take out at the Marys Mine Sportsman's Access on river right.

Levels: Best flows for the stretch from American Falls to Marys Mine are between 3,000 to 20,000 cfs, though it does get more swirly as the water gets higher. Below Marys Mine, the level should be at least 6,500 cfs to cover the ledges. It can be run up to the 20,000 cfs range, but expect squirrelly areas and turbulence from 8,000 cfs and above.

Distance/Time: 9.5 miles / 4 hours for the full run.

Getting to the Take-out. Massacre Rocks State Park. See description on the previous page.

Alternative Take-out. Sportsman's Access at Marys Mine. Marys Mine Access allows boaters to take-out before Duck Point Rapid and Angel Falls, making the trip a class I+ in medium flows. To get to it, start in American Falls and drive over the American Falls Dam. After the dam, turn left on Lamb Weston Road. Follow the signs to the Sportsman's Access.

Another alternative take-out is just below Duck Point Rapid (a class II ledge from 6,500 to 20,000 cfs). Paddlers who want to avoid Angel Falls (class III to III+) at the end of this run can take out at a primitive access point across from Duck Point. You can get to it by taking the Neeley Area Exit (#33) and turning west on Eagle Rock Road which parallels the north side of the Interstate. Watch for a lava rock monument on the right side of the road. Turn right onto the dirt road just before the monument. Follow the dirt road to a "Y" and take the left branch to a point close to the river.

There's no ramp. You'll need to carry boats up to your vehicle. This road is often rutted and a high clearance vehicle is recommended.

Getting to the Put-in. Sportsman's Landing at American Falls. The landing can be reached from the town of American Falls. Or, as we'll describe here, it can be reached from Eagle Rock Road. Eagle Rock Road is the paved road which parallels Interstate 86 on its north side. You can get to it by taking the Rockland Exit (#36). Once on Eagle Rock Road, follow it towards American Falls (east) and watch for the Sportsman's Access signs which point the way.

The Trip. American Falls Section. The stretch from American Falls to Marys Mine has a lot of flat water on it and in the afternoon, strong upriver winds are common. Mornings are the best time to run it, particularly if you are in a raft or inflatable kayak. The rapids on this part of the river are reasonable for open canoes and touring boats in water levels from 3,000 to 20,000 cfs. It's a big, wide river, however, with squirrelly water. You want to make sure that you have adequate flotation in your boat in the event of a capsize.

Beyond Marys Mine access, things get interesting. Duck Point Rapids, about 4 miles from the start, is a rocky, river wide ledge drop. From 6,500 to 20,000 cfs, it's a class II drop, best run near the left shore. (It washes out in flows over 20,000 cfs.) Scout it first from the left. Boaters have capsized here, and it's an ugly place to swim. This and the complicated ledges of the river bed downstream are dangerous in flows under 6,500 cfs. If you are unsure of your skills, avoid Duck Point and take out upriver at the Marys Mine Sportsman's Access, on river right.

If you do run Duck Point, but don't plan to run Angel Falls (class III to III+), you can take out at a primitive road on river left shortly after Duck Point Rapids.

Angel Falls is a long stretch of whitewater with sharp ledges and large waves around an island in the river, called Rattlesnake Island. You'll want to have whitewater experience before undertaking it. Canoeists, in particular, should be experienced and have their boats outfitted for big whitewater. No matter what your craft, all boaters should stop at the top of the island and scout before running the rapid. The normal run is around the right side of the island. One more short class II- to II rapid is found downstream at Eagle Rock, and from there it's smooth sailing to Massacre Rocks.

Shuttle. 15 miles, all paved. To do a bike shuttle, follow the Eagle Rock Road to the west until it ends. You'll have to walk your bike down into a gully and then lift it over a fence at Massacre Rocks Rest Area. From the rest area follow a gravel road to the park.

Craft. Canoes, kayaks, inflatables, drift boats.

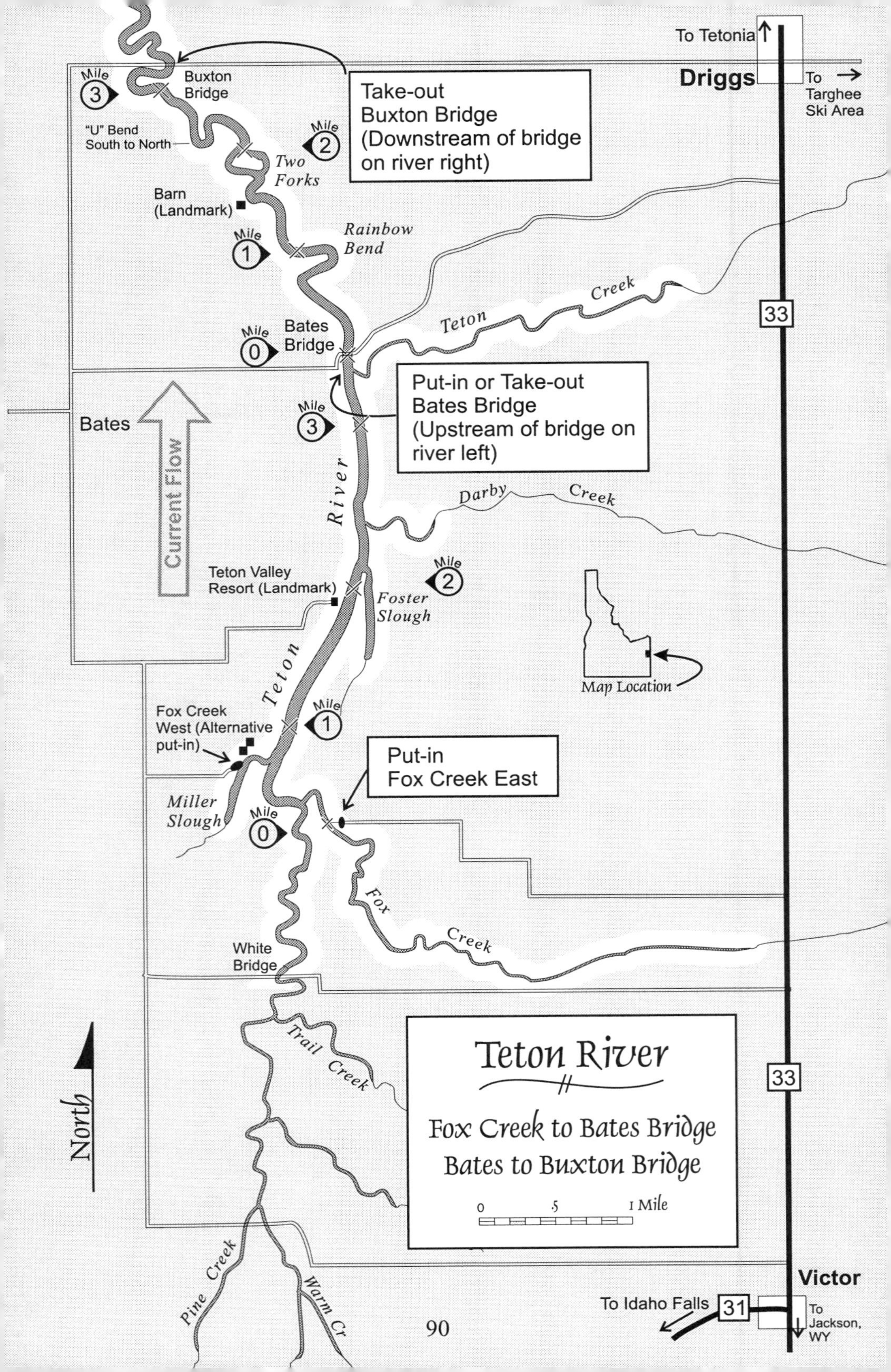
To Tetonia
Driggs
To Targhee Ski Area
Take-out
Buxton Bridge
(Downstream of bridge on river right)
Mile 3
Buxton Bridge
"U" Bend South to North
Mile 2
Two Forks
Barn (Landmark)
Rainbow Bend
Mile 1
Teton Creek
33
Mile 0
Bates Bridge
Put-in or Take-out
Bates Bridge
(Upstream of bridge on river left)
Bates
Current Flow
Mile 3
River
Darby Creek
Teton Valley Resort (Landmark)
Mile 2
Foster Slough
Map Location
Teton
Fox Creek West (Alternative put-in)
Mile 1
Put-in
Fox Creek East
Miller Slough
Mile 0
Fox Creek
White Bridge
Trail Creek
Teton River
Fox Creek to Bates Bridge
Bates to Buxton Bridge
0 .5 1 Mile
North
33
Pine Creek
Warm Cr
Victor
To Idaho Falls
31
To Jackson, WY

Difficulty

Class I
(1.0)

Teton River

Fox Creek East to Bates Bridge and Bates Bridge to Buxton Bridge

THERE ISN'T ANY CLEARER WAY of putting it: the Teton River is simply an outstanding paddling and fishing stream. Meandering through the Teton Basin on the Idaho side of the majestic Tetons, the river can be accessed in many different locations. Idaho doesn't have many rivers with as many easy floating options as the Teton. Two are described in here with three more segments described in the next section.

The first, the river's uppermost floatable segment, is a 3.6-mile stretch starting at a river access known as Fox Creek East. This is the easiest trip that the river offers (class I, 1.0), and it's the stretch to run if you want to do something very safe and very slow. You don't even have to do a shuttle if you're not inclined. By mid summer, the current is slow enough that you can start at the put-in, paddle a short distance down Fox Creek to the Teton River, then paddle up the Teton, fishing and exploring the willow lined banks of the river. When you're ready, you can paddle back to the put-in.

The second stretch starts where the first ends. This is a 3.5-mile reach of river that has a little more current (class I, 1.1) than the Fox Creek section above, but overall it's a gentle and easy going ride. It's on this stretch that you start getting some beautiful views of the central part of the Teton range.

Basic Stats (Fox Creek East to Bates Bridge)

Difficulty: Class I (1.0).

Levels/Season: Below 800 cfs (measured at the Driggs Gauge). Mid summer through fall. We've had several delightful trips at the 375 cfs range, and it can be run even lower.

Distance/Time: 3.6 miles / 1.5 to 3 hours.

Getting to the Take-out. Bates Bridge. To get to Bates Bridge, start at the junction of Highway 33 and the road to Targhee Ski Area in the middle of Driggs. Drive .7 mile to the south on Idaho 33 to South Bates Road. Turn right and continue another 3.4

miles to the bridge over the Teton River. A boat ramp is located on the upstream side of the bridge on river left.

Getting to the Put-in. Fox Creek East Sportsman's Access. The turn-off to the access road is marked with a highway sign, 5.4 miles south of Driggs. Follow the access road to the west. It jogs to the north twice, and eventually, 3.4 miles from the highway, it reaches the put-in at Fox Creek, a tributary of the Teton River.

The Trip. Fox Creek East to Bates Bridge. From the put-in, paddle downstream and within .2 mile Fox Creek joins the Teton River. The current here is very slow and in low water conditions it is possible to paddle up or downstream. This is a good area for fishing and you may want to wet a line before continuing any farther.

From the confluence, the river makes a right hand bend (called Big Bend) and then straightens and heads north. You'll see homes along the left side of the river for about a mile stretch and then the river leaves them behind. The take-out is signaled by Teton Creek coming in from the right followed by Bates Bridge. The take-out is on the upstream side of the bridge on river left.

Shuttle. 12 miles, mostly paved. Bike shuttlers, you'll love this one. It is on a bike path on the west side of Idaho 33 between Victor and Driggs.

Craft. Canoes, kayaks, drift boats. Inflatable boaters may find this segment a bit sluggish and may want to opt for one of the other Teton River stretches.

Mileage Chart
Fox Creek East to Bates Bridge

0	Put-in. Fox Creek East. Right shore of Fox Creek.
.2	Confluence of Fox Creek and Teton River.
.5	Midpoint of Big Bend.
.8	Miller Slough (left). Fox Creek West Boat Access is upstream in Miller Slough. Just past Miller Slough on the left are 2 identical, modified A-frame houses with rough cedar siding.
1.7	Teton Valley Resort (left).
2.2	Foster Slough (right).
2.5	Mouth of Darby Creek (right).
3.2	Mouth of Dick Creek (right).
3.5	Mouth of Teton Creek (right).
3.6	Take-out. Bates Bridge. Ramp located upstream of bridge on river left.

Bates Bridge to Buxton Bridge

> **Basic Stats (Bates Bridge to Buxton Bridge)**
>
> **Difficulty:** Class I (1.1).
>
> **Levels/Season:** Below 1,000 cfs. Mid summer through fall. We've often run it in the 375 cfs range, and it can be run lower.
>
> **Distance/Time:** 3.5 miles / 1.5 to 3 hours.

Getting to the Take-out. Buxton Bridge. From the center of Driggs at the junction of Highway 33 and the turn-off to Targhee Ski Area follow the road leading towards Bates (the opposite direction from Targhee). Continue following this paved secondary road to the west until it crosses over a bridge over the Teton River, 3.8 miles from Driggs. The take-out is on the downstream side of the bridge on river right.

Getting to the Put-in. Bates Bridge. See directions to the take-out for Fox Creek East to Bates Bridge on page 91.

The Trip. Bates Bridge to Buxton Bridge. This section of the river has a more natural feel to it than the previous section. You won't see any structures, other than a barn about midway through. You'll need some basic paddling skills to keep away from the river banks which are brushy with overhung willows, but in medium or low water conditions, the current is not forceful. At a U-bend called Rainbow Bend, about a mile from the start, you'll have a beautiful view of Mt. Owen, the Grand Teton and the Middle Teton above the right shoulder of Teton Canyon.

Just before the 2-mile point the river separates at a junction called Two Forks. Take the deeper and wider right fork. The take-out is 3.5 miles from the start at a small boat ramp on river right, just downstream of Buxton Bridge.

Shuttle. 8 miles, all paved. Bike shuttle: paved secondary roads.

Craft. Canoes, kayaks, small inflatables and drift boats.

Mileage Chart
Bates Bridge to Buxton Bridge

0	Put-in. Bates Bridge. Upstream of bridge on river left.
.8	Rainbow Bend, U-turn bend to left.
1.5	Barn (left).
1.7	Two Forks. Take right channel.
2.5	U-turn bend. River heads due south then due north.
3.5	Take-out. Buxton Bridge. Downstream of bridge on river right.

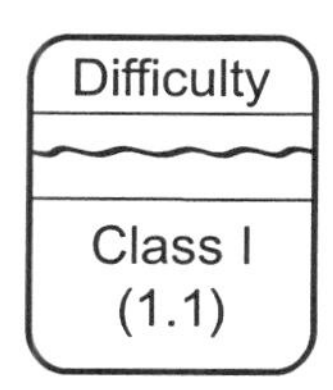

Teton River

Buxton Bridge to Rainier,
Rainier to Cache Bridge,
and Cache Bridge to Highway 33

FROM BUXTON BRIDGE west of the town of Driggs, the Teton River continues its sinuous journey across the lovely Teton Valley. This section looks closely at three more trips on this extraordinary river. These are particularly scenic trips, offering some of the best river views of the Tetons.

Two of the segments are laid-back, easy-going floats (class I, 1.1), like the upstream sections described previously. The third stretch, however, is more difficult (class I+, 1.3). It has swifter, sharper corners and more overhanging brush and trees. Wait to do this run until you are comfortable with your boating techniques and the river has dropped to late summer levels.

Buxton Bridge to Rainier

Basic Stats (Buxton to Rainier)

Difficulty: Class I (1.1).

Levels/Season: Below 1,000 cfs (measured at the Driggs gauge). Mid summer through fall. We've had some wonderfully relaxed trips in the 375 cfs range, and it can be run even lower.

Distance/Time: 3.4 miles / 2-3 hours.

Getting to the Take-out. Rainier Access. From Driggs, drive north on Idaho 33. Four miles north of Driggs, turn left on the Packsaddle Road. At 4.9 miles from the highway, Packsaddle Road crosses over the river at Cache Bridge. Continue another .3 mile past the bridge and turn left on 400 N. At 1.5 miles from the Packsaddle Road, watch for a sign indicating Rainier access and a road heading off to the left. Follow the road down to a concrete boat ramp.

Getting to the Put-in. Buxton Bridge. See directions to the take-out for the Bates to Buxton Bridge segment on page 93.

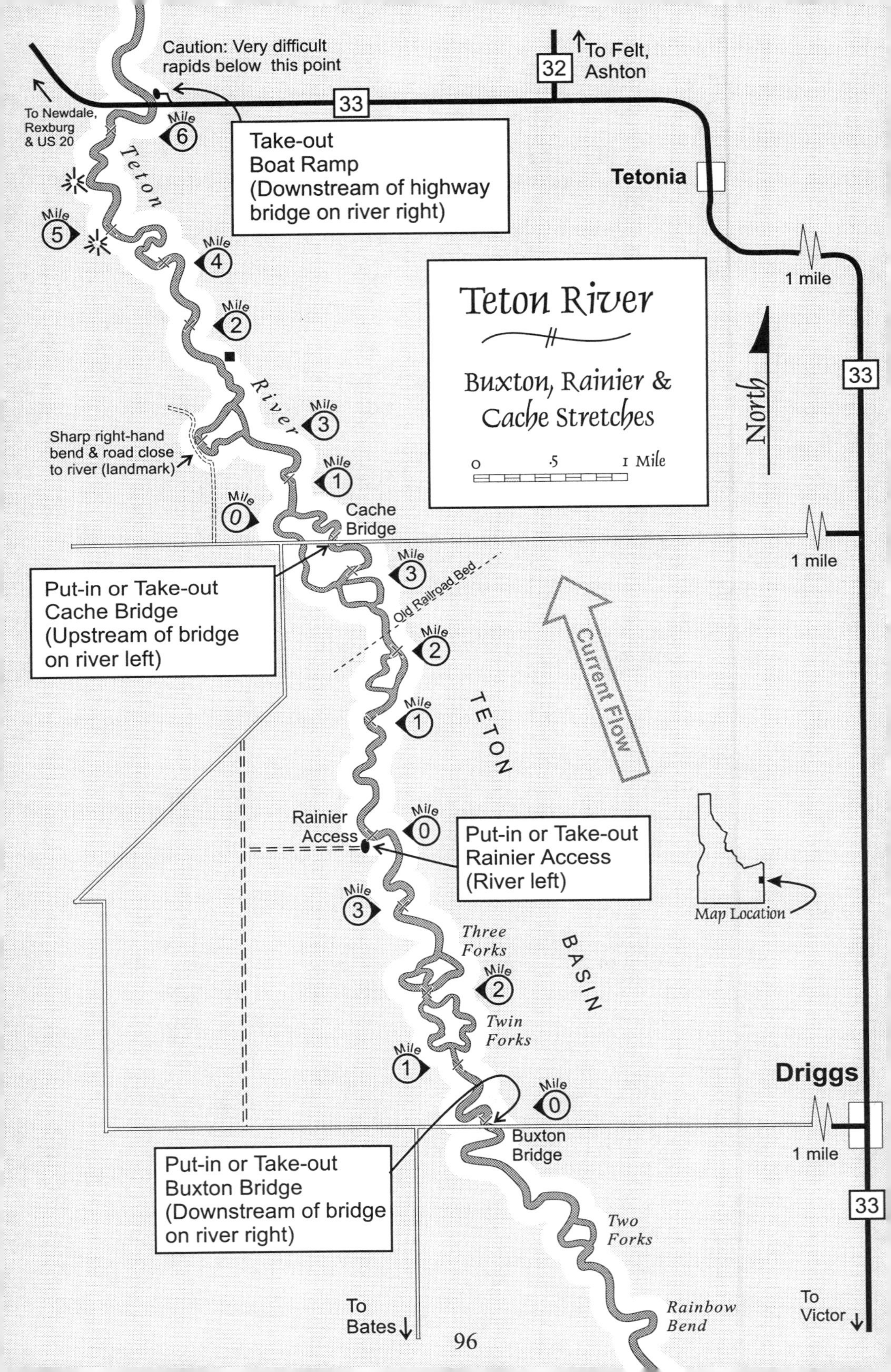

Caution: Very difficult rapids below this point
To Felt, Ashton
32
33
To Newdale, Rexburg & US 20
Mile 6
Take-out Boat Ramp (Downstream of highway bridge on river right)
Teton
Tetonia
Mile 5
Mile 4
1 mile
Teton River
Buxton, Rainier & Cache Stretches
0 .5 1 Mile
Mile 2
North
33
River
Mile 3
Sharp right-hand bend & road close to river (landmark)
Mile 1
Mile 0
Cache Bridge
1 mile
Mile 3
Old Railroad Bed
Put-in or Take-out Cache Bridge (Upstream of bridge on river left)
Current Flow
Mile 2
Mile 1
TETON
Rainier Access
Mile 0
Put-in or Take-out Rainier Access (River left)
Mile 3
Map Location
Three Forks
BASIN
Mile 2
Twin Forks
Mile 1
Driggs
Mile 0
Buxton Bridge
1 mile
Put-in or Take-out Buxton Bridge (Downstream of bridge on river right)
33
Two Forks
To Bates
Rainbow Bend
To Victor

The Trip. Buxton to Rainier. Shortly after getting underway, a house appears downstream and to the right. The river is winding back and forth so much in this section that it seems to take forever to pass it. Eventually, however, the house is passed, and from here to the take-out, the river banks are free of development.

A little more than a mile from the start, you'll come to Twin Forks. When we ran the river, we took the left channel which was wider and was easier to maneuver our canoe. As soon as the two channels come back together, the river again separates; this time into three channels, called—you guessed it—Three Forks. Here the choice is up to you. We took the middle channel. Just before the middle channel joined the left channel, we found a tucked-away gravel bar for lunch.

The Rainier take-out is obvious. The concrete boat ramp is on the left just before a steep bank, the only steep bank on the left on the entire run.

Shuttle. 16 miles, paved and dirt. Enjoyable bike shuttle. Except for 4 miles on the highway, the shuttle is on paved and dirt secondary roads.

Craft. Canoes, kayaks, small inflatables, and drift boats.

Mileage Chart
Buxton Bridge to Rainier

0	Put-in. Buxton Bridge (downstream of bridge on river right).
1.2	Twin Forks. River separates into two channels.
2	Three Forks. River separates into three channels.
3.4	Rainier Access. Boat Ramp (left).

Rainier to Cache Bridge

Basic Stats (Rainier to Cache Bridge)

Difficulty: Class I (1.1).

Levels/Season: Below 1,000 cfs (measured at the Driggs gauge). Mid summer through fall. Also see comments under the Buxton to Rainier stretch.

Distance/Time: 3.5 miles / 1-2.5 hours.

Getting to the Take-out. Cache Bridge. From Driggs, drive north on Idaho 33. Four miles north of Driggs, turn left on Packsaddle Road. At 4.9 miles from the highway, Packsaddle Road crosses over the river at Cache Bridge. The take-out is on the upstream side of the bridge on river left.

Getting to the Put-in. Rainier Access. See directions to the take-out for the Buxton Bridge to Rainier Stretch on page 95.

The Trip. Rainier to Cache Bridge. We really enjoyed this part of the Teton River. No houses have been built along the river and the views of the Idaho side of the Tetons can't be beat. Middle Teton, Grand Teton and Mt. Owen are visible in all their glory though the U-shaped opening of Teton Canyon to the east.

It's all flat water on this stretch, and in some places, the current is barely perceptible. This is a good stretch for hard shelled boats such as canoes, kayaks and drift boats. Because of the idle current, those with inflatables may want to do other parts of the Teton River.

Shuttle. 3.5 miles, some paved, some dirt. Easy bike shuttle on paved and dirt secondary roads.

Craft. Canoes, kayaks, drift boats. Inflatable boaters may bog down on some of the slow parts and may want to try one of the other Teton River stretches.

Mileage Chart
Rainier to Cache Bridge

0	Put-in. Rainier access. River left.
1.3	River splits into 2 channels.
2	The two channels rejoin.
2.2	Piers from old railroad bridge.
2.5	River splits into 2 channels.
3	The two channels rejoin.
3.5	Take-out. Cache Bridge (upstream of bridge on river left).

Cache Bridge to Highway 33

Basic Stats

Difficulty: Class I+ (1.3). Overhanging brush and some sweepers.

Levels/Season: Below 900 cfs (measured at the Driggs gauge). Mid summer through fall. This is one stretch that you want to stay off during high water in May or June. Also see comments under the Buxton to Rainier stretch.

Distance/Time: 6.5 miles / 3-4 hours.

Getting to the Take-out. Highway 33 bridge. From Driggs drive north on Idaho 33 to Tetonia. Continue through Tetonia and stay on Idaho 33 when you come to the junction of Idaho 32. At 2.6 miles from the Idaho 32 and 33 junction, you'll come to a bridge over the Teton River. On the right just before the bridge is a road which leads down to a boat ramp and an outhouse.

Getting to the Put-in. Cache Bridge. See directions to the take-out for the Rainier to Cache Bridge Stretch on page 98.

The Trip. Cache Bridge to Highway 33. Compared to the upstream stretches the Teton River is much swifter here. The brush along its banks is heavier. In places, you'll see cottonwood trees, the first time they make their appearance along the river. Because of swift corners and the presence of some sweepers and snags in the river, this is more difficult than upper portions of the river.

When we ran the river, we came across a family that had just flipped their canoe and were fishing their wet gear out of the river. They were fine, but their unexpected swim points out that you want to make sure you have your paddling technique down before undertaking it. This stretch would be very dangerous during the high water period from May through June.

Because of the brushy banks, however, the river seems more removed and isolated from the busy Teton Valley. Birds were plentiful along this stretch and we saw moose tracks at more than one location. For a change of pace, the last couple of miles the river edges up against the dry foot hills of the Big Hole Mountains.

Shuttle. 14 miles, all paved. Bike shuttle: Much of the shuttle is on Idaho 33, a busy highway with a small to medium shoulder.

Craft. Canoes, kayaks, small inflatables and drift boats.

Mileage Chart
Cache Bridge to Highway 33

0	Put-in. Cache Bridge. Upstream of bridge on river left.
1.8	Sharp right-hand bend. Dirt road very close to river on the bank on river left.
2.5	House visible briefly through brush to right.
5	Steep cut-bank above river on left. (Steep banks are on river left for the next 2 miles).
6.5	Take-out. Highway 33 bridge. Downstream of bridge on river right. Note: Be sure to take-out here. Some distance below this take-out are some very difficult rapids.

Teton River Overnight Trip. It is possible to do a long day trip or, better yet, an overnight trip on the river. Start at the Fox Creek East access point described in the previous section and end at the Highway 33 bridge. Most of the land is private, but not at Rainier. Rainier is located in an ideal position (about midway through the trip at 10.5 miles from the start) for an overnight stay. After Rainier, it's about 10 miles to the Highway 33 bridge.

Help for the Teton River. Join and support the Teton Regional Land Trust: PO Box 247, Driggs, ID 83422. This spirited, grass-roots group is dedicated to the conservation and protection of lands along the Teton River and throughout the Upper Snake River Valley.

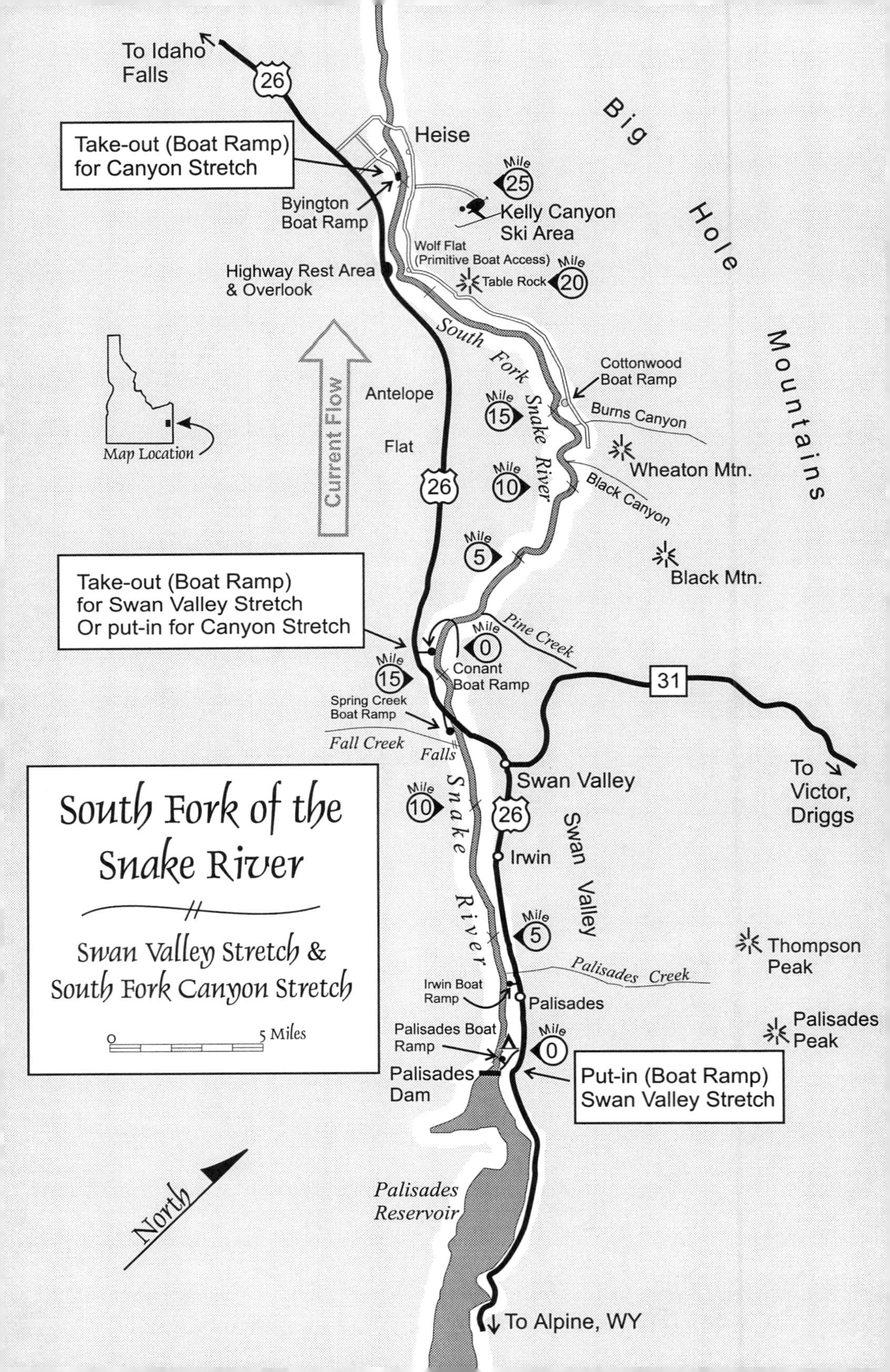
To Idaho Falls
26
Take-out (Boat Ramp) for Canyon Stretch
Heise
Big Hole Mountains
Mile 25
Byington Boat Ramp
Kelly Canyon Ski Area
Wolf Flat (Primitive Boat Access)
Highway Rest Area & Overlook
Table Rock
Mile 20
South Fork Snake River
Current Flow
Antelope Flat
Cottonwood Boat Ramp
Burns Canyon
Mile 15
Wheaton Mtn.
Map Location
Mile 10
Black Canyon
26
Mile 5
Black Mtn.
Take-out (Boat Ramp) for Swan Valley Stretch Or put-in for Canyon Stretch
Pine Creek
Mile 0
Mile 15
Conant Boat Ramp
31
Spring Creek Boat Ramp
Fall Creek
Falls
Swan Valley
To Victor, Driggs
South Fork of the Snake River
Swan Valley Stretch & South Fork Canyon Stretch
0
5 Miles
Mile 10
Snake River
26
Irwin
Swan Valley
Mile 5
Thompson Peak
Palisades Creek
Irwin Boat Ramp
Palisades
Palisades Boat Ramp
Mile 0
Palisades Peak
Palisades Dam
Put-in (Boat Ramp) Swan Valley Stretch
North
Palisades Reservoir
To Alpine, WY

Difficulty
Class I+ (1.4)

South Fork Snake River

Swan Valley & South Fork Canyon

THIS IS ONE RIVER that has it all: fabulous fishing, outstanding scenery and great floating and camping. Gathering much of its water from the Tetons, the South Fork of the Snake flows out of Wyoming into Idaho's Palisades Reservoir, east of Idaho Falls. The two stretches described here are both located below the reservoir and are easily accessed at a number of developed boat ramps.

Both stretches are rated class I+, but the Snake is a big and powerful river. Water flows are controlled by Palisades Dam and through much of the summer season, flows are kept fairly high to meet the demands of irrigators in the fertile Snake River plains downstream. Running this river during the summer is fine if you're experienced, but if you want an easier, more relaxed trip, we recommend that you paddle the South Fork in the fall when releases from the dam are cut back considerably and the river is not as forceful.

Whatever time you choose to run the river, you'll find it a beautiful trip. The upper stretch which flows through Swan Valley has panoramic views of the surrounding mountains and is a particularly colorful place to be when the leaves are changing. The lower, canyon stretch cuts back away from the busy highway and is largely removed from roads. The canyon can be run in one day, but there are lots of nice places to camp along the way and it makes a wonderful overnight outing.

Swan Valley Stretch

Basic Stats (Swan Valley Stretch)

Difficulty: Class I+ (1.4). Some waves (which become larger as the water level gets higher) and some downed and overhanging trees.

Levels: Water is quite high and powerful during much of the summer (over 14,000 cfs). Fall to late fall (3,000 to 8,000 cfs) is best time for canoeists and less experienced boaters. Flows are measured at the Swan Valley gauge.

Distance/Time: 16 miles / 4-5 hours at 4,000 cfs. Can be combined with the Canyon stretch for a longer, overnight trip.

Getting to the Take-out. The take-out is the Conant Valley Boat Ramp, a large, well maintained, concrete boat ramp with restrooms. A small fee is charged for its use. It is located just off of US 26, some 30 miles from Idaho Falls or 1.9 miles from the highway bridge over the Snake River west of the town of Swan Valley. A highway sign marks the turn-off to the ramp. An alternative boat ramp that may be used is located at the highway bridge (river left, upstream of the bridge).

Getting to the Put-in. The put-in is a small concrete ramp just below Palisades Dam. The turn-off to the ramp is located 9.9 miles southeast of the town of Swan Valley on US 26. After you turn on the access road, drive past the campground and you find the ramp situated to the right before reaching the Palisades power plant. An alternative boat ramp that may be used is the Irwin Ramp, about 2 miles closer to Swan Valley off of US 26.

The Trip. Swan Valley Stretch. After being confined by Palisades Dam, the Snake seems anxious to get on its way again. For the first 3.5 miles of this stretch, the current moves along at a good clip, finally culminating in a series of rolling waves near the mouth of Palisades Creek. After the creek, things slow a tad, giving you an opportunity to enjoy the surrounding view. On river right, rising above the cottonwood trees which fringe the river banks are the peaks of the Snake River Range with the lordly Thompson Peak dominating. Throughout the first part of the trip, the river stays in one channel, but beyond the trip's mid point, the river begins braiding, separating into a number of channels.

While it is less of a problem in low water, you'll encounter places where the river flows through downed cottonwood trees and brush. The last part of the trip from the highway bridge to the Conant ramp is probably the worst stretch for trees and snags, and even in low water, use caution and give them a wide berth.

One attraction along the way is Fall Creek Falls, 12.4 miles from the start, which drops into the river over multiple cascades. To get the best view, paddle your boat into the eddy at the base of the falls.

This stretch is a little more civilized than the Canyon stretch, described next. You'll see houses here and there, but the Snake's natural beauty still takes precedent and the bird life, fishing and surrounding mountain scenery can't be beat.

Shuttle. 15 miles, all paved. It can be biked. US 26 has wide shoulders, but be prepared for heavy traffic.

Craft. Because the fishing is good and a variety of boat ramps are available, this is drift boat heaven. But almost any boat can be taken on this stretch including canoes, kayaks and small and large inflatables.

Mileage Chart
Swan Valley Stretch

0	Put-in. Base of Palisades Dam (right).
2.8	Irwin Boat Ramp (right).
3.4	Palisades Creek (right).
7.2	Old Bridge abutments.
12.4	Fall Creek Falls (left).
13.6	Highway 26 Bridge & Spring Creek Boat Ramp.
15.7	Conant Boat Ramp (left).

Phil Merritt / Idaho State Historical Society

The top half of this 1953 aerial photo shows the upper South Fork valley now under the waters of the Palisades Reservoir. The dam site is in the middle of the photo just above the bridge. Palisades townsite, in center foreground, is where the workers lived during the dam's construction. To the left of the townsite is one of the "borrow" areas which provided fill material for the dam.

South Fork Canyon

Basic Stats (South Fork Canyon)

Difficulty: Class I+ (1.4) and class II- for the short rapid and diversion just before Byington take-out. Frequent mini-rapids where the river drops over rocky bars. Downed trees and sweepers scattered throughout.

Levels: See comments under the previous stretch, Swan Valley.

Distance/Time: 23 miles / 7-10 hours at 4,000 cfs. Makes a very pleasant overnight trip.

Getting to the Take-out. The Byington Boat Ramp is a large, well-maintained ramp with restrooms. Fees are charged for its use. The turn-off to Byington is located off of US 26, about 17 miles out of Idaho Falls. Watch for the sign indicating the boat ramp or 175th Street and turn left. If you reach the highway rest area and overlook, you'll need to backtrack 3.6 miles. Once you're on 175th Street, drive 1.1 miles, and take a right on the Old Ririe Highway, follow it .3 mile until it ends at the boat ramp.

Alternative take-outs. Two alternative boat ramps are located on the other side (north) of the river upriver from Byington. Additionally, boats can be hand-carried off the river at many points along the dirt road which parallels the river on its north bank.

Getting to the Put-in. Conant Valley Boat Ramp (see directions to the take-out for Swan Valley Stretch on the previous page).

The Trip. South Fork Canyon. This is one of the finest stretches of water on the upper Snake. It is largely primitive, particularly the first part of the trip, and it's contained within a canyon for the entire length except at the very end where its western side gives way to the edge of the great Snake River agricultural plain.

The river is an outstanding wildlife corridor: mule and whitetail deer, elk, moose and dozens of species of birds. Moreover, it's one of Idaho's most important bald eagle nesting areas, and you'll see their solitary forms sitting high in cottonwood trees scanning the river for fish.

Having said all this, we want to caution you. The South Fork is not a beginner's river. The river flows through overhanging trees and brush along the shores. Occasional snags are found in midstream. While not considered a whitewater stretch, it still has mini-rapids where the river slides down off of gravel bars into deeper water. Just before the take-out, one rapid and a diversion (which are both short, but nevertheless rated as class II-) must be negotiated. Note, however, that both of these can be avoided by taking out at one of the boat ramps higher on the river. In high water which occurs most of the summer, the river is powerful, but even in low water, it is not a stretch to take lightly.

Ron adds the following: I've boated many whitewater rivers throughout the west, but I've only been in one raft that flipped. Most people are surprised when I tell them that it occurred on a class I river, the South Fork of the Snake, but it's true. It was in high water conditions one spring in the early 1970s. Our paddle raft had drifted close to the shore and nudged against a tree. The boat suddenly caught a branch and abruptly it stopped in the current. That's all that was needed. The upriver side immediately went under water, and before I could even shout, the boat was upside down and all four of us were swirling down the river. Quick work from my friend and long-time outdoorsman "H" Hilbert got me and my boating companions out of the river and around a fire before hypothermia set in.

It was a lesson well learned early in my boating career that one needs to have respect for all rivers, even the so-called easy, class I rivers.

If you're new to the South Fork, we recommend that you wait until the fall season and start out with the Swan Valley stretch first. If you feel comfortable on that, then try the canyon stretch. With a little caution and respect, you'll find the South Fork a very special place.

Camping. This is a long stretch and the best way to do the trip is to break it up into two days. The BLM has designated a number of camping areas. Shortly before reaching Pine Creek (2.3 miles from the start), you'll start seeing small signs posted by the BLM indicating campsite locations. The signs are spaced at frequent intervals all the way down the river. We like to camp somewhere between Pine Creek and Black Canyon (9.5 miles from the start) which is in the roadless part of the canyon.

Shuttle. 19 miles, all paved. Bike shuttle: it can be biked, US 26 has a decent shoulder, but be prepared for heavy traffic.

Craft. All river craft are suitable including canoes, kayaks, and small and large inflatables. With a number of boat ramps, this stretch is particularly well suited for drift boats.

The South Fork Canyon has it all: outstanding floating, fishing, and camping.

Mileage Chart (South Fork Canyon)

0	Conant Boat Ramp (left).
2.3	Mouth of Pine Creek (right).
6.2	Mouth of Gormer Canyon & BLM Campsite (right).
9.5	Mouth of Black Canyon (right).
11.9	Boat ramp on right.
16.7	Steep face of Table Rock on right.
19.5	Highway Rest Area & Overlook on canyon rim (left).
20.3	Small diversion (water diverts to left). Middle run.
21.9	I+ to II- rapid just after sharp right bend.
22.1	Gauging Station (cable across river).
22.3	Diversion (water diverts to left). Middle run in low water.
23.4	Byington Boat Ramp (left).

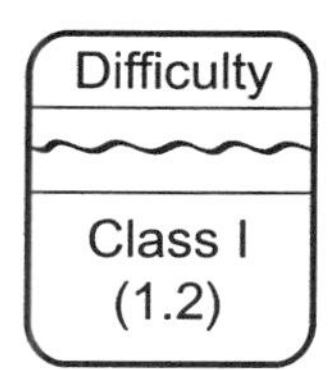

Buffalo River

Headwaters to the Henrys Fork

ALONG WITH BIG SPRINGS, the Buffalo River ranks right up there among Idaho's finest canoe trips. It's a class I (1.2) run which is a bit more difficult than Big Springs. That's because you may need to portage around a fallen tree in the upper stretch, and on the lower part, you'll need to get out and slip your boat under a fence. But the water is unhurried, and there's no danger of being swept into a fence or a log. What obstructions you do run across are only minor distractions in what is otherwise a marvelous trip.

Basic Stats

Difficulty: Class I (1.2).

Season: Wait until the spring high water has passed. The usual paddling season begins in June and continues through the fall.

Distance/Time: 6.4 miles to Highway 20 bridge / 4 hours. It is a 7.4-mile trip (5 hours) to the alternative take-out at Buffalo River Dam.

Obstructions/Fences: Watch for possible downed trees on upper portion. You will have to slip the boat under one or two fences on the lower section. The river, however, is very slow and there's little danger of being swept into obstructions.

Getting to the Take-out. Highway 20 bridge. The Highway bridge over the Buffalo River is adjacent to Pond's Lodge, located about 5 miles south of Macks Inn in Island Park. You can take-out on any side of the bridge. The most used take-outs are upstream of the bridge on river right and left.

Alternative Take-out. Upstream of Buffalo River Dam. You can add another mile to the trip and slightly more difficult water (class I+, 1.3) by continuing past the bridge and taking out just above the Buffalo River Dam. To get there, take the turn-off to Island Park Dam, .3 mile north of Pond's Lodge on US 20. Turn left here and drive .9 mile until coming to a "T" in the road. Take a left at the "T" and continue .5 mile.

About 500 feet before reaching the Island Park Dam, take a left on the road which provides the boat ramp and parking area for the Box Canyon

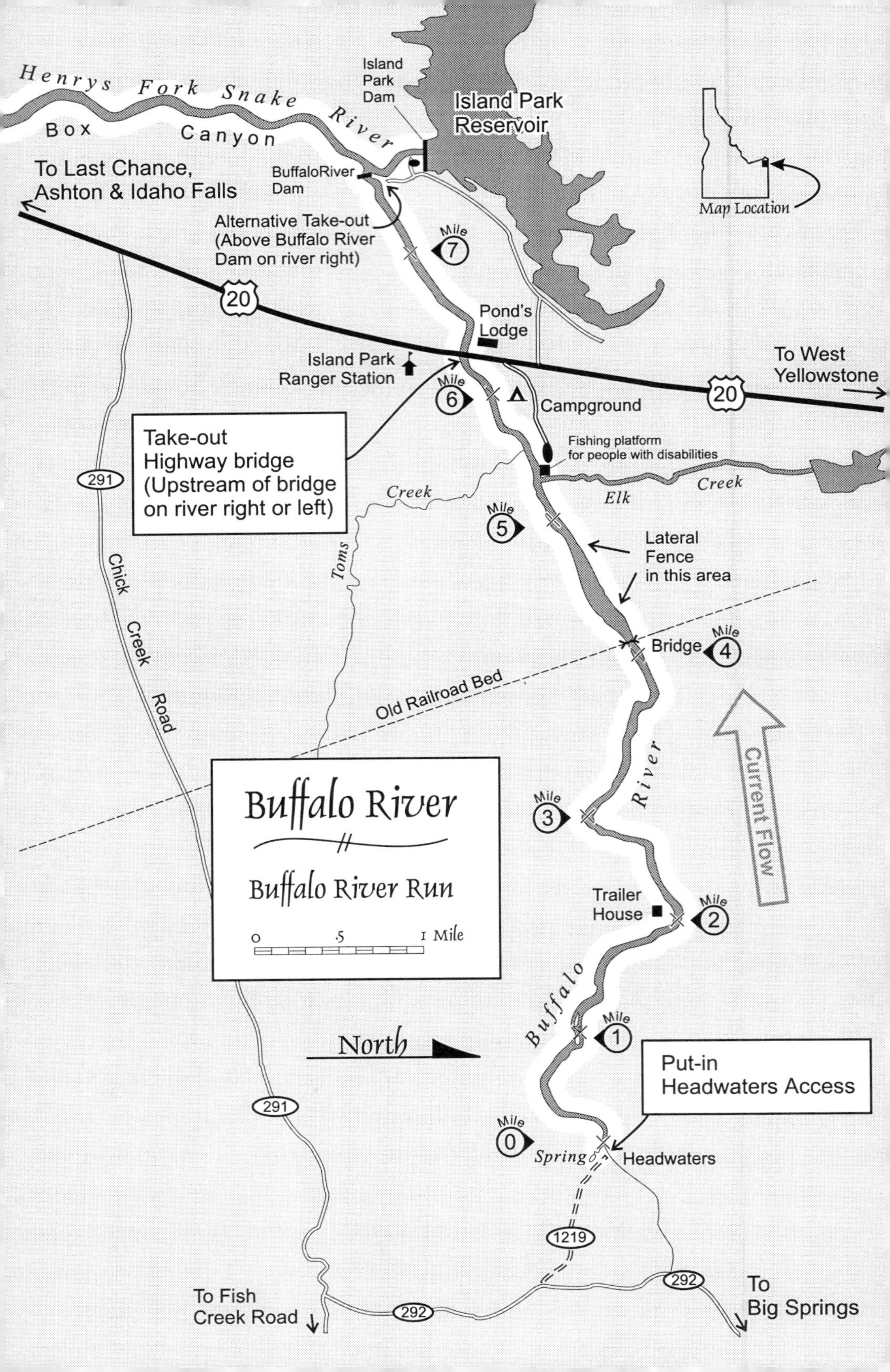

Henrys Fork Snake River
Box Canyon
Island Park Dam
Island Park Reservoir
Map Location
To Last Chance, Ashton & Idaho Falls
BuffaloRiver Dam
Alternative Take-out (Above Buffalo River Dam on river right)
Mile 7
20
Pond's Lodge
Island Park Ranger Station
To West Yellowstone
20
Mile 6
Campground
Take-out Highway bridge (Upstream of bridge on river right or left)
Fishing platform for people with disabilities
291
Creek
Elk
Creek
Mile 5
Toms
Lateral Fence in this area
Chick Creek Road
Bridge
Mile 4
Old Railroad Bed
River
Current Flow
Buffalo River
Buffalo River Run
0 .5 1 Mile
Mile 3
Trailer House
Mile 2
Buffalo
Mile 1
North
Put-in Headwaters Access
291
Mile 0
Spring
Headwaters
1219
292
To Fish Creek Road
292
To Big Springs

stretch of the Henrys Fork (described later). Instead of taking the curve and going all the way to the Box Canyon parking area, continue straight through a gate, and in .2 mile you'll come to a small place to park. From here a trail goes down to the Buffalo River. At the end of your trip, you'll have to hump your boat about 400 feet up a hill.

Getting to the Put-in. Headwaters of the Buffalo River. Note: the last .8 mile of the access road to the headwaters is very rutted. High clearance vehicles are recommended. From Pond's Lodge, drive to the south on US 20. At .2 mile from Pond's, you'll pass the Island Park Ranger Station. Then, 2.1 miles past the Ranger Station, take a left on Chick Creek Road.

Check your odometer. Stay on Chick Creek Road and drive 6.7 to 6.8 miles to the intersection with Forest Road 292. Check your odometer again. Take a left on 292 and drive 1.3 miles to Forest Road 1219. Take another left and follow Forest Road 1219 a little less than a mile to where it ends in a small parking area.

The Trip. Launch your boat on the small stream (Buffalo River) near the parking area. Once the large spring joins the Buffalo River about 40 feet below where you launch, you'll have a little more maneuvering room. The first half of this trip is the most beautiful, and you'll want to take your time here. Normally, small rivers such as the Buffalo which pass through thick forests are not runnable since deadfall invariably blocks the river, but in the Buffalo's case, all the deadfall has been cut away, and the waterway is clear.

However, new trees can fall across the river at any time. Be prepared to portage. The water is slow enough that you don't have to worry about going around a corner and getting broached, but you do want to undertake the trip with the understanding that it may require some work here and there.

The Buffalo runs through a small, intimate canyon with water so clear that you can nearly see each and every individual grain of sand on the river's bed. The only sign of man on the first half of the trip is one trailer house located on river right at the 2-mile point.

From mile 4 downriver, things change. You'll see houses along the river and just below the old railroad bridge, you'll encounter a fence. This barbed wire fence is particularly annoying since it runs laterally down the middle of the river. Bring some heavy leather gloves. You'll have to get out and pass your boat under the fence as the current moves right to left, then once again as the current moves left to right. There's no danger of being swept into the fence. The current is slow and the river is shallow enough to get out and wade.

The fence is the last of the obstructions, and it's home free from here to the Highway 20 bridge.

If you float the mile section of the Buffalo below the bridge, you will encounter one mini-rapid (I+, 1.3) midway down which is easy to run. Shortly after the rapid, the water slows in the backwaters of a dam. Your take-out point is easily located. On the right side of the river is a sign which warns of the approaching dam. At the sign is the trail which leads to the parking area.

Shuttle. 11 miles, mostly dirt. Bike shuttlers will find the short portion on Highway 20 busy but with a wide paved shoulder. Because of dirt roads and the length of the shuttle, give yourself plenty of time.

Craft. Canoes and kayaks.

Mileage Chart

0	Put-in. Headwaters of Buffalo River.
1	Several islands.
2	Trailer house (left).
4	Houses on right.
4.2	Old railroad bridge.
4.4	Lateral fence in river begins.
5.3	Elk Creek (right).
6.2	Take-out. Highway bridge (river right or left).

The Buffalo River is a unhurried and contemplative paddle through the quiet forests of the Island Park area.

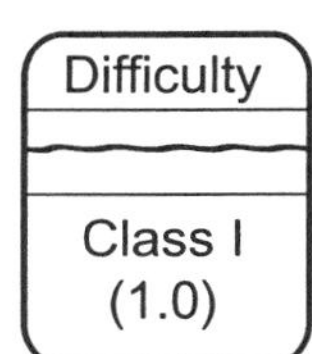

Big Springs

Big Springs National Water Trail

THIS TRANQUIL AND MAGICAL FLOAT through the high lodgepole forests and meadows of the Island Park area is perhaps Idaho's most well-known canoe trip. It's a trip that anyone can do (class I, 1.0) on water that is as clear as gin. Moreover, this stretch of river is a great place to view wildlife so pack your binoculars. In the mornings, you're likely to see moose, deer, maybe elk, osprey, bald eagles, herons and an assortment of ducks.

The water is slow, and if the wind is blowing, it can take forever to get down the river. It's best to get started early in the morning before the afternoon winds come up.

The Forest Service has recognized the importance of this stretch of water and has designated it as the Big Springs National Water Trail. It's named for the huge springs less than a mile upstream from the put-in where an incredible 186 cfs of water pours from the ground at a constant temperature of 52 degrees. If you haven't seen Big Springs it's well worth a side trip.

Basic Stats

Difficulty: Class I (1.0).

Season: Wait until the spring high water has passed. The usual paddling season begins in June and continues through the fall.

Distance/Time: 3.7 miles / 2-3 hours to the Big Springs Water Trail Take-out. If you go to Upper Coffee Pot Campground, the trip is 6.8 miles (3-4 hours). The water is slow, and in windy conditions, the trip can take much longer.

Getting to the Take-out. Big Springs Water Trail Take-out. From Macks Inn, which is located in the middle of the Island Park area, drive to the north on US 20 over the bridge spanning the Henrys Fork and take the first right. Check your odometer at the corner and drive .4 mile to a pull-off to the right. This is the take-out.

Alternative Take-out. Upper Coffee Pot Campground. An alternate take-out is Upper Coffee Pot Campground. The river from Macks Inn to Upper Coffee Pot is also slow, class I (1.0) water. (Note that below the campground, however, things change. Coffee Pot Rapid, a tight class III+

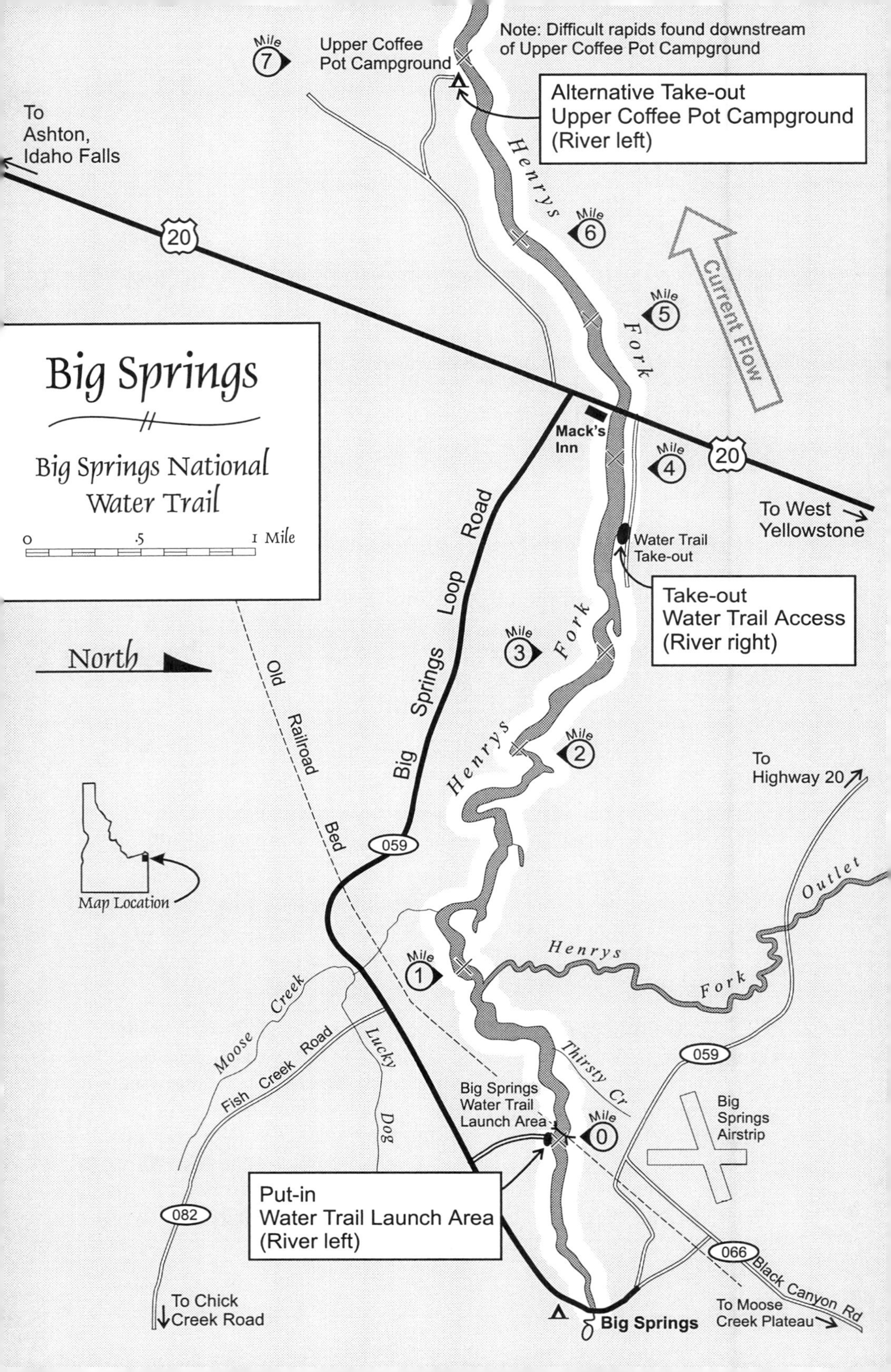

Big Springs
Big Springs National Water Trail
0 .5 1 Mile
North
Map Location
Note: Difficult rapids found downstream of Upper Coffee Pot Campground
Upper Coffee Pot Campground
Alternative Take-out
Upper Coffee Pot Campground
(River left)
To Ashton, Idaho Falls
20
Henrys Fork
Current Flow
Mile 7
Mile 6
Mile 5
Mile 4
Mile 3
Mile 2
Mile 1
Mile 0
Mack's Inn
To West Yellowstone
Water Trail Take-out
Take-out
Water Trail Access
(River right)
Big Springs Loop Road
Old Railroad Bed
059
To Highway 20
Outlet
Henrys Fork
Moose Creek
Fish Creek Road
Lucky Dog
Thirsty Cr
Big Springs Water Trail Launch Area
Big Springs Airstrip
Put-in
Water Trail Launch Area
(River left)
082
066
Black Canyon Rd
To Chick Creek Road
Big Springs
To Moose Creek Plateau

rapid is not too far below it, so you want to make sure that you take out at Upper Coffee Pot Campground and not any lower on the river.)

The turn-off to the campground is off of US 20, .3 mile south of the Big Springs turn-off. The route to the campground is well marked and is just a matter of following signs. As you enter the campground, turn right. The take-out site is a turn-around loop in the east end of the campground. You'll need to carry your boat about 100 feet from the river to the turn-around loop. Don't leave your vehicle here, however. Park in the parking area just outside the entrance of the campground.

Getting to the Put-in. Water Trail Launch Area. At Macks Inn, turn on to the well-marked paved road which leads to Big Springs. It's 3.9 miles from Highway 20 to a road leading off to the left and the boat launch for the water trail. Drive to the end of the road (about a half mile) and unload your boat, then park in the parking lot which is about 300 feet from the launch area.

The Trip. The Targhee National Forest Service really needs to be complimented for the unobtrusive and attractive wooden deck and dock at the put-in from which you can load and launch canoes and kayaks. Once on the water, the river's character becomes immediately obvious: slow and easy going, a pace that remains the rest of the trip.

You'll initially pass through a lodgepole forest but then things open up as the river meanders through meadows. About a mile from the end, you'll start seeing cabins and docks. The take-out is on river right, .4 mile before reaching the Highway 20 bridge.

If you're making a longer trip to Upper Coffee Pot Campground, continue past the highway bridge. Here the river slips into a heavily forested area of lodgepole intermixed with firs and spruce. We particularly enjoyed running this part of the river since it leaves behind the development around Macks Inn and is usually less crowded than the upper stretch. The take-out is at Upper Coffee Pot Campground on river left. Be sure to make this your ending point. Below the campground is a long and difficult rapid.

Shuttle. 5.5 miles, mostly paved, some dirt. Easy bike shuttle: Mostly on a paved secondary road.

Craft. Canoes and kayaks (including lake kayaks). Inflatables will be sluggish in the slow lake-like current.

Mileage Chart

0	Put-in. Big Springs National Water Trail. Launch site. River left.
.7	Henrys Fork enters from right.
3.7	Water Trail Take-out on river right. This is the usual take-out for Big Springs trips.
4.2	Highway 20 bridge.
6.8	Alternative take out. River left. Upper Coffee Pot Campground. (Last take-out before Coffee Pot rapids.)

Packing up for a trip down the Big Springs National Water Trail—and guess who gets to go!

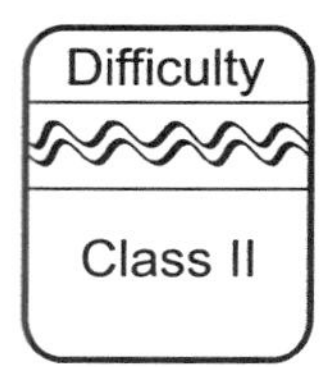

Henrys Fork Snake River

Box Canyon

THE BRISK AND DELIGHTFUL RUN through Box Canyon is another gem in the river-rich Island Park area. It's a playful class II stretch of water which is runnable in open canoes, kayaks, drift boats and inflatables.

Like any class II water, you'll want to have some river experience first, but when you're ready to try a little whitewater, this is a good learning stretch. Moreover, the river runs through a small and elegant lava canyon (Box Canyon) which is hemmed in by a thick conifer forest. This is a very well-known fly fishing stretch and with a boat, you can sample all of its remote riffles and eddies. Moreover, it's broad enough that as you run the river, you can give fly fishers a wide berth.

Basic Stats

Difficulty: Class II. Swift water, occasional rocky rapids, some waves.

Levels/Season: Low to medium flows (less than 800 cfs at the Island Park gauge). Mid-summer through fall.

Distance/Time: 3.7 miles / 1 to 2 hours.

Getting to the Take-out. Last Chance boat ramp. Start in the town of Last Chance located along US 20, 10 miles south of Macks Inn in Island Park. Look for the road sign "Old Hwy 191" near the Edgewater Inn and White Swan Bistro. Get on Old Hwy 191 and drive .4 mile upriver to a small river access area with a ramp.

Getting to the Put-in. Boat ramp just below Island Park Dam. Drive north of Last Chance on US 20 to Pond's Lodge. At .3 mile north of Pond's Lodge on US 20, turn left on the road leading to Island Park Dam. Drive .9 mile until coming to a "T" in the road. Take a left and continue .5 mile, taking a left 500 feet before reaching the Island Park Dam. Follow the road as it curves down to the put-in just below the dam. After unloading your boat by the river, park your vehicle in the parking area up the road a short distance. Restrooms are available.

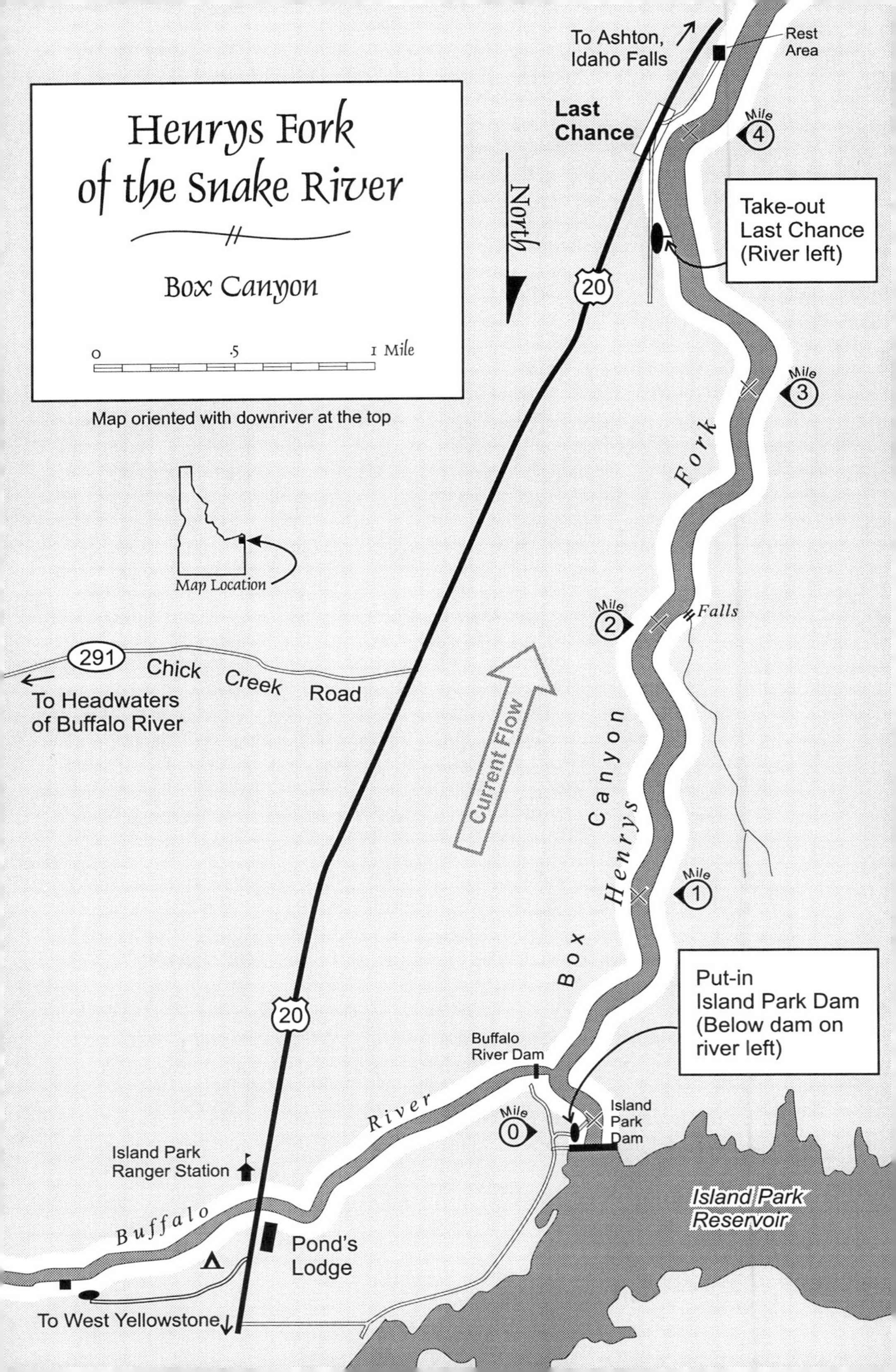
Henrys Fork
of the Snake River
Box Canyon
0
.5
1 Mile
Map oriented with downriver at the top
Map Location
North
To Ashton,
Idaho Falls
Rest
Area
Last
Chance
Mile
4
Take-out
Last Chance
(River left)
20
Mile
3
Fork
Mile
2
Falls
291
Chick
Creek
Road
To Headwaters
of Buffalo River
Current Flow
Canyon
Henrys
Mile
1
Box
Put-in
Island Park Dam
(Below dam on
river left)
20
Buffalo
River Dam
River
Mile
0
Island
Park
Dam
Island Park
Ranger Station
Island Park
Reservoir
Buffalo
Pond's
Lodge
To West Yellowstone

The Trip. The Henrys Fork through Box Canyon is swift with occasional rocks to maneuver around. It starts with some moderately sized waves at the beginning, but the river gradually eases up and the water becomes more rippled and then eventually flattens as it approaches the take-out. You'll see lots of fly fishers, and you'll want to give them plenty of space as you pass by.

Just past the 2-mile mark is a waterfall that comes in from the right. You'll know you're getting near the end when houses start appearing on the left shore. If desired, you can add some more miles to this run by combining it with the next stretch of river through Harriman State Park. The Harriman segment is mostly slow water, but, in addition to excellent fly fishing, it's an outstanding float trip for bird watching.

Shuttle. 7 miles, mostly paved. For bike shuttling, the highway has a wide, paved shoulder, but it is very busy and has lots of truck traffic.

Craft. Canoe, kayaks, inflatables and drift boats.

Mileage Chart

0	Put-in. Base of Island Park Dam, Boat Ramp. River left.
.2	Buffalo River (left).
2.1	Waterfall (right).
2.9	Residential area begins (left).
3.7	Last Chance Boat Ramp (left).

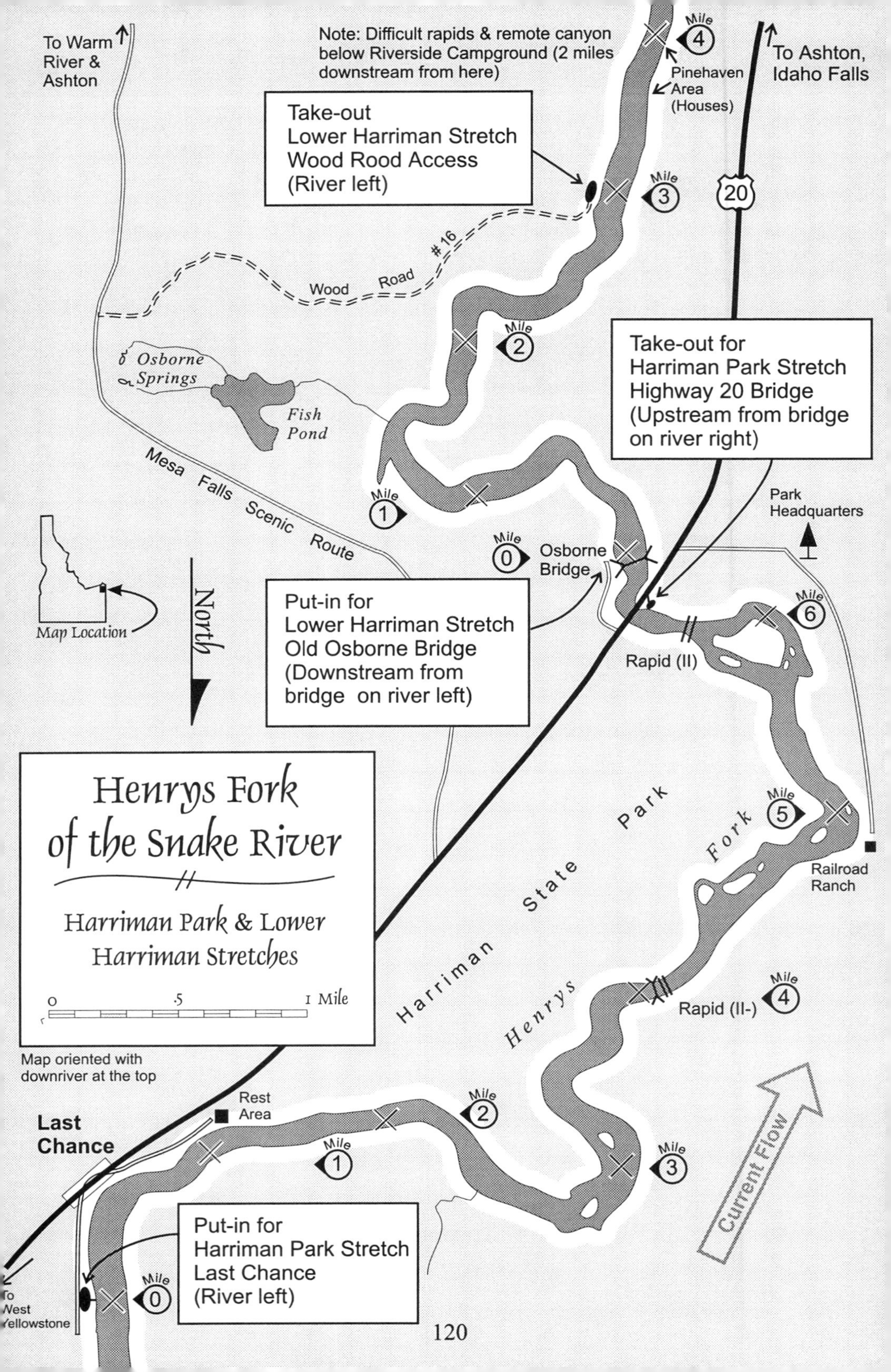

Henrys Fork of the Snake River
Harriman Park & Lower Harriman Stretches
0
.5
1 Mile
Map oriented with downriver at the top
Note: Difficult rapids & remote canyon below Riverside Campground (2 miles downstream from here)
To Warm River & Ashton
To Ashton, Idaho Falls
20
Pinehaven Area (Houses)
Take-out Lower Harriman Stretch Wood Rood Access (River left)
Wood Road #16
Osborne Springs
Fish Pond
Mesa Falls Scenic Route
Take-out for Harriman Park Stretch Highway 20 Bridge (Upstream from bridge on river right)
Osborne Bridge
Park Headquarters
Put-in for Lower Harriman Stretch Old Osborne Bridge (Downstream from bridge on river left)
Rapid (II)
North
Map Location
Harriman State Park
Henrys Fork
Railroad Ranch
Rapid (II-)
Current Flow
Rest Area
Last Chance
Put-in for Harriman Park Stretch Last Chance (River left)
To West Yellowstone
Mile 0
Mile 1
Mile 2
Mile 3
Mile 4
Mile 5
Mile 6

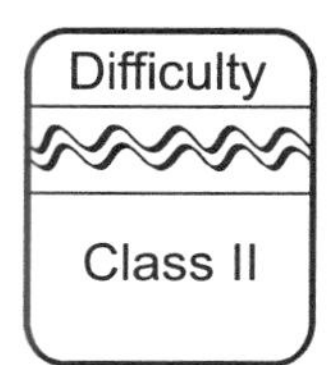

Henrys Fork Snake River

Harriman Park Stretch

EVERY STRETCH of the Henrys Fork through Island Park has some outstanding feature for which to lay claim. This stretch of the river through Harriman State Park is no exception. This is the supreme bird-watching float trip of the Island Park area. Among other birds, you'll see osprey, eagles, hawks, flocks of ducks and geese and the magnificent trumpeter swan. Moreover, it's one of the Henrys Fork's most famous fly fishing stretches. The river is quite wide and it is easy to give fly fishers plenty of room as you float by.

Although the river is very slow (class I, 1.0), it does have two rapids. One is at a bridge midway through the park that has a class II- rapid underneath it. The second is a class II- to II rapid just before the take-out at Osborne Bridge. Other than these two interruptions in the current, it is a tranquil float through sweeping meadows with unfettered views of mountains, near and far.

Basic Stats

Difficulty: Class II. (Two class II rapids, but otherwise the trip is a very easy class I, 1.0). It's open country; watch out for wind.

Season: Mid June through the fall.

Distance/Time: 6.5 miles / 3-5 hours.

Getting to the Take-out. Osborne Bridge. Osborne Bridge is located on US 20 about 3 miles south of Last Chance. The take-out is on the upstream side of the bridge on river right.

Getting to the Put-in. Last Chance Boat Ramp. Start in the town of Last Chance located along US 20, 10 miles south of Macks Inn in Island Park. Look for the road sign "Old Hwy 191" near the Edgewater Inn and White Swan Bistro. Drive .4 mile upriver on Old Hwy 191 to the small river access area with a ramp.

The Trip. Since this is a great bird watching trip, you'll want to do this one in the morning. Additionally, you're less likely to encounter upriver winds. Wind can be a real factor on this trip since the river flows sluggishly across a large wide-open flat.

At 4 miles from the start, a bridge crosses the river. Underneath the bridge is a rapid. The rapid is complicated by the supporting bridge piers. If you are rusty on your whitewater technique, you'll want to get out on the left side and have a look. Every so often somebody wraps a boat on the piers. By scouting and running it carefully, they can be avoided. Even so, if you feel uncomfortable running the rapid, don't be afraid to walk your boat down along the shore.

Just before reaching the take-out at Osborne bridge is one last patch of rapid water. We found that it wasn't too much of a problem picking our way down it, but there are some rocks to avoid. The take-out is on river right, upstream of the bridge.

Shuttle. 3.5 miles, all paved. For bike shuttling, Highway 20 has a wide, paved shoulder but it is extremely busy with lots of truck traffic.

Craft. Canoes, kayaks, drift boats. Inflatables are not recommended because of sluggish current and the possibility of upriver winds.

Mileage Chart

0	Put-in. Last Chance boat ramp (left).
2.3	Beginning of a 1-mile long oxbow bend.
4.1	Bridge. Class II- rapid under bridge. Scout on left.
5	Railroad Ranch (right).
6.3	Class II rapid.
6.5	Take-out. Osborne Bridge (upstream of the bridge on river right).

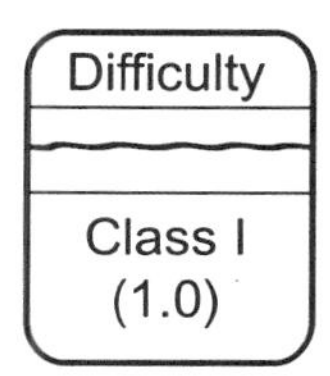

Henrys Fork Snake River

Lower Harriman
(Map on page 120)

THIS 3-MILE SEGMENT of the Henrys Fork is a relaxed beginner's float with good fishing and great views of the surrounding countryside. While the river flowing through the main part of Harriman Park (described in the previous section) has two class II rapids, this one through lower Harriman has no surprises. It is a pure class I (1.0) that can be enjoyed by the entire family.

Basic Stats

Difficulty: Class I (1.0).

Season: Mid June through the fall.

Distance/Time: 3 miles / 1.5 to 3 hours.

Getting to the Take-out: Wood Road Access. From Osborne Bridge along Highway 20, drive to the north .4 mile until reaching the turn-off (to the right) for the Mesa Falls Scenic Route. Check your odometer and drive down the Mesa Falls road for 2.5 miles. Just past Osborne Springs is a sign marked: Wood Road #16. Turn right here and follow the road, 1.6 miles towards the river. At places the road is rutted and a high clearance vehicle is recommended. Drive down to the river and park. This is a primitive take-out point with no privies or a boat ramp.

Alternative Take-out. Riverside Campground. An alternative take-out is Riverside Campground which adds 3 miles. Most of the water from the Wood Road access to Riverside is class I, however, just before the campground is a stretch of class I+ (1.4) water. It's also less natural since a number of homes have been built alongside the river in the Pinehaven area. Since the river is more difficult just above Riverside, family floaters should take-out at the Wood Road access point.

Getting to the Put-in. The old Osborne Bridge. The new Osborne Bridge is located on US 20 about 3 miles south of Last Chance. Just on the north side of the bridge is a fishing access road which provides access to the old bridge. Carry your boat through a gate and down to the river below the bridge. (Downstream of the old bridge on river left).

The Trip. The river starts out with a few riffles at first but it quickly slows down and flows around a large arc to the south. The entire trip is through open pasture and meadow land and nothing blocks the view. From the northwest to the northeast, you'll see the Centennial, Targhee and Henrys Lake Ranges. Almost due north is the prominent Sawtell Peak recognized by the radio tower on its summit.

At times, in the absence of wind, the surface of the river becomes glassy and mirror-like. Since the water is slow, you'll want to do this trip in the morning before afternoon heating starts kicking up the wind. It's a great stretch for families, and as long as there isn't any wind, it can be easily done in a couple of hours.

Like other stretches on the Henrys Fork, you'll see lots of people out fly fishing, but the river is wide and spacious, and it's easy to give them plenty of room as you float by.

Shuttle. 5 miles. Paved and dirt. Bike shuttle: part of the shuttle is on Highway 20 which has a wide, paved shoulder. The rest is on a paved secondary road and a dirt road.

Craft. Canoes, kayaks, drift boats. (Drift boats have a better put-in upstream of the "new" Osborne Bridge on river right.) Inflatables are not recommended because of slow water.

Wide and lazy: the Henrys Fork through Lower Harriman.

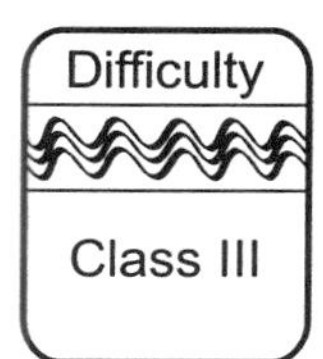

Henrys Fork Snake River

Riverside to Hatchery Ford

THIS IS A CLASS III stretch of moderately difficult and mostly continuous whitewater. We haven't included too many class III stretches of whitewater in this book since our purpose is to concentrate on the easier runs in the state. But we hope to clear up a misconception: this segment of water is often described as class II—and that can get people into trouble.

It can be run in an open canoe, but canoeists should have put in an apprenticeship on class II water first, particularly continuous class II water. A rafter can bounce down this stretch with less skill than a canoeist. In fact, in the past, Ron has used this stretch to help people learn rafting skills on rocky rivers.

Keep in mind that the river moves along at a good clip. If you take a spill, you'll have to swim through some very rocky water before you can get off the river. Nonetheless, if you're prepared and approach the river with respect and caution, this is an invigorating run through a beautiful and remote canyon.

Basic Stats

Difficulty: Class III (continuous).

Levels/Season: Low to medium water flows. Below 800 cfs at the Island Park Dam gauge. Mid June through the fall.

Distance/Time: 4.3 miles / 2-3 hours.

Getting to the Take-out. Hatchery Ford. Take the Mesa Falls Scenic Road which is located about .5 mile north of the entrance to Harriman State Park on US 20. Check your odometer and drive about 8 miles. Watch for the Hatchery Ford Road (Forest Road # 351) going off to the right. Turn onto road 351 and follow it for 3.5 miles to where it ends at a boat ramp. The last .5 mile is down a steep hill. A 4-wheel drive is recommended. Note that this is the last take-out before several major waterfalls on the river. You don't want to go any farther down the river than Hatchery Ford.

Getting to the Put-in. Riverside Campground. Riverside Campground is 3.5 miles south of Osborne Bridge. Turn to the east and drive .9 mile into the campground. On the western edge of the campground is a road which leads down to the river and the launching area.

The Trip. The rapids start just below the campground and continue unabated for most of the run. Much of the whitewater can be scouted from the seat of your boat, but pull off if something looks uncomfortable and scout it first. The take-out can't be missed. Several signs have been posted along the river warning of the unrunnable falls that are located downstream.

Shuttle. 16 miles. Paved and dirt. Bike shuttle is possible, but allow plenty of time.

Craft. Canoes, kayaks, inflatables and drift boats.

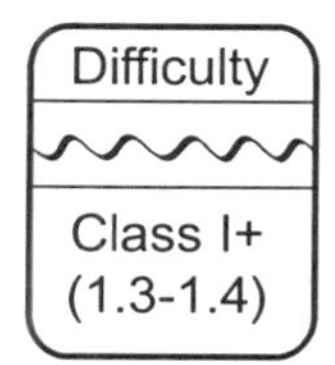

Henrys Fork Snake River

Warm River Stretch
(Stone Bridge to Backwaters of Ashton Reservoir)

THIS IS A TRANSITION ZONE for the Henrys Fork. Flowing out of the high plateau northeast of the town of Ashton, the river is changing from a snow and spring-fed mountain stream to a riffle and pool, flatland river. The vegetative patterns also reflect the change with one side of the river shaded by a conifer forest and the other open to the sun with eroded lava cliffs and sagebrush hills.

From a river running standpoint, it is class I+ (1.3 to 1.4) with some rock avoidance here and there, but very little overhanging brush and trees. Like other parts of the Henrys Fork, there are fish here. Though the trout are smaller than elsewhere, they are numerous—and hungry when the conditions are right.

Basic Stats

Difficulty: Class I+ (1.3 to 1.4).

Levels/Season: Low to medium flows (less than 800 cfs at the Island Park gauge). Mid summer through fall.

Distance/Time: 6.8 miles / 3 to 4 hours.

Getting to the Take-out. County Boat Ramp, backwaters of Ashton Reservoir. From Ashton, drive north on US 20. Three miles north of Ashton, you'll cross over the Henrys Fork. Just beyond the bridge take a left (west) and drive .3 mile to the county boat ramp.

Getting to the Put-in. Stone bridge, downstream from Warm River. From Ashton, take Idaho 47 to the east (towards Warm River). You'll drop down into the Henrys Fork canyon and at 8 miles from Ashton, turn left on the intersection of North River Road with South River Road. About .5 mile from the intersection, cross the bridge over the river and drive .2 mile downriver from the bridge until coming to a small pull-off and a place to launch boats.

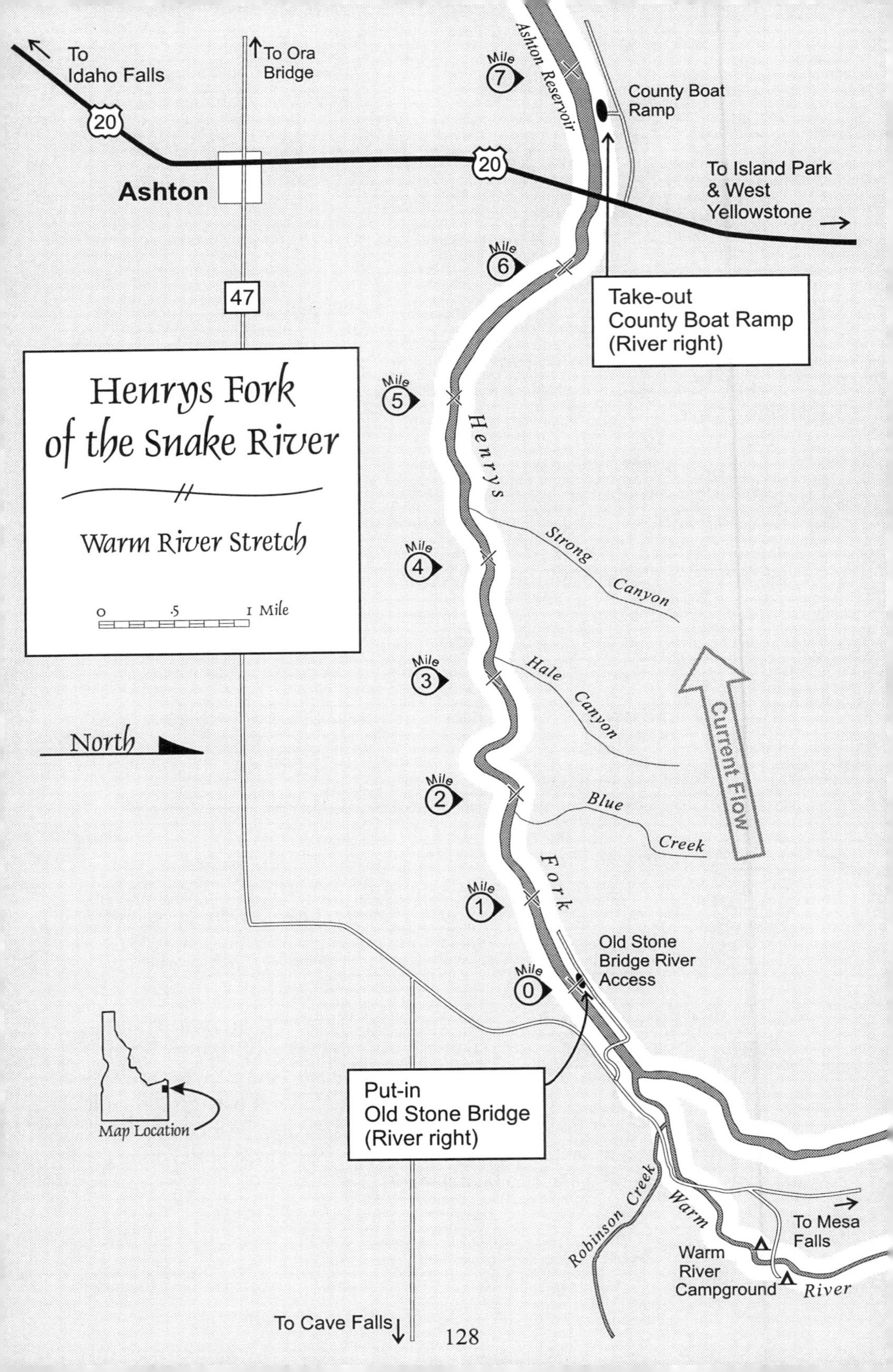

To Idaho Falls
20
To Ora Bridge
Ashton
20
47
Ashton Reservoir
Mile 7
County Boat Ramp
To Island Park & West Yellowstone
Mile 6
Take-out
County Boat Ramp
(River right)
Mile 5
Henrys Fork of the Snake River
Warm River Stretch
0 .5 1 Mile
Henrys
Strong Canyon
Mile 4
Mile 3
Hale Canyon
Current Flow
North
Mile 2
Blue Creek
Fork
Mile 1
Old Stone Bridge River Access
Mile 0
Put-in
Old Stone Bridge
(River right)
Map Location
Robinson Creek
Warm River
To Mesa Falls
Warm River Campground
To Cave Falls

The Trip. This is an enjoyable and attractive float trip. It has a fair amount of swift water, but most of the time you can run it down the middle without much maneuvering either direction. The water is clear and crystalline and fed by a multitude of springs along the way. The fact that there are plenty of fish in the river is indicated by the presence of bald eagles and one particularly fat and brazen river otter that we passed about 5 miles from the start.

You'll know that the end is coming as the trees become sparser and the canyon lowers. After passing under the highway bridge, it's only .2 mile to the take-out on the right.

Shuttle. 12 miles, mostly all paved. Bike shuttle: 3 miles is on Highway 20 which is very busy but has a moderately wide, paved shoulder. The rest is a paved secondary road. Give yourself plenty of time.

Craft. Canoes, kayaks, inflatables and drift boats.

Mileage Chart

0	Put-in. Old stone bridge downstream from Warm River. River right.
1.9	Mouth of Blue Creek (right). Secondary road alongside river on the right turns and climbs away from river.
3	Rock formations on river right.
3.3	Mouth of Hale Canyon (right).
4.5	Mouth of Strong Canyon (right).
5.8	Stream enters on left.
6.5	Highway 20 bridge.
6.8	Take-out. County boat ramp (right).

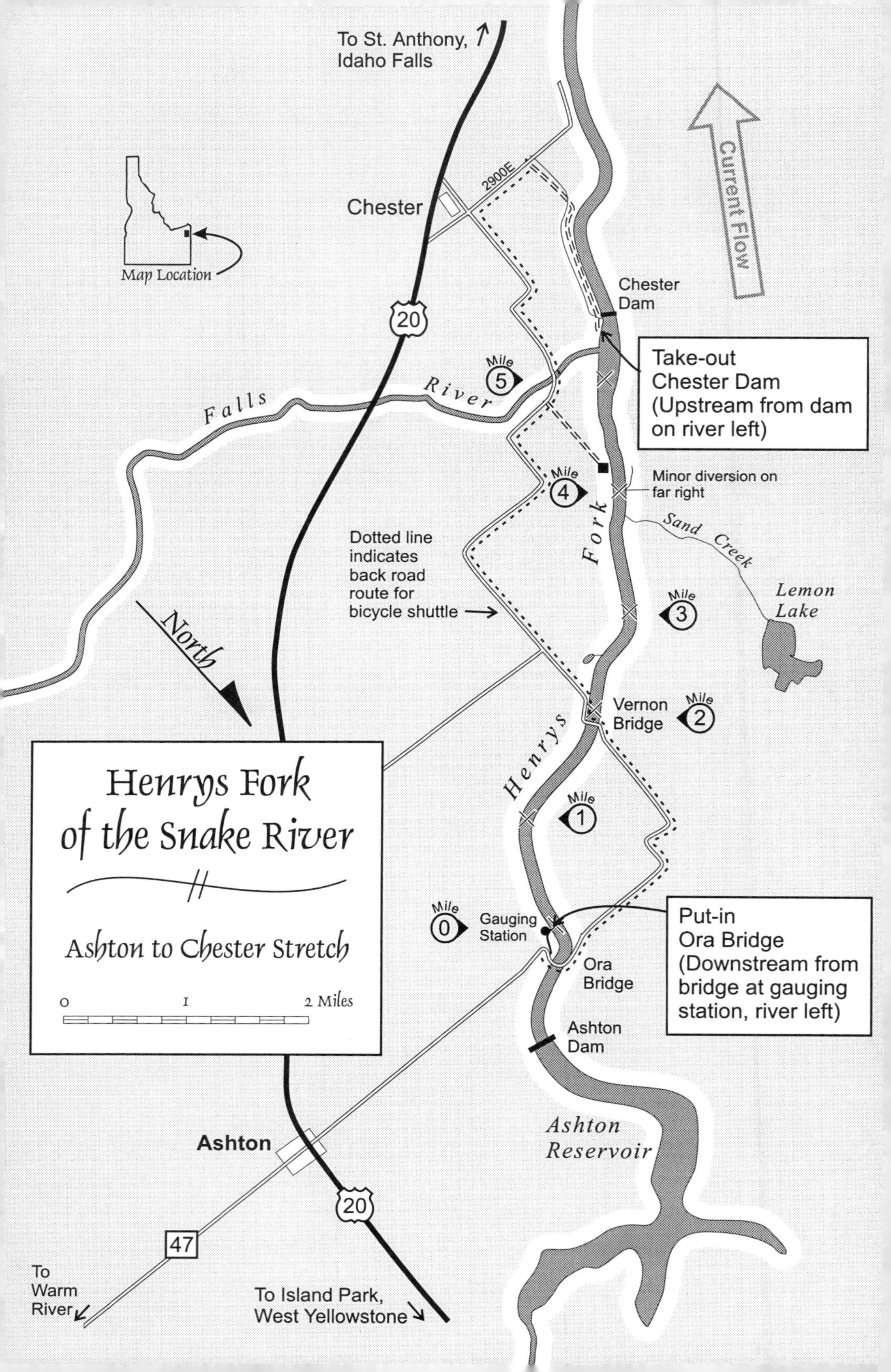

To St. Anthony, Idaho Falls
Current Flow
2900E
Chester
Map Location
Chester Dam
20
Take-out
Chester Dam
(Upstream from dam on river left)
Mile 5
Falls River
Mile 4
Minor diversion on far right
Sand Creek
Fork
Dotted line indicates back road route for bicycle shuttle
Lemon Lake
Mile 3
North
Vernon Bridge
Mile 2
Henrys
Mile 1
Henrys Fork of the Snake River
Ashton to Chester Stretch
0
1
2 Miles
Mile 0
Gauging Station
Put-in
Ora Bridge
(Downstream from bridge at gauging station, river left)
Ora Bridge
Ashton Dam
Ashton Reservoir
Ashton
20
47
To Warm River
To Island Park, West Yellowstone

Difficulty

Class I
(1.1-1.2)

Henrys Fork Snake River

Ashton to Chester Stretch

THE HENRYS FORK just downstream from Ashton Reservoir flows through the undulating lands, and wide open spaces, of the upper Snake River Valley. This an easy stretch (class I, 1.1 to 1.2), a good one for families or beginners that are comfortable in a boat.

It doesn't have any cantankerous snags or overhanging brush, only some riffles and a couple of rocks to paddle around. One of the attractions of this segment of the Henrys Fork is the good trout fishing. Good habitat combined with the cold water released from the dam support a sizable population of trout. Consequently, you'll see a fair number of fly fishers in drift boats early and late in the season. The river, however, is wide enough that paddlers passing by can give them their space.

Basic Stats

Difficulty: Class I (1.1 to 1.2).

Levels/Season: Below 2,000 cfs. Mid summer through fall.

Distance/Time: 5.5 miles / 2-3 hours.

Getting to the Take-out. Chester Dam. The small town of Chester is located just off of Idaho 20, about 8 miles south of Ashton. From Chester, follow a secondary road (2900 E) which heads straight west, towards the river. At 1 mile from US 20 in Chester, a rough dirt road leads off to the right (north) to Chester Dam. Follow the road for 1.5 miles until it comes to the dam. Drive across a rickety bridge over a canal to an area where boats can be taken out in the small reservoir which forms behind the dam.

Getting to the Put-in. Ora Bridge. From the US 20 and Idaho 47 intersection in Ashton, turn to the west and drive towards the river. Stay on the main road and drive 2.6 miles from Ashton to the bridge over the Henrys Fork. About 300 feet before reaching the bridge take a left on a dirt road which leads down to the river. The place to launch boats is next to a round gauging station.

The Trip. The river starts in a shallow lava canyon. A couple of houses are visible from river-level, but the surrounding country is mostly open and rural. Some patchy wild rose and willow grow in the riparian zone, but largely the banks are free of brush. Close to the end, the openness of the country allows a far-off view of the Tetons to the east.

The take-out is obvious. The river slows in the small reservoir behind Chester Dam. Just after reaching the slow water, the Falls River enters from the left. A fun side trip is to paddle up the Falls to a small rapid.

The take-out is located on river left, just after the mouth of the Falls River, about 25 yards above the dam.

Shuttle. 12 miles, paved except 1.5 miles of dirt access road to Chester Dam. This has a pleasant bike shuttle on paved secondary roads. The route is marked with a dotted line on the map.

Craft. Canoes, kayaks, inflatables and drift boats.

Mileage Chart

0	Put-in. Ora Bridge. River left, .2 mile downstream of the bridge.
2	Vernon Bridge.
2.5	Stream enters from left.
3.8	Mouth of Sand Creek (right).
4	Diversion on far right—minor diversion, no rapids.
5.4	Mouth of Falls River (left).
5.5	Take-out. Just above Chester Dam on left.

Difficulty		Difficulty
Class I (1.0)	or	Class I+ (1.4-1.5)

Salmon River

Salmon City, North Fork and Deadwater Stretches

THE SALMON RIVER has traversed a varied landscape by the time it flows under the Salmon City bridge: through the high, cool and beautiful Sawtooth Valley, by great sweeping slopes of talus near Clayton, and under the banded, bluish-green cliffs outside Challis. The portion of river described in this section is passing through its last unconfined valley and is beginning a journey through a deep canyon across the River of No Return Wilderness.

Most boaters coming to this part of Idaho are heading farther downstream, beyond the town of North Fork to the River of No Return stretch where the Salmon is best known for its whitewater. So many people clamor to get on the River of No Return that the Forest Service conducts an annual lottery to decide who will receive permits.

But no lottery is necessary for the part of the river described here. There are no crowds, no permits (thank heaven!) and some mighty fine scenery.

We have chosen three trips on this part of the Salmon. The first one (Salmon City to Donnelly Gulch just past North Fork) requires previous river experience. Rated class I+ (1.4-1.5), the water moves quickly and there are lots of willow and cottonwood snags to avoid. As an easier option, we have included a short 3-mile section just below the town of North Fork which is slower and less technical at a class I (1.2-1.3).

Finally the easiest stretch (class I, 1.0) is found downstream from North Fork in an area called Deadwater. It's very short and is mostly suitable for canoes or lake kayaks, but you won't have to do a shuttle. The water is slow enough that you can put in at the Deadwater boat ramp and paddle up or downstream, watching for wildlife and exploring something that is very rare on the Salmon: quiet water.

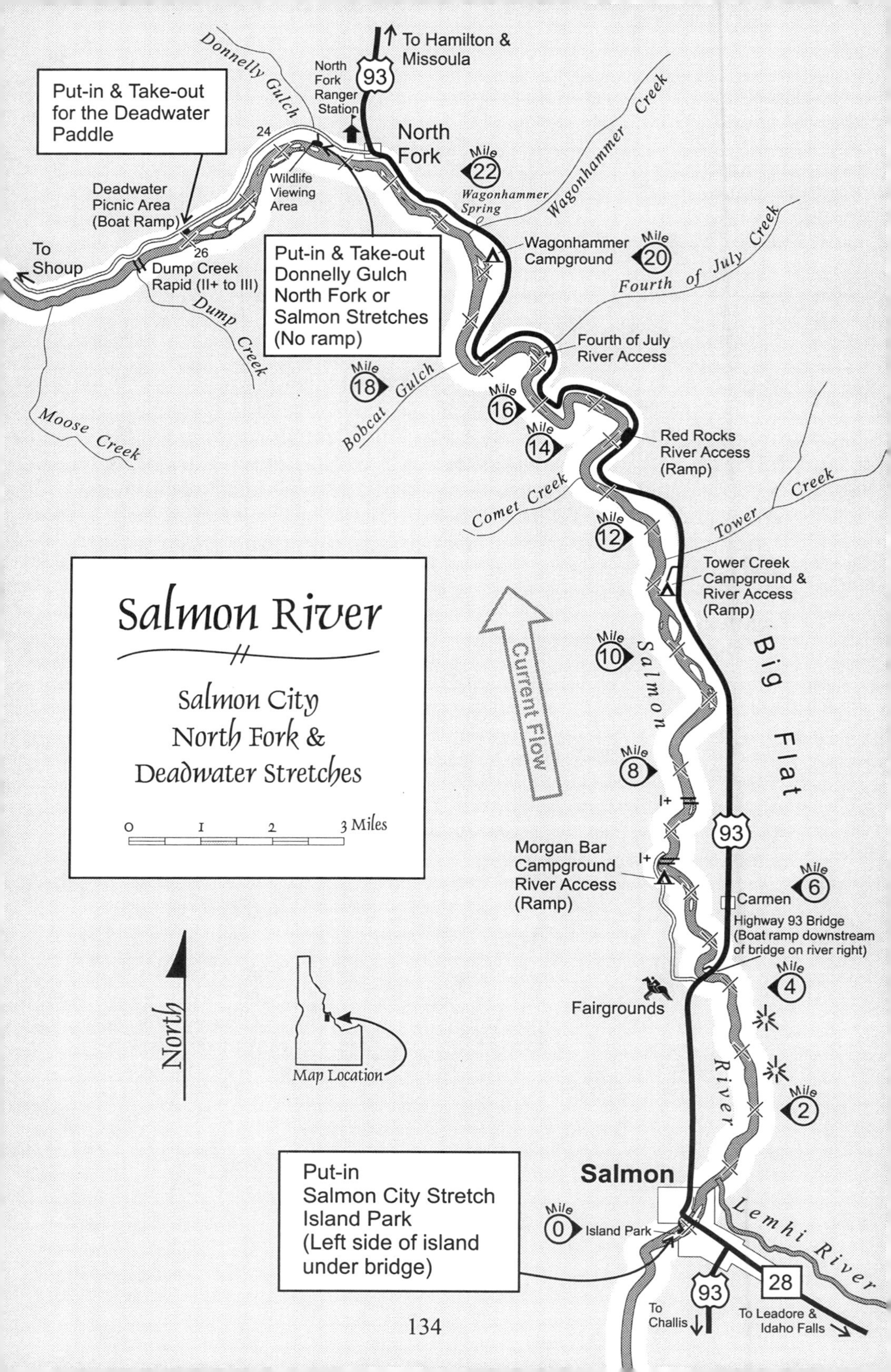

Salmon River
Salmon City
North Fork &
Deadwater Stretches
0
1
2
3 Miles
Put-in & Take-out for the Deadwater Paddle
Put-in & Take-out Donnelly Gulch North Fork or Salmon Stretches (No ramp)
Put-in Salmon City Stretch Island Park (Left side of island under bridge)
To Hamilton & Missoula
North Fork Ranger Station
North Fork
93
Donnelly Gulch
24
Wildlife Viewing Area
Deadwater Picnic Area (Boat Ramp)
To Shoup
26
Dump Creek Rapid (II+ to III)
Dump Creek
Moose Creek
Mile 22
Wagonhammer Spring
Wagonhammer Creek
Wagonhammer Campground
Mile 20
Fourth of July Creek
Fourth of July River Access
Mile 18
Bobcat Gulch
Mile 16
Mile 14
Red Rocks River Access (Ramp)
Comet Creek
Mile 12
Tower Creek
Tower Creek Campground & River Access (Ramp)
Current Flow
Mile 10
Salmon
Big Flat
Mile 8
I+
I+
Morgan Bar Campground River Access (Ramp)
Mile 6
Carmen
Highway 93 Bridge (Boat ramp downstream of bridge on river right)
Mile 4
Fairgrounds
River
Mile 2
North
Map Location
Salmon
Mile 0
Island Park
Lemhi River
28
93
To Challis
To Leadore & Idaho Falls

Salmon City Stretch
(Salmon City to Donnelly Gulch—Wildlife Viewing Area)

Basic Stats (Salmon City to Donnelly Gulch)

Difficulty: Class I+ (1.4 -1.5) Some small rapids, occasional rocks to avoid and frequent snags and sweepers.

Levels: The Salmon River can get very high and dangerous during high water which usually comes in June. During this time, water levels measured at the Salmon gauge may go way above 10,000 cfs. This trip is best done in late summer or fall when the flows have dropped to the 3,000 cfs range or lower.

Distance/Time : 24 miles / 6-7 hours in low water. Two shorter runs may be done: Salmon City to Red Rock, 14 miles (3 hours) or Red Rock to Donnelly Gulch, 10 miles (3 hours). A nice overnight trip can be made by floating all the way to Deadwater.

Getting to the Take-out. Donnelly Gulch. Drive to North Fork, 21 miles north of Salmon on US 93. At North Fork, take a left on the paved secondary road which follows the Salmon River towards Shoup. At .6 mile from North Fork, turn left on a road which leads down the river and ends at the remains of an old bridge. This road is marked with the sign: "Wildlife Viewing Area." It is located just before Donnelly Gulch which comes in from river right. There's no ramp here and the bank drops off several feet into the river, but canoes, kayaks and small inflatables can take out—or put in—here. Drift boaters will want to use the ramp located 3 more miles downriver at Deadwater Picnic Area.

Alternative Take-outs. A number of other access points are also available. One suggested alternative take-out which cuts the trip in half is the Red Rock Boat Ramp. Red Rock is marked with a highway sign, 7.9 miles south of North Fork or 9 miles north of the Salmon River bridge in the town of Salmon on US 93.

Getting to the Put-in. Island Park in the town of Salmon. To get to Island Park, drive through Salmon heading northwest on US 93. Cross over the bridge spanning the Salmon River. Take the first left on the other side of the bridge. This road leads to a municipal park called Island Park which has parking, restrooms and a concrete boat ramp. The ramp is located almost under the bridge. Other put-in points are accessed off US 93 and are indicated on the map.

The Trip. (Salmon City to Donnelly Gulch.) The Salmon River doesn't lollygag, and once on the water, you'll find yourself quickly whisked through town. At the beginning of the run, you will be running down the left channel of a long island. One diversion is encountered in this channel about 500 feet from the start. We found the diversion which draws water off to the left to be easily run by staying in the middle of the channel.

Shortly after the diversion, you'll reach the end of the island. At .8 mile from the start, the Lemhi River enters from the right. The currents at the junction of the two rivers can be a little tricky, and if you're in a canoe you'll want to stay in the middle and move on through.

The next three miles is an attractive portion of the trip with white chalky cliffs rising up on the right side of the river and a protective stand of cottonwoods and willows on the left. At times, the dry gullies which cut through the cliffs almost resemble dry arroyos of Southwest canyon country. Among the birds on this stretch, we spotted a falcon and a bald eagle. Cliff swallows are numerous and their prolific dark nests show up plainly against the surrounding light-colored rock.

The river passes under the Highway 93 bridge, 4.4 miles from the start and stays on the western side of the highway for the remainder of the trip. At 6.4 miles from the start, you'll pass the Morgan Bar Campground which has two boat ramps—one in the upper part of the campground and one in the lower. Just after the campground is a small rapid, class I+ (1.4-1.5). Another small rapid is found in another mile. Both rapids are fairly easy, but have some waves and some minor rock dodging.

You'll see a few homes along this area of the river, but for the most part, the cottonwood forest blocks out a good part of the development that has occurred north of town. Now and then through breaks in the trees, you catch a glimpse of the impressive Beaverhead Mountains to the east on the continental divide between Idaho and Montana.

For the next half of the trip, the river character is very similar to the first. Throughout the entire run, watch carefully for overhanging trees and brush. Be particularly careful for snags on the outside of bends. Follow the safe river running technique of entering bends on the inside.

The river takes a major bend at North Fork, heading west and beginning its journey from one side of the state to the other. Once you pass the town of North Fork, you're almost there. The take-out is at the site of an old bridge, slightly more than 1 mile from North Fork on the right.

Idaho State Historical Society

A boating party ready to depart from the bridge at Salmon City. *Circa* 1915.

Camping. This stretch of river makes a very nice overnight trip. Even though lots of private land is found along it, river campers have a number of good choices. One option is to spot your vehicle with camping gear at one of the developed campsites along the river including Morgan Bar, Tower Rock, and Wagonhammer. Primitive (and free) camping is also available. One such place is the Sportsman's Access at Fourth of July Creek. On our overnight trip from Salmon to Deadwater, we found a nice place to camp on a small island across from Donnelly Gulch.

Shuttle. 22 miles, all paved. Bike shuttle is possible, but Highway 93 is very busy and the shoulder is narrow.

Craft. Canoes, kayaks, large and small inflatables, and drift boats (plenty of ramps are available). Late summer and fall is the best time for canoeing the river.

Mileage Chart
Salmon City to Donnelly Gulch

0	Put-in. Island Park in Salmon City.
.1	Diversion. Diverts to left. Middle run.
.8	Lemhi River enters from the right.
4.4	Highway 93 bridge. A boat ramp is located downstream of the bridge on river right.
6	Morgan Bar Campground (river left). Two boat ramps are located in the campground.
6.4	Class I+ (1.4-1.5) rapid.
7.5	Class I+ (1.4-1.5) rapid.
11	Tower Creek Campground (right). Boat ramp.
14.4	Red Rocks boat ramp (right).
16.9	Fourth of July Creek River Access—not easily seen from the river (right).
19	Wagonhammer Campground (right).
22.3	North Fork (right). Note: the North Fork boat ramp is private.
23.5	Take-out. Remains of old bridge. Wildlife viewing area near Donnelly Gulch (right).

North Fork Section
Donnelly Gulch to Deadwater Picnic Area

Basic Stats (Donnelly to Deadwater)

Difficulty: Class I (1.2 to 1.3). Some possible overhanging trees and a couple of mini-rapids where the river slides down over gravel bars, but all-in-all easier than the previous stretch.

Levels: Same comments as the previous stretch.

Distance/Time: 3 miles / 1 hour.

Getting to the Take-out. Deadwater Picnic Area. The Deadwater Picnic Area is located 3.6 miles from North Fork on the paved secondary road which leads to Shoup.

Getting to the Put-in. Wildlife Viewing Area at Donnelly Gulch. See previous stretch (page 135) for directions. Note that there is also a boat ramp at North Fork, but it is on private land, and the public is asked to use Donnelly or other public access points along the river.

The Trip. Donnelly Gulch to Deadwater Picnic Area. This is a shorter and easier option to the Salmon City to Donnelly Gulch stretch described previously. On this trip, you'll encounter some corners and mini-rapids at gravel bars and possibly some overhanging brush and trees. With the observance of normal river running precautions, you'll find it a pleasant, moderately easy run, removed from the hustle and bustle of Highway 93.

You'll also find this part of the river more hemmed in than the Salmon City stretch, with grass and sage-covered slopes rising from 3,500 at river level to high points over 7,000 feet. Several islands dot the river and are good places for bird watching. From a fishing standpoint, the primary attraction are steelhead which run in the spring and fall.

About a half mile from the take-out, the current slows and enters the slow, lake-like waters of Deadwater, a natural impoundment, formed by a downriver ledge.

Shuttle. 3 miles, all paved. Easy bicycle shuttle on a paved, secondary road.

Craft. Canoes, kayaks and all-sized inflatables. Drift boats are very common on this stretch, but since Donnelly does not have a ramp, drift boaters will want to put in at ramps located along US 93 above North Fork.

Deadwater Paddle

Basic Stats (Deadwater Paddle)

Difficulty: Class I (1.0). Flat, lake-like water.

Season: Avoid the high water period which usually occurs in mid June. Spring, summer and fall are fine.

Distance: Out and back trip, 1 to 1.5 miles.

Accessing the Put-in and Take-out. Deadwater Picnic area, located 3.6 miles from North Fork on the road to Shoup.

The Paddle. Deadwater. Deadwater, the slow, lake-like stretch on the Salmon River between North Fork and Shoup only occupies about a mile of the river, but if you are looking for a safe place to canoe or kayak without worrying about snags or rapids this is the place. Boats can be launched at the concrete ramp at the Deadwater Picnic area.

From the picnic area, you can paddle upstream or downstream about a half mile in either direction. If you paddle downstream, you'll want to stay in the slow moving water since Dump Creek Rapid (class III) is located .3 mile below where the flat water ends. If you have children with you, the safest option is to have them paddle upstream from the picnic area. Even though this is flat, easy water, make sure everyone wears a life jacket.

Craft. Canoes and lake kayaks.

The Salmon River Canyon near North Fork.

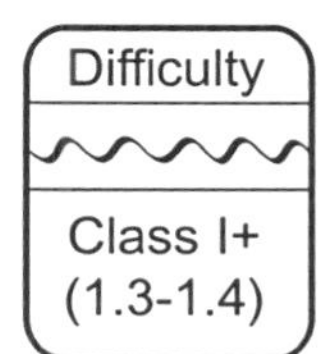

Salmon Falls Creek

Salmon Falls Canyon Overnight Trip

SALMON FALLS CREEK, located south of Twin Falls, is a wonderful overnight trip through a mostly roadless desert canyon. Once you leave the launching area alongside Highway 93, you'll find yourself in another world with cliffs that rise up from the river and volcanic canyon walls which have been eroded into bizarre shapes and forms.

There's no significant whitewater on this stretch other than a few waves and swift sections, but you'll want to make sure that you have river boating experience before undertaking it. You'll need to feel comfortable in your boat and be able to handle rivers that twist and turn—which Salmon Falls Creek likes to do a lot. It's also a river which after peaking from run-off, goes down quickly, and you'll need to time your trip so it occurs after high water but before the river gets too low and unrunnable later in the season. One portage must be made around a fish check dam, but it's fairly short and can be done without too much effort.

Basic Stats

Difficulty: Class I+ (1.3 to 1.4) at around 300 cfs. No real rapids. Some swift current here and there.

Levels: Good levels are around 300 cfs (becomes more pushy in higher levels). Season is dependent on water: late June to mid July. Gauge: Salmon Falls near San Jacinto, NV.

Distance/Time: 11 miles / 6-8 hours at 300 cfs. Best done as an overnight trip.

Portages: One. Fish check dam 3.2 miles from the start.

Accessing the Take-out. Drive to Rogerson, Idaho on US 93 about 25 miles south of Twin Falls. Check your odometer at Rogerson. Between 9 and 10 miles from Rogerson, you'll pass the turn-off to Norton Bay (a boat launch and recreation site on Salmon Falls Reservoir) marked by a highway sign. Keep driving until you have gone 10.3 miles from Rogerson and look for a dirt road heading off to the right (west). This is the road that goes to the Backwaters Recreation Site on Salmon Falls Reservoir. It may not be marked. (It wasn't when we ran the river.) If you end up in Jackpot, back track on US 93, 7.7 miles from the stoplight at Cactus Pete's, and you should find it.

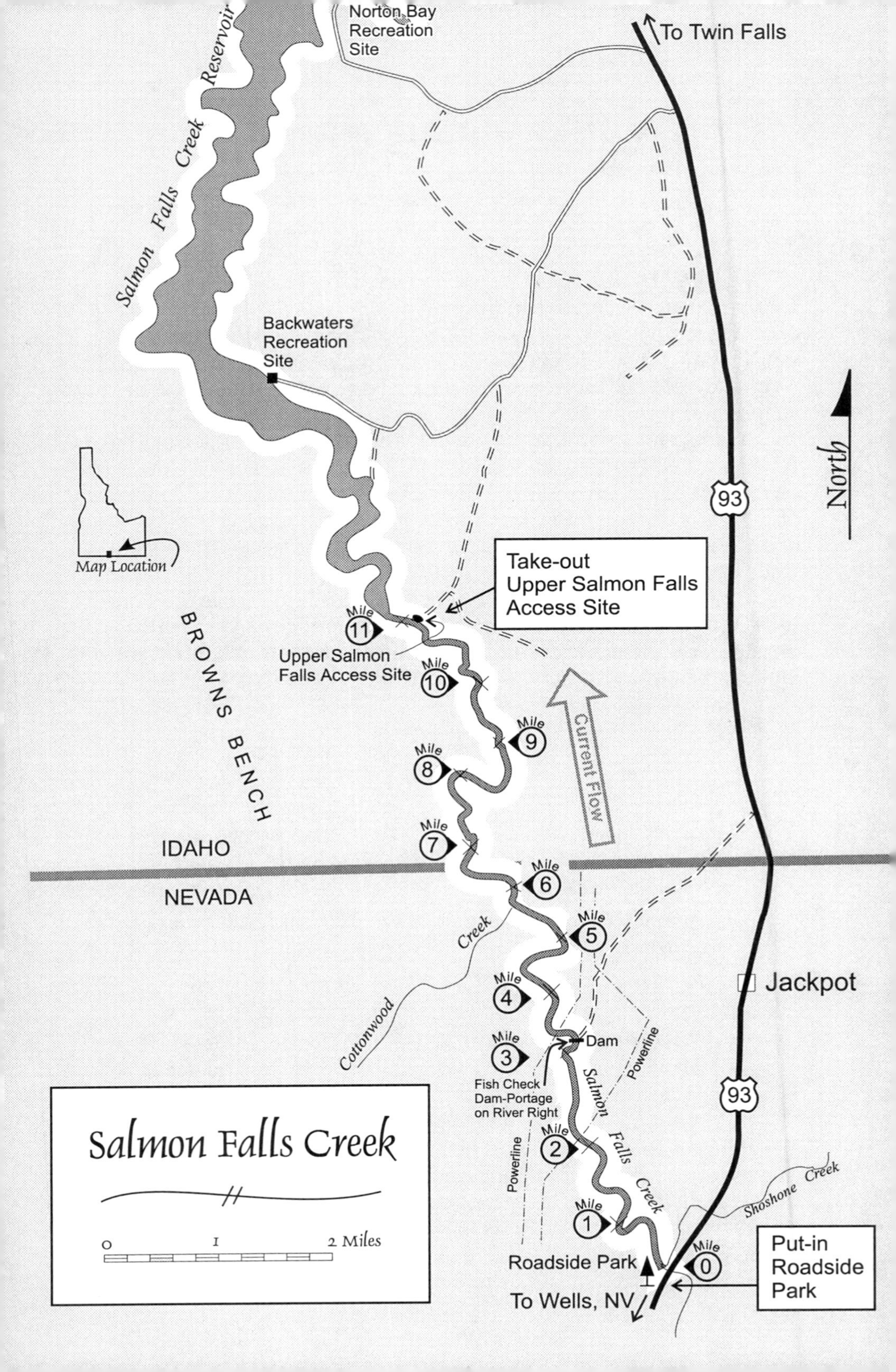
Norton Bay
Recreation
Site
To Twin Falls
Salmon Falls Creek Reservoir
Backwaters
Recreation
Site
North
93
Map Location
Take-out
Upper Salmon Falls
Access Site
Mile 11
Upper Salmon
Falls Access Site
Mile 10
Mile 9
Mile 8
Current Flow
BROWNS BENCH
Mile 7
IDAHO
NEVADA
Mile 6
Cottonwood Creek
Mile 5
Jackpot
Mile 4
Mile 3
Dam
Powerline
Fish Check
Dam-Portage
on River Right
Salmon Falls Creek
93
Mile 2
Powerline
Shoshone Creek
Mile 1
Mile 0
Roadside Park
Put-in
Roadside
Park
To Wells, NV
Salmon Falls Creek
0
1
2 Miles

As you turn off the highway on the road leading to Backwaters, check your odometer again. Drive exactly 3 miles and take a left on a side road. In dry conditions this road is passable by two wheel drive, but if it's wet or if a recent storm has eroded the road, you'll be more secure in a pickup or four-wheel drive vehicle. Follow this road 2.5 miles to the river. The take-out place is a pleasant grassy bench alongside the river with a picnic table. Leave your shuttle vehicle or mountain bike here.

Accessing the Put-in. Drive to Jackpot, Nevada on US 93 and continue south on the highway for 3 miles until coming to a bridge over Salmon Falls Creek. Just on the south side of the bridge is a roadside rest area. This is the launch site.

The Trip. Salmon Falls Creek is a relatively easy run, but it is not a boring river. It bends back and forth like an erratic sine wave, swinging, twisting and turning by sandy and rocky bars, cliffs and brushy bends. By the time you finish the trip, you'll be an expert at handling a curvy river.

There is some swift water, but the main technique on this river is straightforward: enter bends on the inside and paddle away from overhanging brush or cliffs on the outside of bends. At 300 cfs, the current is not forceful, and with basic skills, canoeists and other boaters won't find it too hard to maneuver the corners. At higher flows, however, the current becomes more forceful, and it takes quicker reaction times and more powerful strokes. Running the river is not recommended during peak flows.

The banks of the river are filled with willows, dogwood, and wild rose. At the end of June, rose is in bloom and a pleasant aroma is all along the river. The canyon never exceeds more than a couple hundred feet deep, but it is a fascinating place with volcanic walls eroded into columns and spires. At night, the ragged edge of the canyon turns into the forms of a menagerie backlit by the incomparable desert sky.

It is possible to do the trip in one day, but when you figure driving and shuttle time, your experience on the river will be much more relaxed if you spread it over a 2 day period. Plus, there are not many easy overnight trips, particularly primitive desert trips, and it would be a shame to rush down the river without taking time to really enjoy—and spend a night in—this delightful place.

The Portage. A fish check dam is located 3.2 miles from the start. The dam is not runnable and must be portaged. You'll pass under one powerline crossing, and just before the second, you'll come to the backwaters of the dam. You don't have to worry about being swept over it. The water is slow

Salmon Falls Canyon near Cottonwood Creek: a number of small gravel and sand bars are available for camping in this area.

and lake-like, but as a precaution when you reach the slow water, stay close to the right (east) shore of the river. Pull off approximately 30-40 feet above the dam. You'll find a path which goes around the impoundment. The normal put-in is just below the dam, but it involves running a small rapid. If you don't like the looks of the rapid, carry your boat a little farther downstream to where the water is more to your liking.

Camping. A good area for your river camp is just past Cottonwood Creek (5.7 miles from the start). Cottonwood Creek is signaled by a large valley coming in from the left, 2.5 miles below the fish check dam. The reason we like the Cottonwood Creek area is because it is out of sight of the two powerlines which cross high above the river, but it's still in an interesting part of the canyon. Moreover, at medium flows, a number of gravel and sand bars are available in this area for camping. If you go too much farther below Cottonwood Creek for your campsite, the canyon starts flattening out some.

At our camp, we sat and watched a band of night hawks zipping through the sky and were serenaded by the melodic song of a canyon wren. During the day, we saw great blue herons, killdeers, mergansers, mallards, swallows, red tail hawks and a muskrat.

From a camp in the Cottonwood Creek area, it's only a couple of hours down to the upper Salmon Falls take-out. If desired, you can make the trip longer by paddling the backwaters of Salmon Falls Reservoir and take out at the Backwaters Boat Launch. A word of caution, however. The reservoir can produce strong up-canyon winds, particularly in the afternoon. It's best to catch a reservoir paddle early in the morning before the day warms up and starts stirring up the winds. Once you get into the reservoir proper, stay a few feet off of the right shore, so you're close to safety should you run into trouble.

Shuttle. 16 miles. Involves dirt roads and paved highway. Can be done on a mountain bike.

Craft. Canoes are the craft of choice for Salmon Falls Creek. With a canoe you can carry overnight gear and have a light enough craft to do the portage easily. Kayaks and small inflatables also are suitable for the trip. Drift boats can make it down, but you'll have to carry the boat around the fish dam. Additionally, there are no developed boat ramps for the river trip, but with a little effort boats can be slipped in and out of water.

Mileage Chart

0	Put-in at highway rest area, 3 miles south of Jackpot on US 93.
2.1	Cross under first powerline.
3.2	Fish check dam (must be portaged on right).
3.4	Cross under second powerline.
5.7	Cottonwood Creek comes in from left.
6.9	Cross the state line between Idaho and Nevada.
11.1	Take-out. Upper Salmon Falls Access Site (right).

Salmon Falls Creek twists and turns through the southern Idaho desert.

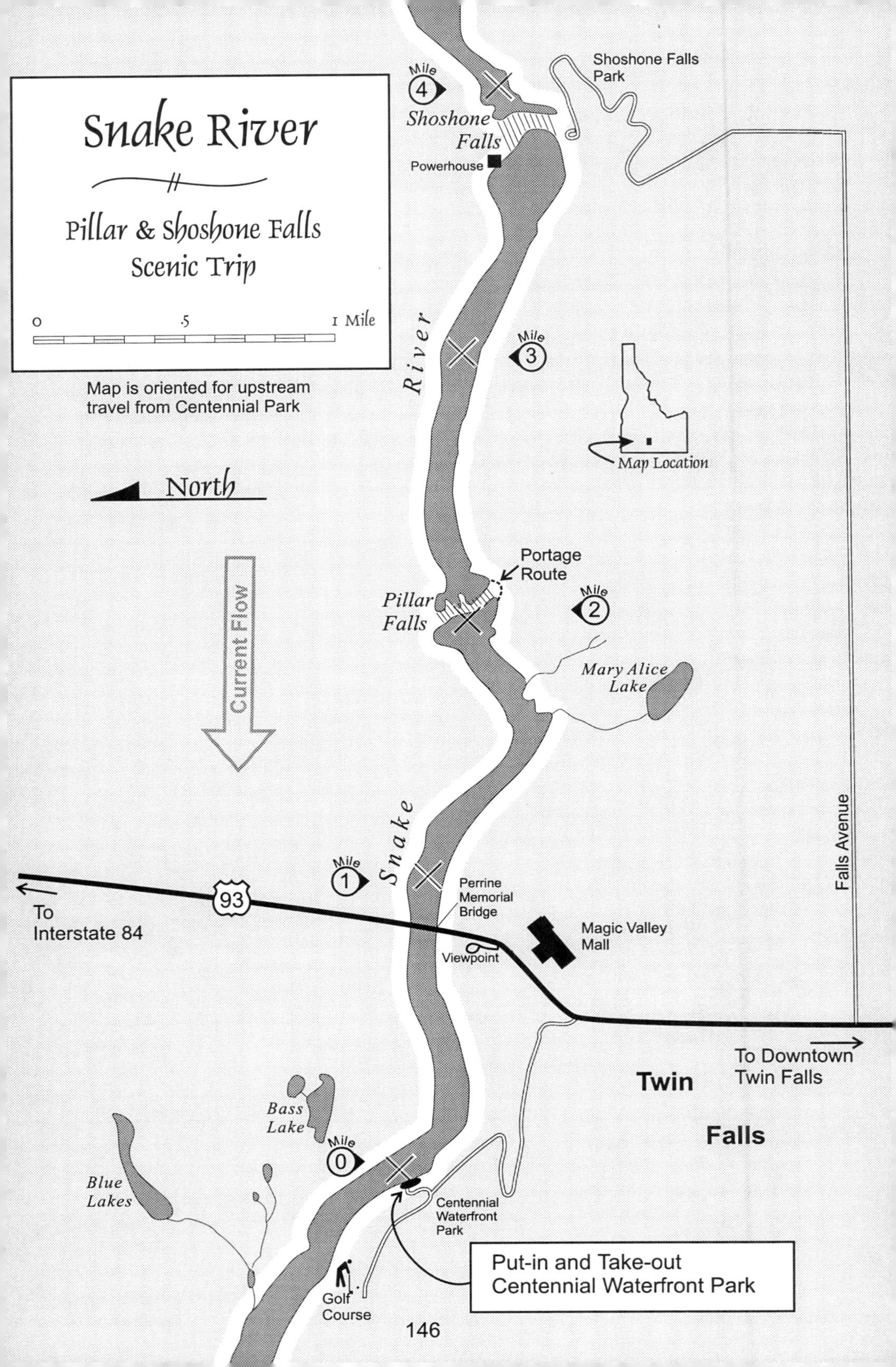
Snake River
Pillar & Shoshone Falls
Scenic Trip
0
.5
1 Mile
Map is oriented for upstream travel from Centennial Park
North
Current Flow
Mile 4
Shoshone Falls
Shoshone Falls Park
Powerhouse
River
Mile 3
Map Location
Portage Route
Pillar Falls
Mile 2
Mary Alice Lake
Snake
Mile 1
93
To Interstate 84
Perrine Memorial Bridge
Viewpoint
Magic Valley Mall
Falls Avenue
To Downtown Twin Falls
Twin Falls
Bass Lake
Mile 0
Blue Lakes
Centennial Waterfront Park
Put-in and Take-out Centennial Waterfront Park
Golf Course

Difficulty

Class I
(1.0)

Snake River

Pillar Falls and Shoshone Falls Scenic Trip

THIS SECTION OF THE SNAKE RIVER near Twin Falls is one of Idaho's most interesting paddle trips. It's an easy trip which can be done by the whole family—and it is spectacular.

The trip starts at Twin Falls Centennial Park, a park and boat ramp on the Snake River. It's an easy paddle upstream on lake-like water. Along the way, dozens of clear spring rivulets enter the river. Scattered here and there among the springs are little enchanting alcoves framed with lush, verdant greenery.

Two miles from the start is Pillar Falls, an awesome geological feature where the river tumbles around huge, teeth-shaped spires of lava jutting into the air. At Pillar Falls, you can turn around—or, better yet, when the water is low, make a short portage and continue paddling upstream until reaching the base of Idaho's Niagara Falls: Shoshone Falls.

Shoshone Falls spills over the edge of a ragged bowl of lava, dropping 212 feet and thundering into the river. You can view the falls from the canyon rim, but nothing compares to the view from the seat of a canoe or a kayak.

This trip took us completely off guard. For years we had heard about it, but just never got around to doing it. When we finally did, we couldn't stop talking about it. Put it on your list of trips to do—and do it soon.

Basic Stats

Difficulty: Class I (1.0). Flat, lake-like water.

Levels: Since it's flat water, the river can be paddled in all water levels. In order to do the portage around Pillar Falls (to view Shoshone Falls), the water level should be less than 3,500 cfs. The Milner gauge on the Snake River is used to judge flows in the Twin Falls area.

Distance/Time: 4 miles round trip to Pillar Falls (2-3 hours). 7-miles round trip to the base of Shoshone Falls (5-6 hours).

Portage: To visit Shoshone Falls, Pillar Falls must be portaged on river left (the right side of the river as you paddle upstream).

Getting to the Put-in and Take-out. Centennial Park, Twin Falls. If you are on Interstate 84, take the Twin Falls Exit (US 93). At 3.3 miles from I-84, you'll cross a bridge over the Snake River Canyon. Check your odometer on the Twin Falls end of the bridge. Drive .4 mile and take a right at the sign pointing the way to Centennial Park. Drive down the road to the park which has restrooms, paved parking, a dock, and a boat ramp. It's an attractive park, nicely designed and well maintained.

Shoshone Falls: the destination of one of Idaho's most spectacular paddle trips.

The Trip. From Centennial Park, it is difficult to tell which is upstream and downstream since the water is very still. As you face the river from the boat ramp, upstream is to the right. This is the direction you want to go. (Although you can paddle downstream, not too far down is a class III stretch of water—and below that is Auger Falls, a rarely run and hazardous falls.)

As you paddle upstream, stay close to the right shore. Because of all the springs that come in, this is the most interesting side of the river. If the wind comes up or anybody in your party has difficulty, you are always close to safety. Early on you'll pass under the graceful arch of Perrine Bridge, a brilliantly designed bridge which harmonizes with the environment of the Snake River Canyon.

Two miles from the start you'll come to Pillar Falls. As you paddle around viewing the falls, keep back a couple hundred feet from the base of the falls to avoid the turbulence. For some folks a visit to Pillar Falls will be enough. But if you want to continue, look at the river left side of the falls (that means to the far right as you are paddling upstream). You'll see a channel that Pillar Falls has cut through the lava rock. If there's no water going through this channel, then the portage route is open. Usually water flows through here at levels above 3,500 cfs. It is also possible to do a portage on the hillside on river right (left as you look upstream) in high water conditions, but it's long and difficult.

If you have a plastic boat, the portage is simple. The rock in the dry channel is polished and smooth, and you can easily drag your boat up it. At the upstream end of the channel, you'll need to walk your boat out through a shallow pond, but once beyond the pond, you're on your way again.

Shoshone Falls is another 1.5 miles—and is well worth the trip. Depending on flows, part or all of the curving arc of the falls' face will have water pouring over it. During certain times of the day, spray from the falls will create a rainbow which rises from the base of the falls. It's a dazzling view which is accompanied by the pounding and crashing of water. For safety's sake and to avoid turbulence, stay back 500 or 600 feet—the length of a couple of football fields.

If you have beginning boaters with you, make sure that everyone stays close to the far left (river left) shore on the return trip from the Shoshone Falls. That way you don't have to worry about getting anyone from one side of the river to the other as you get close to the portage around Pillar Falls.

Shuttle. None required. Up and back trip.

Craft. Canoes and kayaks, including lake kayaks. Drift boats can do the trip up to the base of Pillar Falls.

Mileage Chart
(Mileages start at Centennial Park and work upstream)

0	Put in and take-out. Centennial Park Boat Ramp.
.8	Perrine Memorial Bridge.
2	Pillar Falls. Portage is on river left—or the right side as one paddles upriver.
3.7	Shoshone Falls.

Idaho State Historical Society

Shoshone Falls from the canyon rim about 100 years ago.

Difficulty

Class I
(1.0-1.1)

Silver Creek

Silver Creek Preserve and Silver Creek West to Picabo Bridge

SILVER CREEK. The name says it all: water as clear as it comes, trout fishing known throughout the world, and canoeing among Idaho's best. Located just south and east of the Sun Valley-Ketchum area, Silver Creek arises from scores of springs and meanders through an agrarian valley. It is a laid-back canoe or kayak trip, a pure class I (1.1) which can be enjoyed by everyone no matter what their ability.

Two stretches are described in detail here. One is a beautiful 2.9-mile stretch through the Nature Conservancy's Silver Creek Preserve. The other is an equally lovely 4.5-mile segment which ends near the colorfully named town of Picabo.

The Silver Creek Preserve is a real success story in Idaho lands conservation. The Nature Conservancy has safeguarded one of the best remaining examples of a high desert, cold-spring ecosystem—and what better way to view it than from the seat of a canoe. The hard-working and dedicated management of the preserve has also worked closely with area land owners to restore other parts of Silver Creek to its original state.

The Preserve's staff asks that all users of the river—fly fishermen, boaters and hikers—stop at the visitor's center to sign-in. A donation is requested to help defray costs of maintaining the preserve. Give generously. As boaters, we really need to support outstanding programs such as the Silver Creek Preserve if we want to protect and preserve Idaho's magnificent waterways.

Silver Creek Preserve

Basic Stats (Silver Creek Preserve)

Difficulty: Class I (1.0 to 1.1).

Season: Fed by springs, it is floatable all year. Since Silver Creek is a world renowned fly fishing stream, the best time for boat trips and to avoid conflicts with fishermen is prior to Memorial Day, the start of the fishing season.

Distance/Time: 2.9 miles / 2 hours.

Sign-in: All users of Silver Creek Preserve must sign-in at the visitor's center. Leave a generous donation.

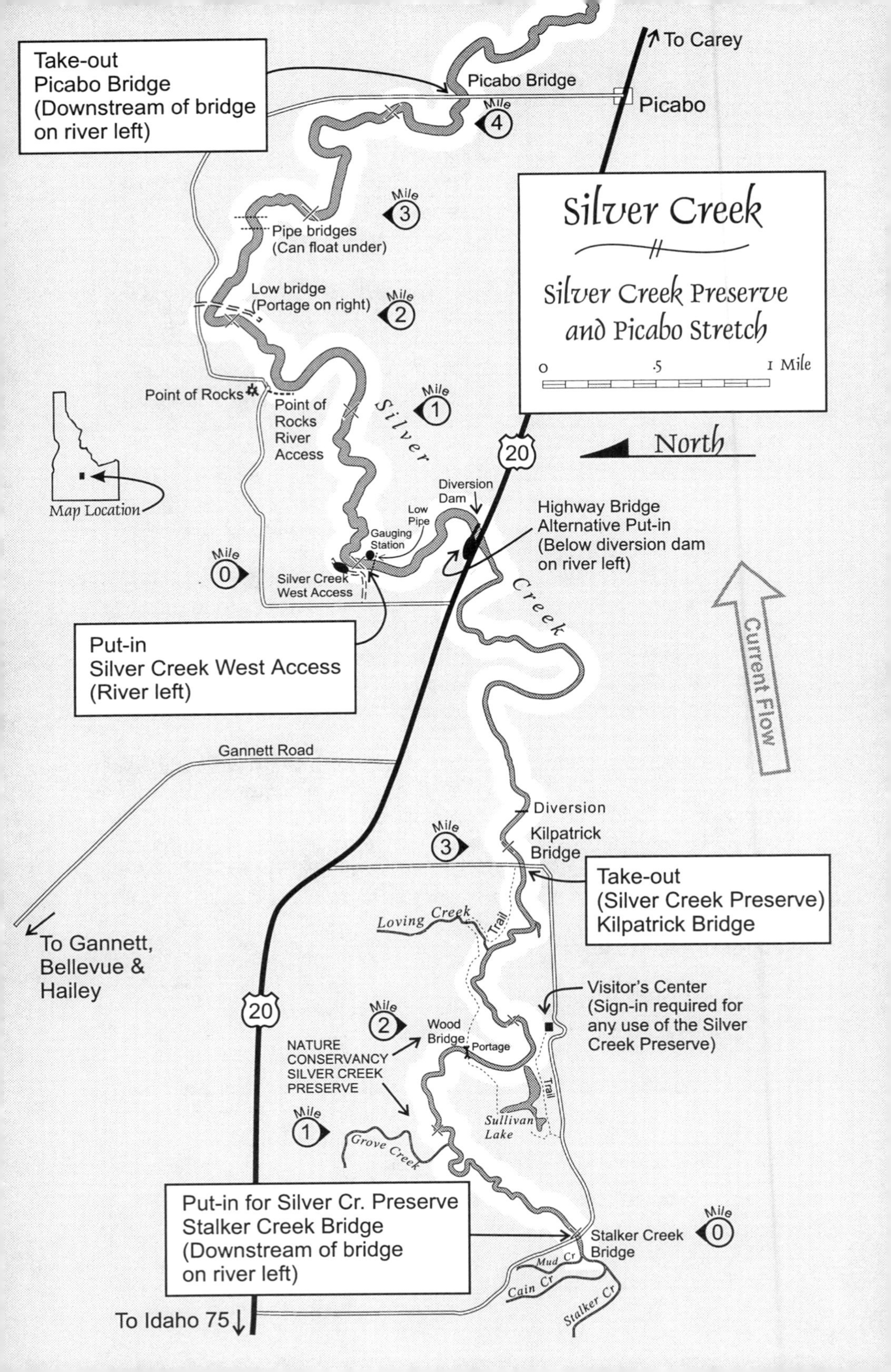

Silver Creek
Silver Creek Preserve and Picabo Stretch
0
.5
1 Mile
North
Current Flow
To Carey
Take-out
Picabo Bridge
(Downstream of bridge on river left)
Picabo Bridge
Picabo
Mile 4
Mile 3
Pipe bridges
(Can float under)
Low bridge
(Portage on right)
Mile 2
Point of Rocks
Point of Rocks River Access
Mile 1
Silver
Map Location
20
Diversion Dam
Low Pipe
Gauging Station
Highway Bridge
Alternative Put-in
(Below diversion dam on river left)
Mile 0
Silver Creek West Access
Creek
Put-in
Silver Creek West Access
(River left)
Gannett Road
Diversion
Kilpatrick Bridge
Mile 3
Take-out
(Silver Creek Preserve)
Kilpatrick Bridge
Loving Creek
Trail
To Gannett, Bellevue & Hailey
20
Mile 2
Wood Bridge
Portage
Visitor's Center
(Sign-in required for any use of the Silver Creek Preserve)
NATURE CONSERVANCY SILVER CREEK PRESERVE
Trail
Sullivan Lake
Mile 1
Grove Creek
Put-in for Silver Cr. Preserve
Stalker Creek Bridge
(Downstream of bridge on river left)
Stalker Creek Bridge
Mile 0
Mud Cr
Cain Cr
Stalker Cr
To Idaho 75

Getting to the Take-out. Kilpatrick Bridge. From the Sun Valley-Ketchum area, drive south on Idaho 75 to the US 20-Idaho 75 junction, about 10 miles south of Bellevue. Turn left (east) on US 20 and follow it 7 miles until coming to a sign indicating the Silver Creek Preserve. Turn right (south) and drive about .8 mile to a bridge over Silver Creek (Kilpatrick Bridge), the take-out. The Preserve's visitor center is about another .7 mile farther down the road.

Getting to the Put-in. Stalker Bridge. After signing in at the visitor's center, drive up the hill behind the center. Continue to the west for a mile until coming to a bridge over the creek (Stalker Bridge). Put in downstream of the bridge on river right.

The Trip. Silver Creek Preserve. This very relaxed trip ambles through the heart of the Silver Creek Preserve, one of the bright spots in Idaho river conservation. When you stop at the visitor's center to register, be sure to pick up a bird list and a nature guide. They provide helpful information on identifying birds, river bank plant communities and understanding the ecology of the area. Plan on one easy portage about midway through at a wooden bridge.

Because of the river's worldwide fishing reputation, fly fishers congregate in droves here. It's a narrow stream and unlike other popular fly fishing rivers, like the Henrys Fork, it's hard to give fisherfolk much room as you pass by in a boat. To avoid conflicts, the preserve staff encourages canoeists and kayakers to do their trips prior to Memorial Day, the opening of the fishing season. Too, the river never freezes over, and if you bundle-up, Silver Creek is an unforgettable winter trip.

If you must go during the summer, at the least, plan to do your trip in the hot part of the afternoon when the fishing pressure relaxes some. Give the preserve office a call in advance of your trip. They are more than happy to provide you with information that will help make your visit an enjoyable one. You'll find that Silver Creek is a very well-run operation with a topnotch manager and staff.

If you do encounter fishers while on your trip, give them a wide berth. Quietly let them know you're coming and ask which way they want you to float around. Smile and give them a courteous wave.

Note that it is possible to float between the Kilpatrick and Highway 20 bridges. Plan on one portage around a diversion dam. This is private land, but state law allows boaters to make portages around obstructions as long as they re-enter the river immediately below.

Shuttle. 2 miles. Easy bike shuttle.

Craft. Canoes, kayaks and lake kayaks.

Silver Creek West to Picabo Bridge

> **Basic Stats (Silver Creek West to Picabo Bridge)**
>
> **Difficulty:** Class I (1.1).
>
> **Season:** Floatable all year. See information on the Silver Creek Preserve about best times to avoid conflicts with fly fishers.
>
> **Distance/Time:** 4.5 miles / 2-3 hours.

Getting to the Take-out. Picabo bridge. Picabo is located on US 20, 7 miles west of Carey and 13 miles east of the Idaho 75 and US 20 junction south of Ketchum/Sun Valley area. From the west edge of the Picabo store's parking lot is a road heading north. Follow this road for .7 mile until coming to a bridge over Silver Creek. The take-out is on the downstream side of the bridge on river left.

Alternative Take-out. Point of Rocks. If you wish to make the trip shorter (1.7 miles) and avoid a portage around a low bridge, you can take-out at the Point of Rocks river access. To get to it, continue driving past the Picabo bridge 2.5 more miles and look for the access parking area on the left.

Getting to the Put-in. Silver Creek West Access. The turn-off to Silver Creek West Access is 2.3 miles west of Picabo on US 20. Turn right (north) and drive about .3 mile until reaching the access road leading off to the right (east). Park near the large boulders which block an old road leading to the river. The put-in is beyond the boulders.

Alternative Put-in. US 20 Bridge. You can also put-in at the Silver Creek bridge on US 20. The bridge is located 2 miles west of Picabo. Park on the downstream side of the bridge, river left. You'll have to hoist your boat up and over a fence and carry it 50 feet to below a small check dam just downstream of the bridge. Note that on this stretch, you'll encounter a very low pipe just before Silver Creek West. You may need to portage it if your boat sits high in the water.

The Trip. Silver Creek West to Picabo Bridge. During the first part of this float, the river is hemmed in by dogwood, willow and wild rose. While the river bends some, the curves are gentle and the water is never very forceful. The brush falls back within a mile and the river flows placidly through pasture land. In this open area, you'll have some nice views of the surrounding mountains: the foothills of the Pioneers to the North and the Picabo Hills to the south.

A low bridge is located at the 2.2-mile point. Since the bridge has some nails protruding below it (ouch!), a short 30-foot portage must be made on river right. At 2.7 miles are two pipes which cross the river, but we found both high enough to float under. From here, there are no more obstructions, and it's smooth sailing to the Picabo bridge.

Shuttle. 3 miles, mostly paved, some dirt. Bike shuttle: Highway 20 is moderately busy but does have a paved shoulder.

Craft. Canoes & kayaks.

Mileage Chart
Silver Creek West to Picabo Bridge

0	Put-in. Silver Creek West (river left).
1.7	Point of Rocks river access (left). Alternative take-out.
2.2	Low bridge. Portage on right.
2.7	Two pipes cross river.
4.5	Take-out. Picabo bridge (downstream of bridge on river left).

A Strike on Silver Creek: from an old postcard photo.

Idaho State Historical Society

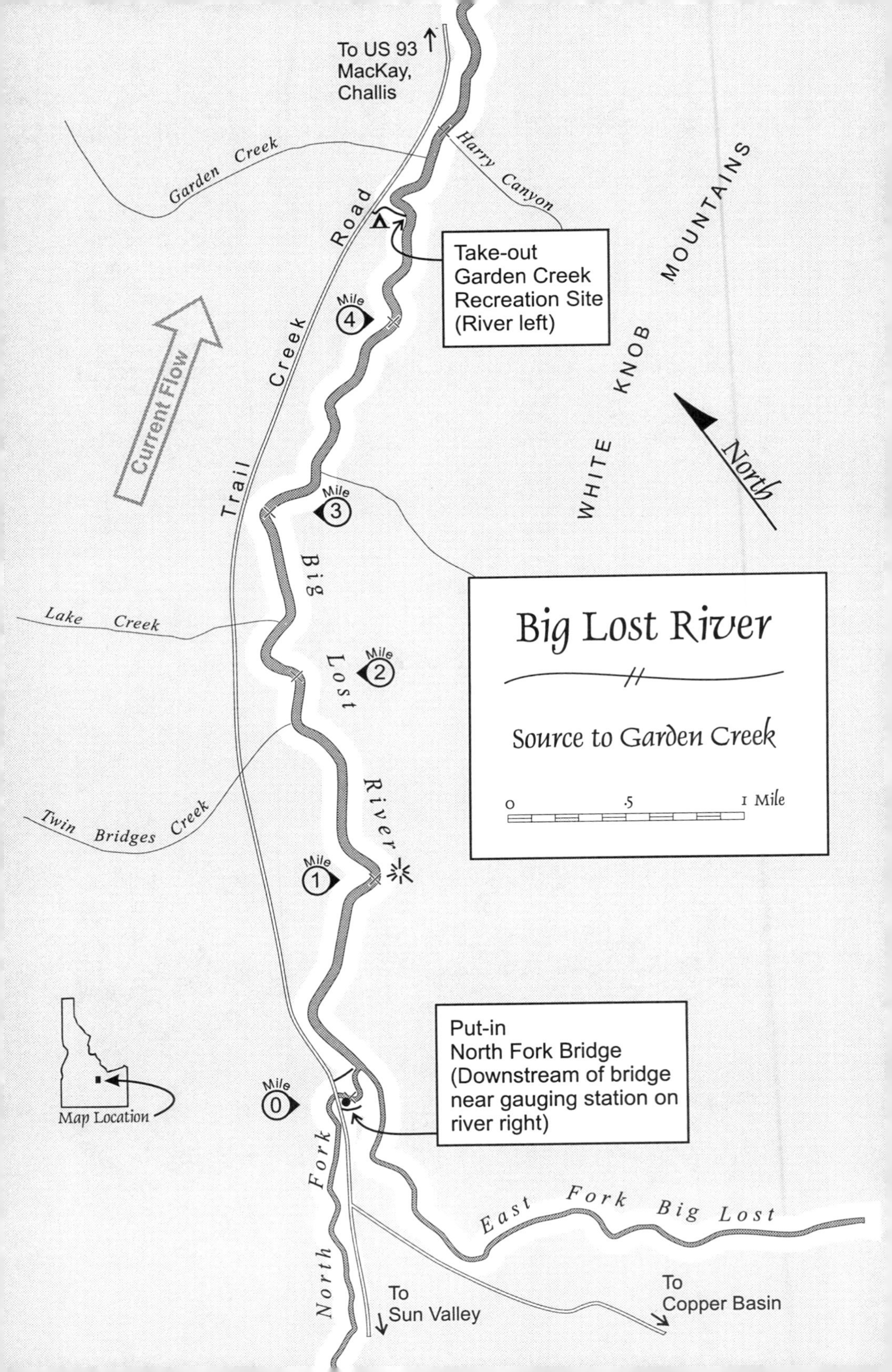

Big Lost River
Source to Garden Creek
0
.5
1 Mile
To US 93
MacKay,
Challis
Take-out
Garden Creek
Recreation Site
(River left)
Put-in
North Fork Bridge
(Downstream of bridge
near gauging station on
river right)
Garden Creek
Harry Canyon
Trail Creek Road
Current Flow
WHITE KNOB MOUNTAINS
North
Big Lost River
Lake Creek
Twin Bridges Creek
Mile 0
Mile 1
Mile 2
Mile 3
Mile 4
North Fork
East Fork Big Lost
To
Sun Valley
To
Copper Basin
Map Location

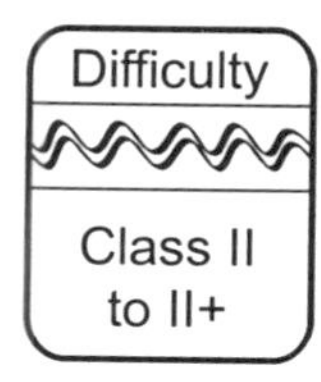

Big Lost River

Source to Garden Creek Recreation Site

THE BIG LOST RIVER, to the east of the Sun Valley area, flows through an open and expansive valley, surrounded by equally expansive mountain ranges. You really feel like you have elbow room in this country. It's a lovely drive through the valley, and along the way you can see portions of the Pioneers, White Knobs and the Lost Rivers.

It's even a better view from the river, but the scenery goes past quickly. The Big Lost River gallops. Starting from its source at the confluence of the North and East Forks and ending just before the river crosses into private lands, this stretch of the river is an exhilarating class II to II+ run. It's canoeable, but you'll want to feel comfortable about running long stretches of rapid water. Kayakers and boaters in small inflatables such as inflatable kayaks, mini-cats and small rafts (12-foot or less in size) will also enjoy this run.

Basic Stats

Difficulty: Class II to II+, a continuous stretch of rapid water with overhanging brush and the possibility of an occasional snag in the river.

Distance/Time: 4.5 miles / 1.5 to 2 hours.

Levels: 500 cfs or less at the Big Lost River gauge at Howell Ranch (under 3.0 feet on the gauge at the put-in).

Getting to the Take-out. Garden Creek Recreation Site. If you're coming from the Arco or Mackay direction, go north on US 93 until coming to Trail Creek Road. Take a left (west) on Trail Creek and drive 13.5 miles until coming to the Garden Creek Recreation Site.

If you're coming from Ketchum, drive out Trail Creek Road, until you reach Garden Creek, about 27 miles from Ketchum.

Garden Creek is a fairly primitive and free BLM campground. Sadly, not many semi-developed campgrounds like Garden Creek are free any more, but this one is. Drive into the small campground area and continue beyond on a dirt road that leads south towards the river. The take-out is located where a powerline crosses the river. There's no eddy here, but as long as you're running the river in low water you should be able to stop a boat in the shallows on river left.

Getting to the Put-in. North Fork Bridge. The bridge is located 3.9 mile west of the Garden Creek Recreation site on Trail Creek Road. You have two choices for launching a boat in the area. The easiest access is to put in just below the bridge and run the North Fork of the Big Lost .2 mile to its confluence with the East Fork (forming the main Big Lost River). To get to this launching point, look for the round gauging station on the downstream side of the bridge on river right and park nearby. Just below the gauging station are the remains of a bridge and you'll find a gravelly beach from which you can get started.

Before launching, take a walk down along the river and scout it down to the confluence. It's very narrow and some rock dodging is involved. It's not more difficult than class II, but if you don't want to start right off with such a tight rapid, you may want to launch at the confluence.

To get to the confluence, look for a dirt road leading to the south on the east side of the bridge. Follow this bumpy dirt road back about a 100 yards to where you can look down at the two forks coming together. Just below here is the launch point. It's gnarly: a steep, 25-foot carry down to the river and plenty of shrubby birch to get in the way, but it can be done. We saw no sign of a trail here which gives you an idea how often people put in at this spot.

The Trip. The river moves away quickly from the put-in and doesn't slow much along the entire stretch. One nice feature of the river from a canoeing standpoint is that it doesn't have any sharp corners. But it does have birch trees overhanging the river, and you'll want to keep the boat in mid stream to keep from getting tangled up in them. While the rapids on this stretch are not more than class I+, we feel that a class II to II+ rating is more appropriate because of brush, constant gradient and some continuous sections. Be sure to do this one in low to low-medium flows.

It's easy to find the take-out. Just keep watching for where the powerline crosses the river and pull off on the left. No fences cross the river and since most of the taller trees are back from the river, the probability of log jams is low. Below the take-out, however, the narrow river braids and goes through a thick cottonwood riparian zone where log jams are frequent.

Shuttle. 4 miles, gravel. It's an easy bike shuttle. The traffic on the graveled Trail Creek Road is moderate, but vehicles speed by, and you'll want to be prepared for dust clouds.

Craft. Canoes, kayaks, small rafts (12-foot size), and small inflatables. No ramps, but with some work, it is possible to get a drift boat in and out.

Mileage Chart

0	Confluence of the East and North Fork of the Big Lost River.
1	Prominent left hand bend. Cliff on right side of the river.
4.4	Take-out. Powerline crossing at Garden Creek Recreation area.

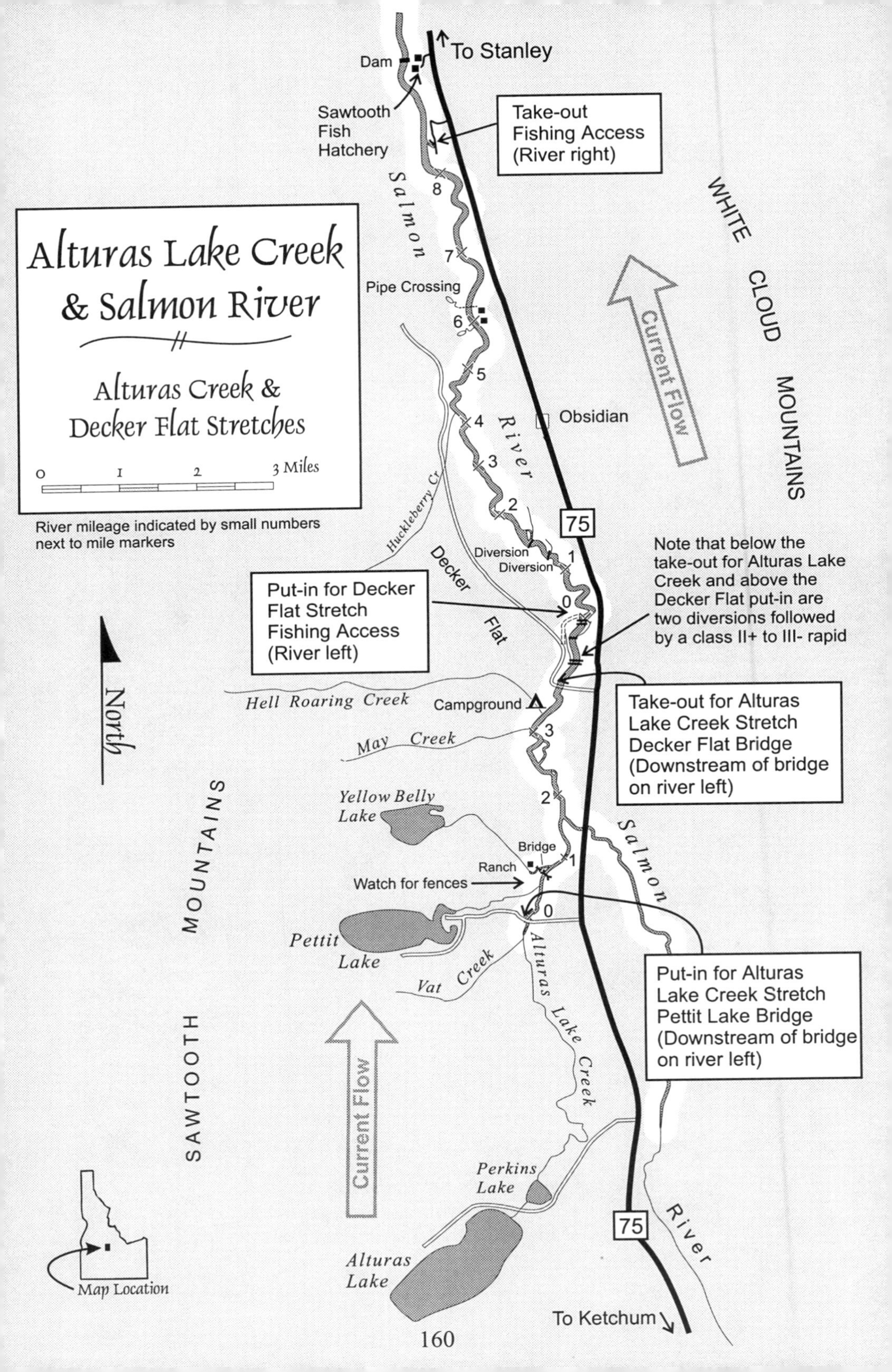

Alturas Lake Creek & Salmon River
Alturas Creek & Decker Flat Stretches
0 1 2 3 Miles
River mileage indicated by small numbers next to mile markers
To Stanley
Dam
Sawtooth Fish Hatchery
Take-out Fishing Access (River right)
WHITE CLOUD MOUNTAINS
Salmon
Pipe Crossing
Current Flow
Obsidian
River
Huckleberry Cr.
75
Diversion
Diversion
Decker Flat
Note that below the take-out for Alturas Lake Creek and above the Decker Flat put-in are two diversions followed by a class II+ to III- rapid
Put-in for Decker Flat Stretch Fishing Access (River left)
North
Hell Roaring Creek
Campground
Take-out for Alturas Lake Creek Stretch Decker Flat Bridge (Downstream of bridge on river left)
May Creek
Yellow Belly Lake
Bridge
Ranch
Watch for fences
Salmon
Pettit Lake
Vat Creek
Alturas Lake Creek
Put-in for Alturas Lake Creek Stretch Pettit Lake Bridge (Downstream of bridge on river left)
SAWTOOTH MOUNTAINS
Current Flow
Perkins Lake
75
River
Alturas Lake
Map Location
To Ketchum

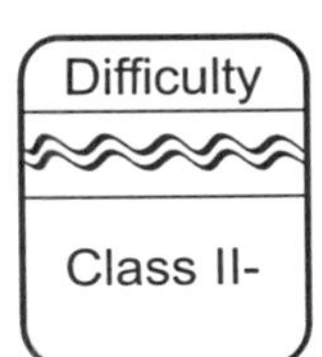

Salmon River

Alturas Lake Creek–Salmon River Stretch

LOCATED IN THE SAWTOOTH VALLEY, this segment of river is the uppermost run that can be made on the Salmon. It actually begins on Alturas Lake Creek, a tributary of the Salmon and then joins the Salmon for the remaining mile to the take-out. Unfortunately, it's not a run for beginners. In fact, because of fences and diversions, the Forest Service doesn't even recommend that it be run. But fences and diversions are common on small class I+ rivers in Idaho, and they can be safely run as long as boaters are comfortable with their boating skills and wait for medium or low water.

We rate the Alturas Lake Creek stretch as class II-. The river slides downhill at a good pace and you have to be able to handle quick corners. It begins as a stream, barely floatable and quickly becomes a small river at the confluence with the Salmon. Passing beneath the eastern flank of the Sawtooths, the river meanders through damp meadows fed by scores of small springs.

Basic Stats

Difficulty: Continuous class II- (continuous class II- requires a higher skill level than short class II- rapids).

Levels/Season: Avoid this stretch during high water in May and June. The best time to run it is from mid July to late July. The season is short and is largely over by early August.

Distance/Time: 3.7 miles / 2-3 hours in low water.

Obstructions: Barbed wire fences. We encountered two places where fences spanned the river. In both cases, we were able to float under them. They were not located on blind corners, nor were they situated in areas of particularly swift current, but new fences can be added, and you should be vigilant.

Permits/Passes: The Sawtooth National Recreation Area (SNRA) has a registration system for other parts of the Salmon, but at the time of this writing did not have one in place for this segment. Check the Stanley Office of the SNRA (208-774-3000) for the latest information.

Getting to the Take-out. Decker Flat Bridge. The turn-off to Decker Flat is located 3.1 miles north of the Pettit Lake turn-off (see below) on Idaho 75. Once off the highway, it's .2 mile to the bridge. Parking is available to the right (river left, downstream side of the bridge). Camping is also available here.

Getting to the Put-in. Pettit Lake Bridge over Alturas Lake Creek. The turn-off to Pettit Lake is located midway through the Sawtooth Valley on Idaho 75. It's 5.8 miles south of the Smiley Creek Lodge—or 6.8 miles north of Obsidian. Turn on the Pettit Lake Road and drive .7 mile to the bridge. This is a primitive boat access, but you'll find a place to park on the downstream side of the bridge on river left.

The Trip. Alturas Lake Creek is a small, shallow stream, which breaks into even smaller channels. To do this stretch you'll want a maneuverable river canoe or whitewater kayak. Since Alturas Lake Creek flows through a meadow you won't have to worry about log jams, but when faced with a choice of channels take the largest channel.

The size of the stream quickly increases. At 1.7 miles from the start, Alturas Lake Creek joins the main Salmon. Before the confluence, both are small streams, but once combined, you'll suddenly find yourself on a real river. A small one, albeit, but a river, nevertheless. From here it's another mile to the take-out at the Decker Flat bridge.

Fences. We encountered two fences. One was located .6 mile from the start, about a .1 mile above a bridge servicing the Clark-Miller Guest Ranch. The other was located about .2 mile above the confluence with the Salmon. Both were high enough to float under and were not located on blind corners. New fences can go up and existing ones sag into the water. Watch for fence posts leading to the edge of the river, always have an eddy that you can stop in, and run it in low water when the current gives you more time to react.

Note that if you decide to continue from here, you'll encounter a diversion just below the bridge. (See the next river segment for details.)

Shuttle. 4 miles. Paved and gravel. Bike shuttle: highway 95 is busy but it has a wide, paved shoulder.

Craft. River canoes and kayaks.

Mileage Chart

0	Put-in. Pettit Lake Bridge over Alturas Lake. Downstream of bridge on river left.
.5	Pettit Lake outlet enters on left.
.6	Fence.
.7	Bridge to Clark-Miller Guest Ranch.
1.5	Fence.
1.7	Confluence with Salmon River.
2.9	Mouth of Mays Creek (left).
3.2	Mouth of Hell Roaring Creek & Campground (left).
3.7	Take-out. Decker Flat bridge (downstream of bridge on river left).

Upper Alturas Lake Creek. If you've driven into Alturas Lake, you may have noticed that Alturas Lake Creek looks runnable where it flows out of Perkins Lake. (Perkins Lake, by the way, is a small lake which is designated as non-motorized and is a nice place for a quick spin in a canoe or kayak with the family.) Some distance below Perkins Lake, however, Alturas Lake Creek is blocked by log jams and beyond that the stream narrows and is considerably obstructed by downed timber. The stream doesn't really become runnable until the Pettit Lake bridge.

Difficulty
Class I+
(1.4-1.5)

Salmon River

Sawtooth Valley–Decker Flat
(Map on page 160)

DECKER FLAT is the second of two runs on the upper Salmon through the Sawtooth Valley. It is slightly easier than the first run (described in the previous section), but it's not for novices. Rated class I+ (1.4 - 1.5), this reach of river has some sharp corners, diversions, and the possibility of a fence spanning it, though we never encountered any. Because of these obstructions, the Forest Service does not recommend running it. But diversions and fences are common on many so-called easy Idaho rivers, and if you have good basic skills and take normal river running precautions, this is a very boatable stretch—*as long as it is done in low flows.*

It's also a beautiful run: the river meanders through the sweeping openness of Decker Flat, and the Sawtooths in all their glory pass on your left, while the graceful slopes of the White Cloud Mountains across the valley pass on your right. Mostly, the river snakes its way through meadows and pastures where you'll see cattle grazing. Occasionally, the river bends close to the highway, but all in all, it is a most agreeable way of getting to know a very special place in Idaho.

Basic Stats

Difficulty: The suggested run, which begins 1 mile below Decker Flat Bridge, is class I+ (1.3-1.4). If you start at Decker Flat bridge, it is class III-.

Suggested Season: Stay off this stretch during the high water in May and June. The best time to run it is from mid July to late July. The season is pretty much over by the first and second week of August.

Distance/Time: 8.4 miles / 3-5 hours in low water. (Note that USGS maps show the river mileage at around 6.3, but 8.4 is more realistic considering the meandering nature of the river.)

Permits: The Sawtooth National Recreation Area (SNRA) has a registration system for other parts of the Salmon, but at the time of this writing did not have one in place for this section. Check the Stanley Office of the SNRA (208-774-3000) for the latest information.

Getting to the Take-out. Fishing access above Sawtooth Fish Hatchery. The fishing access road is not marked. To find it, check your odometer at the entrance to the Sawtooth Fish Hatchery (6.5 miles north of Stanley). Drive south (towards Ketchum) 1.1 miles and take a right onto a bumpy dirt road. One branch of the road goes straight to the river. Avoid that and continue to drive upriver. At about .3 mile from the highway, look for a faint road heading toward the river. It will pass by a large spring and end at a primitive camp site.

Where the large spring joins the river, it forms an eddy and provides a small but natural place to take-out. When you run the river, pull into the spring and paddle up it to where your vehicle is parked. Since no obvious landmarks are found here and you can't see the parked vehicle from the river, you'll want to carefully memorize the location, otherwise, you'll end up at the fish hatchery. You can tie a bright piece of clothing to a bush to help you find the location, but remember to take it down when you leave.

Getting to the Put-in. Decker Flat Bridge. Turn on to the Decker Flat Road, 3.6 miles north of Sessions Lodge in Obsidian or 9 miles south of Smiley Creek Lodge at Sawtooth City. Drive down the Decker Flat Road, cross over the Salmon, and turn right. Continue driving a couple of tenths of a mile, until you see a dirt road leading off to the right. This is a fishing access road which parallels the river downstream and ends at a fence. The put-in is along the grassy and rocky shore of the river at the bottom of a rapid.

The Trip. At the put-in, you are at the tail end of a rapid. The water is a little swift here, but it avoids two diversions and the main part of a class II+ to III- rapid. Even though the water is a bit swift at the put-in, you are in a fairly good position to slip down on the left side of what's left of the rapid. It is a fairly straight shot and it can be done without having to do much maneuvering.

Once past the rapid, the river meanders, braiding here and there and passing around an occasional sharp corner. Since the river flows mostly through marsh and pasture land, there's not much danger of log jams—something that you would normally be concerned about on a small river. While fences are a possibility since this is grazing land, we never encountered any. This part of the Salmon is an excellent birding stretch. You'll see osprey and quite a number of ducks and geese, along with other marsh and river species.

Diversions. Two diversions are found on this stretch. One is located at 1.4 miles from the start and the other at 1.6 miles from the start. Both diversions, however, are easy runs. They are recognized by having a straight line of rocks angling into the current from the right. Both divert water to the right. We found that both could be run on the left down rippling water.

Shuttle. 10 miles. Mostly paved with some dirt. For bike shuttling, Highway 75 is busy but it has a moderately-wide paved shoulder. One warning: don't try to use Decker Flat Road to do the shuttle. It makes a nice mountain bike ride, but as a shuttle at the end of a river trip, the dirt road seems to go on and on and on.

Craft. Canoes, kayaks and small inflatables.

Mileage Chart

(Note: We have deviated from the mileages shown on the USGS topographic map. These are more realistic considering the meandering nature of the river.)

Mile	Description
0	Put-in. Approximately 1 mile below Decker Flat Bridge on river left.
1.4	Diversion. Water diverts to right. Run left side.
1.6	Diversion. Water diverts to right. Run left side.
4.2	Mouth of Huckleberry Creek. Decker Flat Road is close to river on left.
5.8	Pipe crosses the river at Rocky Mountain Ranch.
7.8	Small pull-off next to highway 75 (river right) is visible from the river.
8.4	Take-out. Salmon Spring. Unmarked fishing access at a spring. River right.

Information on Upper Whitewater Stretch. Two diversions are located between the Decker Flat Bridge and the fishing access put-in described above. The first diversion comes .2 mile after the bridge. It is signaled by a line of large boulders angling out from the left shore. The boulders divert water into a canal on the left side of the river. Scout from the right shore. In low water, you'll probably find three drops with the last drop being the steepest. Be certain that you check out the last drop and decide upon the best route. We ran it on the far right.

Another diversion follows .2 mile beyond the first. This one is a little easier than the first, and we had a straightforward run down river left. After the second diversion, the action picks up with quick maneuvering needed in a very rocky rapid (class II+ to III-) on a curve. The suggested put-in described above is near the end of this rapid.

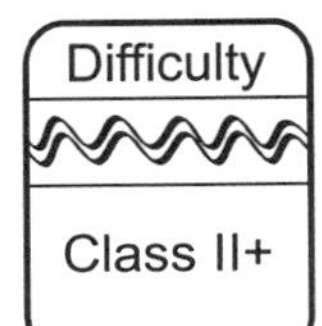

Salmon River

Redfish Stretch (Buckhorn to Stanley)
(Map on page 170)

THIS IS A CONTINUOUS STRETCH of very boney, whitewater (class II+ to III-), located just upstream from Stanley. Since it is swift and continuous, you'll want to have built up some solid river running skills before undertaking it. While rafts and inflatables can bounce down it, open canoeists, in particular, need to approach it cautiously and will want to look it over carefully before running it. Fortunately, much of it can be scouted from driving down the highway and stopping at the campgrounds along the river.

This stretch gets rockier and rockier as the water drops during the summer. Generally, it's runnable from July to early August.

Basic Stats

Difficulty: Class II+ to III-. Continuous and very rocky.

Levels/Season: Low to medium water, July through August. Avoid the high water period in May and June.

Distance/Time: 6 miles / 2-3 hours.

Permits: At the time of this writing, the Forest Service was requiring all boaters to fill out a free, self issuing permit at the Buckhorn launch site. Regulations can change. Check signs at the put-in for information.

Getting to the Take-out. Salmon River Lodge Bridge. See the next segment of the Salmon River (Stanley Scenic Stretch) for a description of how to get there.

Getting to the Put-in. Buckhorn Picnic Area. Buckhorn Picnic Area is just off of Idaho 75, .7 mile south of the Redfish Lake turn-off. (Redfish Lake is located about 4 miles south of Stanley.) A bridge spans the Salmon River at this point, if you are heading south (towards Ketchum/Sun Valley) turn to the right and drive up the river a short distance to Buckhorn. You'll have to carry your boat about 80 feet from the parking area to the river's edge. There is no ramp.

The Trip. This is a very rocky stretch of water, particularly for a couple of miles downstream of Sunny Gulch Campground. We highly recommend that you look at the rapids before launching. Stop at Sunny Gulch and take a look at the river, and then drive down to the primitive camping areas alongside the river just below Sunny Gulch. Thoroughly scout the river in the primitive camping area since this is where most of the action is found. It's a spirited stretch of water, so you'll want to have experience making quick moves in shallow rock gardens before undertaking it.

Shuttle. 5.5 miles, all paved. For bike shuttling, Idaho 75 is very busy with a moderately wide paved shoulder.

Craft. Canoes, kayaks, small to medium inflatables. Drift boats can run it, but there are no ramps, you'll have to carry the boat to the river.

Mileage Chart

0	Put-in. Buckhorn Picnic Area (river left).
.1	Highway 75 bridge.
.9	Redfish Lake Creek enters from left.
1.5	Sunny Gulch Campground.
4.9	Scenic by-way pull-off on Idaho 75 (left). Alternative take-out.
5.9	Take-out. Salmon River Lodge Bridge (downstream of bridge on river left).

This photo of Little Redfish Lake is by Ernie Day, one of Idaho's great conservationists. Day played a key role in protecting such Idaho treasures as the River of No Return and the magnificent Sawtooth Valley.

Ernie Day / Idaho State Historical Society

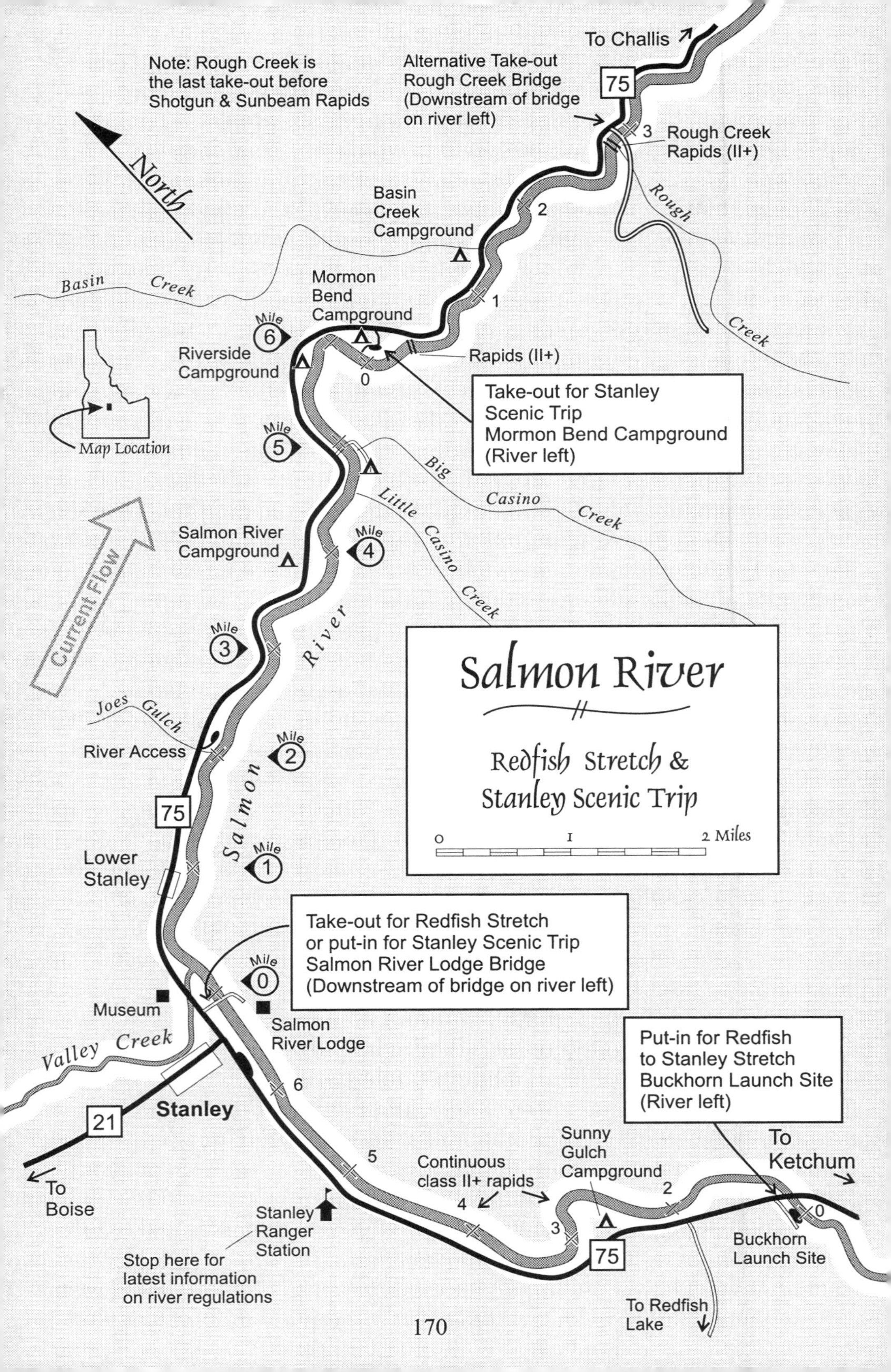
To Challis
Note: Rough Creek is the last take-out before Shotgun & Sunbeam Rapids
Alternative Take-out Rough Creek Bridge (Downstream of bridge on river left)
75
North
3
Rough Creek Rapids (II+)
Rough Creek
2
Basin Creek Campground
Basin Creek
1
Mormon Bend Campground
Mile 6
Riverside Campground
0
Rapids (II+)
Take-out for Stanley Scenic Trip Mormon Bend Campground (River left)
Map Location
Mile 5
Big Casino Creek
Little Casino Creek
Salmon River Campground
Mile 4
Current Flow
Mile 3
River
Salmon River
Redfish Stretch & Stanley Scenic Trip
0
1
2 Miles
Joes Gulch
River Access
Mile 2
Salmon
75
Lower Stanley
Mile 1
Take-out for Redfish Stretch or put-in for Stanley Scenic Trip Salmon River Lodge Bridge (Downstream of bridge on river left)
Mile 0
Museum
Salmon River Lodge
Valley Creek
6
Put-in for Redfish to Stanley Stretch Buckhorn Launch Site (River left)
Stanley
21
To Boise
5
Continuous class II+ rapids
Sunny Gulch Campground
2
To Ketchum
4
3
0
Stanley Ranger Station
75
Buckhorn Launch Site
Stop here for latest information on river regulations
To Redfish Lake

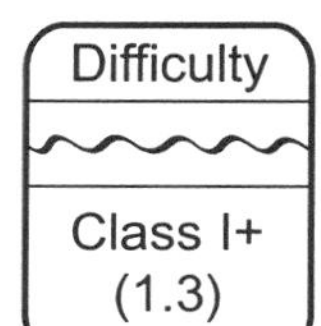

Salmon River

Stanley Scenic Trip (Stanley to Mormon Bend)

IF YOU'RE IN THE SAWTOOTH AREA and you are looking for an easy run without much objective danger this is the one. This 6-mile stretch of the Salmon River, just below the town of Stanley, is about as easy as one can find in the area. We say "easy" in a relative sense. The Salmon is not the best river to run if you've just bought a new boat, and you've never run a river before. This segment is a class I+ (1.3) and has occasional overhanging trees, boulders to avoid here and there, and some maneuvering around shallows, but overall, for someone with rudimentary river skills, it is a benign and easy-going part of the Salmon.

Moreover, it's a pretty stretch starting at the north edge of the Sawtooth Valley and entering a canyon with slopes of sage and pine. It's run in everything: inner tubes, open canoes, kayaks, drift boats, inflatables and rafts. The important thing to remember is to stay off of it during the run-off period (usually in May and June) when the river is powerful and unpredictable. From mid summer on, however, when the water is down and current unhurried, it is a marvelous trip.

Basic Stats

Difficulty: Class I+ (1.3).

Levels/Season: Low to medium water, July through August. Avoid the high water period in May, June and sometimes early July.

Distance/Time: 6.3 miles / 2.5 to 3 hours (medium to low water).

Permits & Registration: At this writing, boaters were asked to self-register using the forms available in a box at the put-in. It is a good idea to check the Stanley Office of the Sawtooth National Recreation Area (208-774-3000) for the latest information.

Getting to the Take-out. Mormon Bend Campground. Mormon Bend is located along Idaho 75, 6.6 miles northeast of the Idaho 75 junction with Idaho 21 on the edge of Stanley. Mormon Bend is an expansive campground, but look for the boat launch sign pointing the way.

Alternative Take-out. Rough Creek Bridge. If you want to include a little whitewater in the run, an alternative take-out is the Rough Creek Bridge. Rough Creek is 2.9 miles beyond Mormon Bend. Parking is available on a pull-off on the left side of the highway across from where the Rough Creek road turns off. The take-out is downstream of the bridge on river left. You'll have to hump your boat up a steep 15-foot embankment.

Getting to the Put-in. Salmon River Lodge Bridge. The turn-off to Salmon River Lodge is just off of Idaho 75, just .5 mile north of the Idaho 75 and Idaho 21 junction on the edge of Stanley. Turn right and park on the grassy area to the left before the bridge (downstream side of the bridge on river left).

The Trip. Compared to its upper reaches, the Salmon River is wide here with room to move around. During the first mile or two—if you look back over your shoulder—you'll have some beautiful views of the Sawtooth Mountains. You may want to bring your fishing rod for this stretch. It's well stocked and the fishing is typically good. You'll have some maneuvering around rocks and a rare tree to avoid which may have fallen into the river, but otherwise, the run is straightforward.

Surprisingly, for being located in one of Idaho's most popular vacation spots, this stretch is relatively uncrowded compared to the busy whitewater stretches downriver from here. You will, however, see lots of people in the heavily-used campgrounds along the way. The campgrounds are handy. With them you can keep track of your progress down the river.

Shuttle. 6 miles, all paved. A bike shuttle is not recommended. Highway 75 is a narrow, curvy, and exceedingly busy road with a narrow shoulder.

Craft. Canoes, kayaks, inflatables of all sizes, and drift boats.

Mileage Chart

0	Put-in. Salmon River Lodge Bridge (downstream of bridge on river left).
.8	Lower Stanley (left).
2.1	River access through heavy willow growth, Joes Gulch (left).
4	Salmon River Campground (left).
5	Big Casino Creek (right) and Casino Creek Bridge.
5.7	Riverside Campground (left).
6.3	Take-out. Mormon Bend Campground (river left).

Mormon Bend to Rough Creek Bridge. Below Mormon Bend is a 3-mile whitewater stretch suitable for open canoes (and kayaks, inflatables and drift boats). The take-out for this stretch is at Rough Creek Bridge. Two rapids are found on this stretch: The first rapid (a short class II+ to III-) is .3 mile below Mormon Bend. You can scout this one easily from the highway when you do the shuttle. The second rapid (class II+) is just before the Rough Creek Bridge. Rough Creek Rapid ends in an eddy on river left on the downstream side of the bridge where you take out.

Be sure to take out at Rough Creek. It's the last place to remove a boat before the whitewater stretch on the river through Shotgun and Sunbeam Dam Rapids (rated up to class IV, depending on water levels). Information on the runs below Rough Creek is available in Idaho whitewater river guides.

Salmon River and Sawtooth Mountains near Lower Stanley

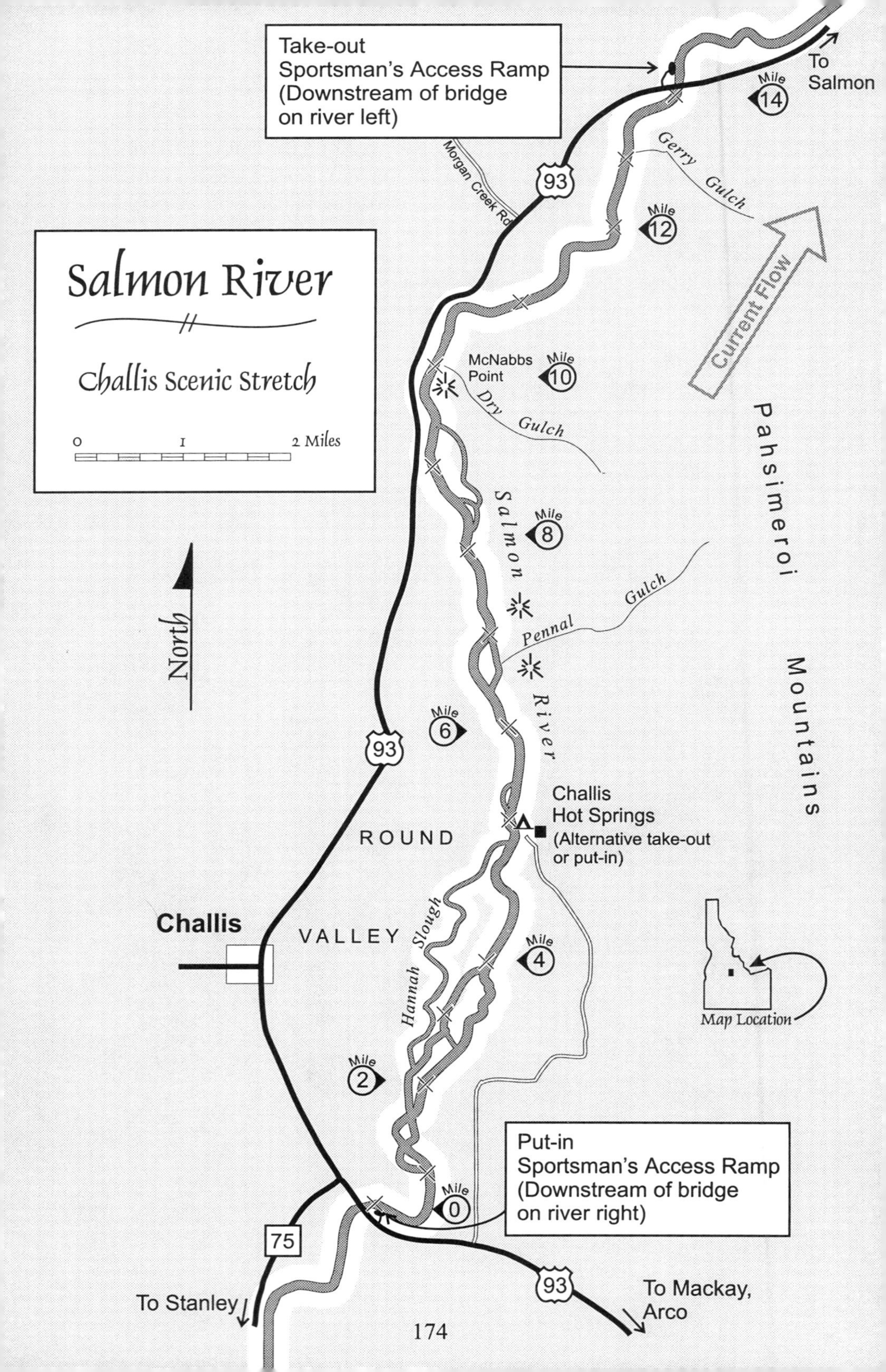
Take-out
Sportsman's Access Ramp
(Downstream of bridge
on river left)
To
Salmon
Mile
14
Gerry
Gulch
Morgan Creek Rd
93
Mile
12
Current Flow
Salmon River
Challis Scenic Stretch
0
1
2 Miles
McNabbs
Point
Mile
10
Dry
Gulch
Pahsimeroi
Salmon
Mile
8
Pennal
Gulch
North
River
Mountains
Mile
6
93
Challis
Hot Springs
(Alternative take-out
or put-in)
ROUND
Challis
VALLEY
Hannah
Slough
Mile
4
Map Location
Mile
2
Put-in
Sportsman's Access Ramp
(Downstream of bridge
on river right)
Mile
0
75
93
To Stanley
To Mackay,
Arco

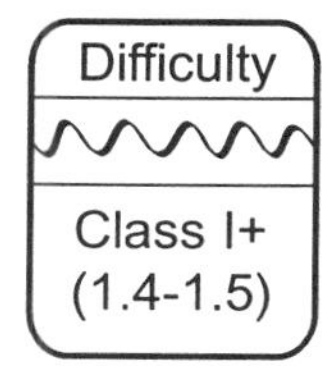

Salmon River

Challis Scenic Stretch

THE SALMON RIVER as it flows through Round Valley near the town of Challis was a surprising experience for us. From the highway, you wouldn't think of the river as being particularly scenic, but indeed, once on it, we were amazed. It is well screened from valley development by a thick layering of cottonwoods. Midway through the trip is Challis Hot Springs which has a campground, showers and a pool—a great base camp for a weekend of river running. You can launch or take out there and have a great soak to boot.

Our favorite stretch was downstream from the hot springs, a sort of half canyon with multicolored, variegated cliffs rising up from the right shore of the river.

Rated at class I+ (1.4 to 1.5), it's not a beginner's stretch. With frequent braiding and a cottonwood forest on either side, snags and downed logs are common, and you need good skills to maneuver your boat around obstructions and to stop when necessary.

Basic Stats

Difficulty: Class I (1.4-1.5) in medium & low water. Lots of braiding, overhanging trees and sweepers.

Levels/Season: Low water in late July through the fall.

Distance/Time: 14.2 miles / 4 to 6 hours in low water.

Getting to the Take-out. Sportsman's Access near Highway 93 bridge north of Challis. From the Main Street and Highway 93 junction in Challis, drive 10 miles north (towards Salmon) on US 93. Just before the bridge over the Salmon is a Sportsman's Access and boat ramp. (Downstream of the bridge on river left).

Getting to the Put-in. River access near Highway 93 bridge, south of Challis. From Main Street and the Highway 93 junction in Challis, drive south. At 2.6 miles from Challis, you'll come to the bridge over the Salmon. Continue another .2 mile and take a left on a dirt road which heads down to the river and a small boat ramp. (Note that this access may not be marked with a sign. It wasn't when we were there.)

The Trip. Not long after the put-in, the river begins braiding and you'll need to keep an eye out for trees and snags in the current. Ease around corners and stay away from the outside of bends where most the overhanging trees and sweepers are found. We never encountered any places where trees completely blocked the river, but blockages could occur in some of the smaller channels. Thus, when the river splits, stay in the largest channel.

This stretch is peppered with little rapids that are easy from a whitewater standpoint, but, nevertheless, keep things interesting and the pace brisk. Stop now and then and scan the shores for wildlife. Beaver sign is everywhere and birds along the river are prolific.

The colorful cliffs just below Challis Hot Springs are a feast for the eyes, something out of Disney's *Fantasia*: red, gray, cobalt blue, green, orange, and all shades of brown. This is a nice area to pull off and have a lunch break.

Towards the last half of the trip, you'll pass by some houses. The take-out is signaled by the highway bridge, followed shortly by the boat ramp at the Sportsman's Access.

Shuttle. 13 miles. Bike shuttle is possible, but the highway is busy and doesn't have much of a shoulder.

Craft. Canoes, kayaks, inflatables of all sizes. Ramps available for drift and row boats.

Mileage Chart

Mile	Description
0	Put-in. River access near Highway 93 Bridge south of Challis. River right.
3.8	Challis Hot Springs (right). Alternative put-in or take-out. Free to patrons of the Hot Springs.
5-8	Colorful cliff area on right.
9.8	McNabbs Point on right.
12	Morgan Creek Canyon enters through the hills on the left.
14.1	Highway 93 Bridge.
14.2	Sportsman's Access and boat ramp (left).

Brisk fall morning in the Salmon River valley near Challis.

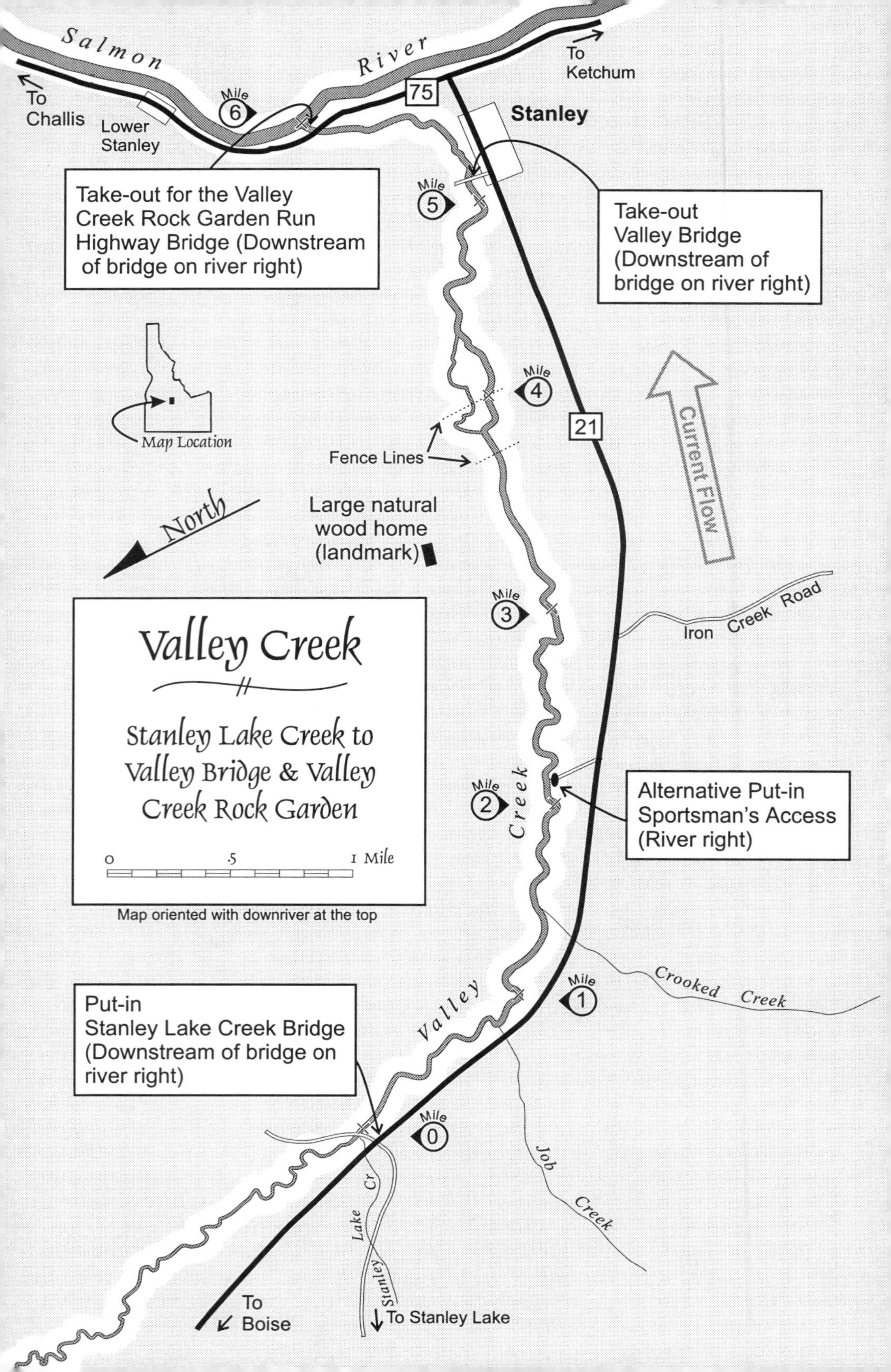
Salmon River
To Challis
Lower Stanley
Mile 6
75
To Ketchum
Stanley
Take-out for the Valley Creek Rock Garden Run Highway Bridge (Downstream of bridge on river right)
Mile 5
Take-out Valley Bridge (Downstream of bridge on river right)
Map Location
Mile 4
21
Current Flow
Fence Lines
North
Large natural wood home (landmark)
Mile 3
Iron Creek Road
Valley Creek
Stanley Lake Creek to Valley Bridge & Valley Creek Rock Garden
0
.5
1 Mile
Map oriented with downriver at the top
Mile 2
Creek
Alternative Put-in Sportsman's Access (River right)
Crooked Creek
Mile 1
Valley
Put-in Stanley Lake Creek Bridge (Downstream of bridge on river right)
Mile 0
Job Creek
Stanley Lake Cr
To Boise
To Stanley Lake

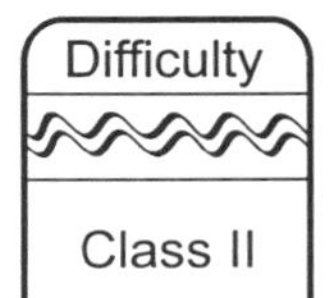

Valley Creek

Stanley Lake Creek to Valley Bridge

VALLEY CREEK, which flows into the Salmon River, just downstream from the town of Stanley, is a real treat. For pure scenic value, few other runs in Idaho can beat it. It flows through a mostly open, high, green mountain valley with the ragged, northern summits of the Sawtooths looming over the river's right shore.

But you'll have to look fast. You'll be busy. While the rapids aren't terribly difficult, it's a fairly swift, class II run with narrow channels that drop continuously and don't allow too much time for sightseeing. But do stop, take a break, and savor the view. From the banks of Valley Creek, the Sawtooths are far more impressive than any place along the highway.

Overall, Valley Creek is a great open canoe stretch and a fun run in a kayak. Small inflatables can do it, but you'll want a minicat or a craft which can make quick eddy turns. Be sure you have experience before undertaking it. The main obstacles that you'll need to watch for are the fences which cross the river (we encountered two on our trip).

Because of the fences, the Sawtooth National Recreation Area doesn't recommend floating it, but there wouldn't be much river canoeing or touring in Idaho if you stayed off all rivers with fences. Local boaters run this stretch all the time. The way to make it relatively safe is to wait until low to low-medium water in mid summer. Then the current is slow enough that you'll have time to pull off and slide your boat under any fences that you encounter.

Basic Stats

Difficulty: Class II with some long, continuous stretches of swift water.

Levels/Season: Best levels are low to medium levels, during mid summer. Avoid high water which usually occurs in early to mid June. At this writing, real-time flows are not available on the Internet for Valley Creek, but a gauge is located on the Sportsman's Access bridge (mentioned below). When we ran the river in late July, it was .2 on the gauge. At that level we found the segment of river from Stanley Lake Bridge to the Sportsman's Access bridge very scratchy, but the .2 flow was more than adequate for the stretch from the Sportsman's Access to Stanley.

Distance/Time: 5.5 miles / 3-4 hours in low water.

Obstructions: Fences across the river. We encountered fences at 3.7 and 4.0 miles from the put-in at Stanley Lake Bridge. There could be others.

Getting to the Take-out. Valley Bridge in Stanley. The most convenient take-out is Valley Bridge, located just behind Creekside Lodge. Creekside Lodge is situated on the north side of Idaho 21, .7 mile west of the Idaho 21 and Idaho 75 junction. Turn at Creekside Lodge and head north one block to the bridge. Valley Bridge is private, so you can't drive across it, but you can fish and take boats out on the downstream side of the bridge on river right.

Alternative take-out. Idaho 75 Bridge over Valley Creek. An alternative take-out is the bridge over Valley Creek on Idaho 75 between Stanley and Lower Stanley. From the Idaho 75 and Idaho 21 junction, the bridge is located .5 mile north (towards Lower Stanley). A small pull-out is located on the downstream side of the bridge (river right) where you can leave a bike or vehicle. The take-out here involves carrying your boat up a 40-foot hill.

Getting to the Put-in. Stanley Lake Creek Road Bridge. To get to the bridge, drive towards Boise (to the west) on Idaho 21. From the Idaho 21 and Idaho 75 highway junction on the edge of Stanley, it is 4.9 miles to the Stanley Lake turn-off. Turn to the *right* (north) and drive a short distance to the bridge over Valley Creek.

Alternative Put-in. (Location of Valley Creek gauge). An alternative put-in is the Sportsman's Access at an old bridge. From the Idaho 21 and Idaho 75 junction, drive northwest (towards Boise) 3.1 miles to a road leading off to the right and the Sportsman's Access. Park in the parking area. At the river, you'll find an old bridge and a water level gauge. You can use this gauge to get an idea of water levels.

Information on Permits. Although not required at the time of this writing, it's possible in the future that you may need a Sawtooth National Recreation Area (SNRA) Pass to run Valley Creek. Check with the SNRA Headquarters (208-726-8291) outside of Ketchum, or the Stanley Office (208-774-3000), located on Idaho 75 a couple miles south of Stanley, for current information regarding regulations.

The Trip. If you start at the Stanley Lake Creek Bridge, you'll encounter about a 100 yard stretch through a meadow, where the river is confined to a fairly straight but narrow chute. It's located about midway between the Stanley Lake Creek Bridge and the Sportsman's Access, 2.1 miles from the start. The water is swift, but on our run, we encountered no major obstacles. Since you can't see very far ahead, however, as a precaution, pull off before you get into the chute and walk down the right bank to make sure it's clean.

You'll find more water at the Sportsman's Access. If things are too low at the Stanley Lake Creek Bridge, you may want to start here instead. We ran at a level of .2 on the gauge. Friends in Stanley tell us that it's not particularly harder in higher water. Nevertheless, we recommend that you stay off it during the high water period in mid to late June.

From the Sportsman's Access, you'll find scattered small rapids which you can pick your way through. As long as the water isn't high, you have time to stop in eddies and read the river from your boat. It's an enjoyable, lively run and very scenic.

You'll see some homes along this stretch, but with the highway a distance away, it's quiet and the river has a relaxed, primitive feel to it.

Fences. We found two fences spanning the river—you can see the approximate location of one by stopping at the Ponderosa Drive Informational Turn-out, 1.5 miles west of the junction of Idaho 75 and 21 in Stanley. From the turn-out, a fence line heads straight north. Although you really can't see the river from here, it's this fence that goes across the river. The other fence crosses the river 1/4 mile upstream from here.

Here are some helpful landmarks that you'll see on the river when in the vicinity of the fences: The hillside which has been on river left from the start will give way to a broad drainage. Up the drainage is a very large, natural wood home with an equally large stone fire place. After you see the home, the river begins to braid, and then reaches the first of the fences.

Other fences can go up, so be alert. As on any river, you never want to go around a swift corner without knowing what's around the bend. Always take corners on the inside where the water is slower and you can stop if need be. If you can't see around the swift corner, get out and take a quick look. Be extra alert when you see a fence line which runs down to the river. We found that Valley Creek, with sensible river running precautions, was an enjoyable run and fences could be spotted early and easily portaged or lined.

Valley Creek Rock Garden. If you would like to try your hand at a rock garden on Valley Creek, you can continue from Stanley to Highway 75, a distance of 1 mile. There's some braiding on the river in Stanley, but when we ran it, we found all the braids clear of obstructions. Nevertheless, you should still approach corners on the inside and keep an eye out for overhanging trees. The rock garden comes as Valley Creek nears its confluence with the Salmon River. In low water, particularly if you are a canoeist, the trick is to try to get through this stretch without brushing against any rocks.

Shuttle. 5 miles, all paved. Bike shuttle: The highway is busy, but it has a wide, paved shoulder and bike riding along it is common.

Craft. Canoes and kayaks.

Mileage Chart

0	Lake Creek Bridge.
.9	Mouth of Job Creek (right).
1.5	Mouth of Crooked Creek (right).
2.1	Sportsman's Access. Old bridge. Water gauge located here.
3.2	A wide drainage comes in from the left. Large, natural wood home visible in the drainage.
3.75	Fence crosses river.
4	Fence crosses river.
5.1	Take-out. Valley Creek Bridge near the Creekside Lodge in Stanley (downstream of the bridge on river right).

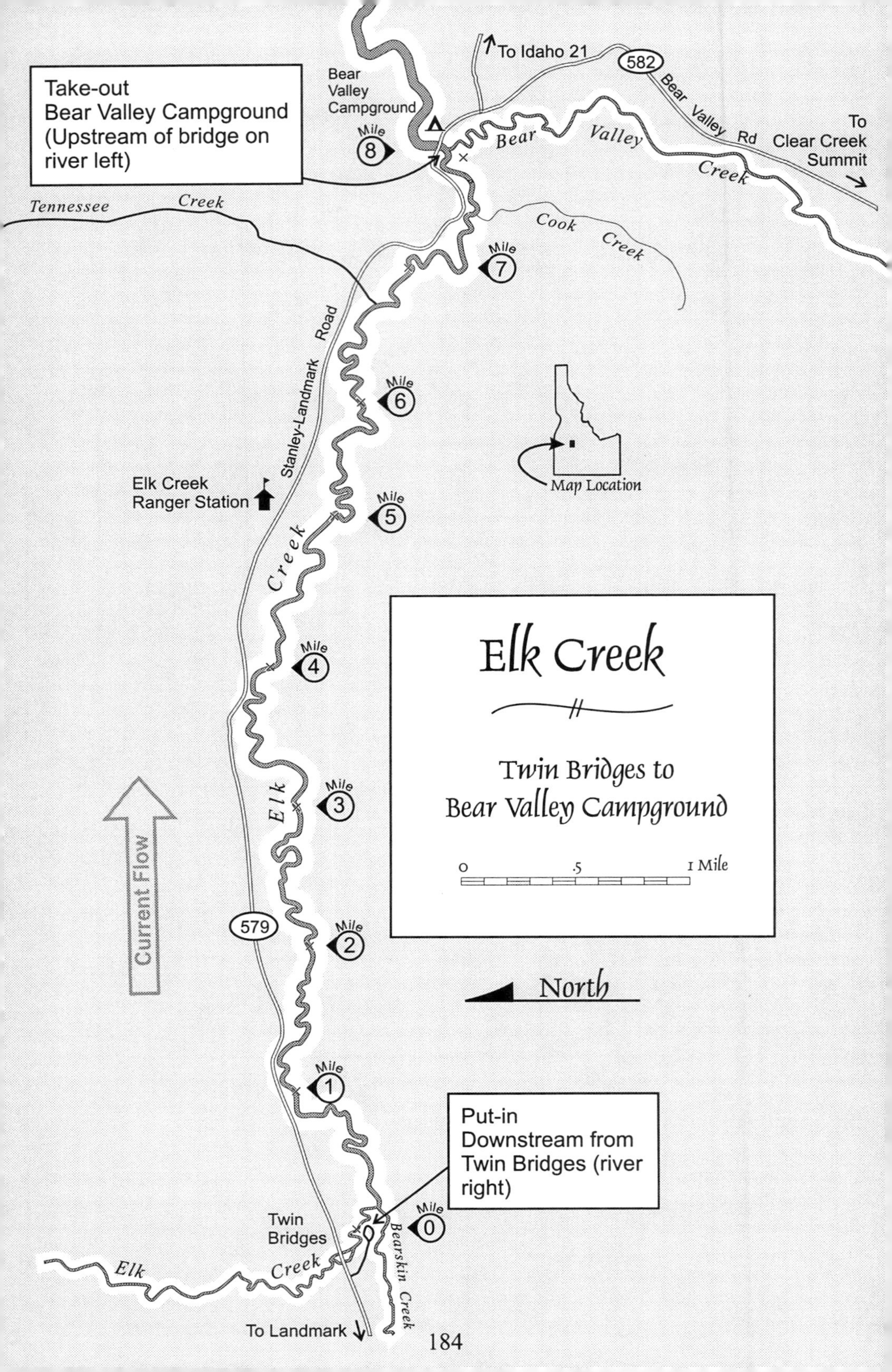
Take-out
Bear Valley Campground
(Upstream of bridge on river left)
Bear Valley Campground
Mile 8
To Idaho 21
582
Bear Valley Rd
To Clear Creek Summit
Bear Valley Creek
Tennessee Creek
Cook Creek
Mile 7
Stanley-Landmark Road
Mile 6
Map Location
Elk Creek Ranger Station
Mile 5
Creek
Elk Creek
Twin Bridges to
Bear Valley Campground
0
.5
1 Mile
Mile 4
Elk
Mile 3
Current Flow
579
Mile 2
North
Mile 1
Put-in
Downstream from Twin Bridges (river right)
Twin Bridges
Mile 0
Bearskin Creek
Elk Creek
To Landmark

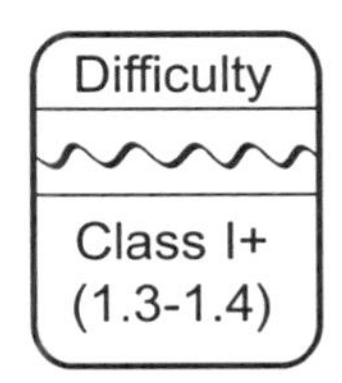

Elk Creek

Twin Bridges to Bear Valley Campground

ELK CREEK IS A SMALL, winding stream which passes through open meadows and patches of forest just outside the southern edge of the River of No Return Wilderness. It has some sharp corners and you're likely to encounter some trees which have fallen across the creek (class I+, 1.3 to 1.4). Because of tree blockages, you'll have to plan to do some portaging. In low water, however, the current is slow enough that you'll have plenty of time to stop and most portages can be made by dragging your boat across rocky bars alongside the river.

Basic Stats

Difficulty: Class I+ (1.3 with brief 1.4 at the beginning).

Distance/Time: 8 miles / 5-7 hours. It's a narrow, slow moving stream with portages. Give yourself a full day.

Season: The best time to run it is July and early August when the water is medium-low or low. Avoid the high water period in May and June.

Fences & Portages: Since this is a small, shallow stream, you will encounter places where trees have fallen across the creek. (We came to one place blocked by several downed trees and made an 80-foot portage by sliding the boat over a sand bar, but you may come across other places.) Two fences also cross the river.

Getting to the Take-out. Bear Valley Campground. The campground is located along a dirt road north of the Cape Horn country between Stanley and Lowman. To get there, start at Stanley and drive on Idaho 21 towards Lowman (and Boise) a little over 15 miles. Look for the turn-off to Bruce Meadows, Boundary Creek and Forest Road #579. Turn right and follow the dirt road as it goes up and over a pass, then down, eventually reaching a large meadows (Bruce Meadows) and an intersection with the road to Boundary Creek and Dagger Falls, 9 miles from Idaho 21.

Check your odometer at the intersection and continue straight, avoiding the turn off to Boundary Creek. At 1.6 miles from the intersection, take a right at a "Y" in the road. Drive 1.2 more miles and you'll come to Bear Valley Campground and the bridge over Bear Valley Creek. The take-out is upstream of the bridge on river left.

Getting to the Put-in. Twin Bridges. From Bear Valley Campground continue driving to the west. At 2.1 miles from the Bear Valley bridge you'll pass the Elk Creek Guard Station and at 5.4 miles from Bear Valley you'll come to two bridges over Elk Creek (called Twin Bridges). Just past the second bridge on the left is a road that turns off and goes down to a small camping area and a place to launch boats. You'll have to carry your boat about 30 feet to the stream's edge.

The Trip. At the beginning, Elk Creek is barely floatable. You need to do a couple of quick turns on this narrow, sharply turning stretch, but within a ¼ mile, Bearskin Creek comes in from the right and the stream widens enough to make maneuvering easier. There are no real rapids on Elk Creek, just riffles and lots of corners, most of them easy to negotiate.

A trip down Elk Creek doesn't seem very far when you drive it, but you need to plan a full day to do this run. The creek is in no hurry and it ambles along, twisting and turning it's way through grassy meadows sprinkled with elephants head and past spotty patches of lodgepole pines. In the distance to the northeast, you'll catch a view of Bear Valley Mountain and beyond that Blue Bunch Ridge, which rises above the canyon of the upper Middle Fork of the Salmon.

The road is close by, but it's only moderately traveled (most of the traffic turns off at the road heading to Boundary Creek), and you'll find it a very peaceful and relaxing way of spending the day.

Portages/Fences. We encountered two fences. One at 4.5 miles from the start just before the Elk Creek Ranger station. And the second was nearly at the end, just before the take-out bridge. Both fences were made of belting material—not barbed wire—and were easily pushed up and out of the way as we floated by. We also made one portage 7.5 river miles from the start. Several trees were across the river, but it was an easy drag of the canoe over a pebbly bar on river left.

Shuttle. 5.5 miles, all dirt. It's a short, easy bike shuttle on back roads which are moderately traveled.

Craft. Canoes and kayaks.

Mileage Chart

0	Put-in. Just below Twin Bridges on river right.
.2	Bearskin Creek enters on right.
1	Elk Creek curves close to road.
3.7	Elk Creek curves close to road, again.
4.5	Fence across river.
4.7	Elk Creek Ranger Station (left).
6.7	Mouth of Tennessee Creek (left).
7.9	Fence across river.
8	Bear Valley joins from the right.
8.1	Take-out. Bridge over Bear Valley (upstream or downstream of bridge on river left).

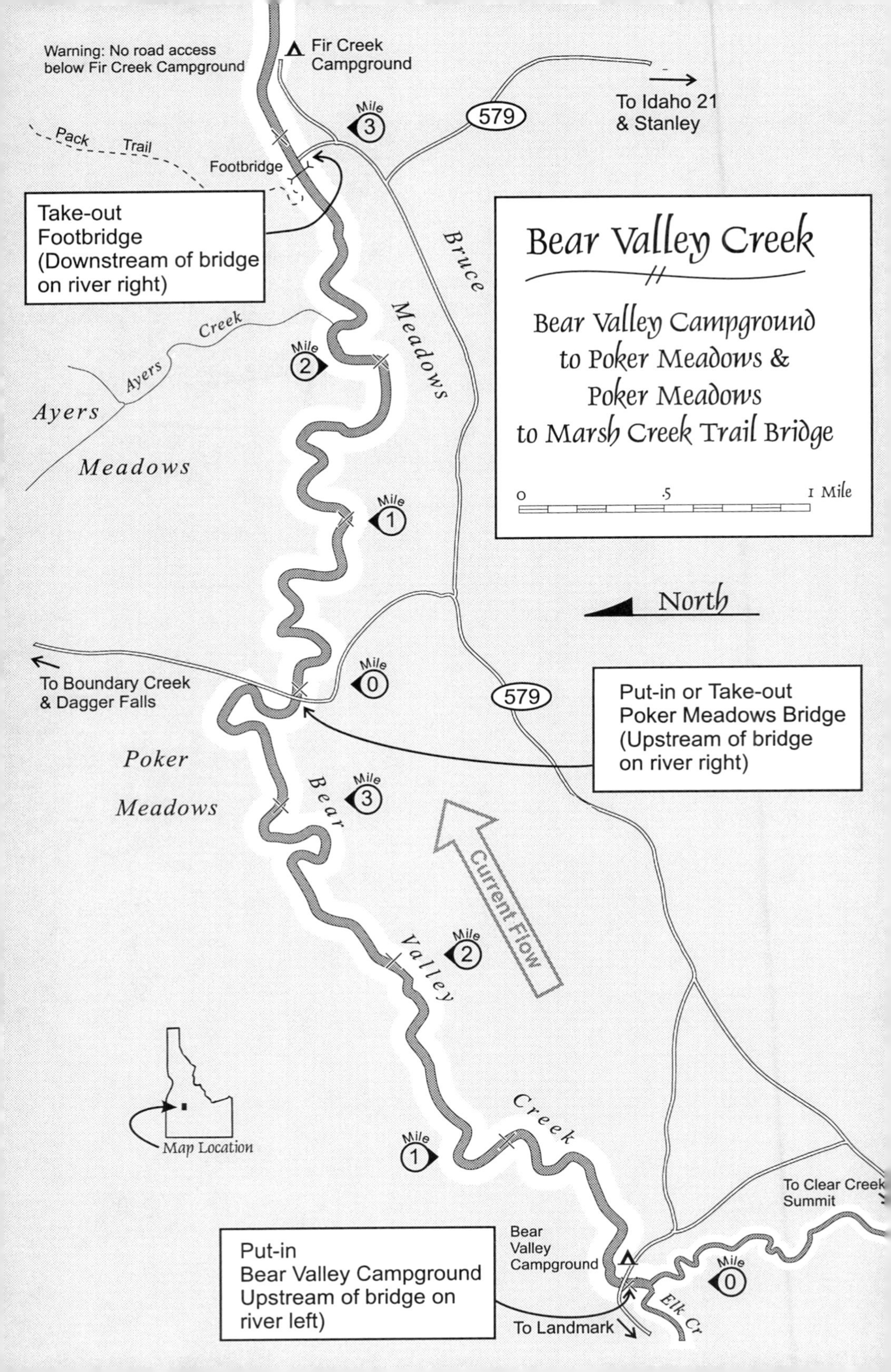

Bear Valley Creek
Bear Valley Campground to Poker Meadows & Poker Meadows to Marsh Creek Trail Bridge
0
.5
1 Mile
North
Warning: No road access below Fir Creek Campground
Fir Creek Campground
To Idaho 21 & Stanley
579
Pack Trail
Footbridge
Take-out Footbridge (Downstream of bridge on river right)
Bruce Meadows
Ayers Creek
Ayers Meadows
Mile 3
Mile 2
Mile 1
Mile 0
To Boundary Creek & Dagger Falls
Put-in or Take-out Poker Meadows Bridge (Upstream of bridge on river right)
Poker Meadows
Bear Valley Creek
Current Flow
Map Location
To Clear Creek Summit
Bear Valley Campground
Put-in Bear Valley Campground Upstream of bridge on river left)
To Landmark
Elk Cr

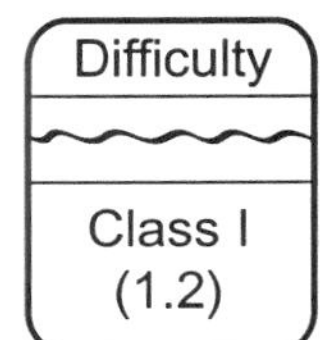

Bear Valley Creek

Bear Valley Campground to Poker Meadows Bridge and Poker Meadows to Marsh Creek Pack Bridge

UPPER BEAR VALLEY CREEK has some of the easiest runs in the central Idaho region. The first stretch (Bear Valley Campground to Poker Meadows Bridge) is a non-curving, class I (1.2) which starts with tree-lined banks and ends in the large Poker Meadows.

The second run starts where the first ends. It is a bit more difficult, class I+ (1.3) since it has a couple of sharp curves, and short, but swift sections. Yet, it's straightforward with little objective danger. Flowing through the northern edge of the expansive Bruce Meadows, it is wide open, and no downed or overhanging trees obstruct the river.

The country in this part of Idaho is undeveloped national forest land with no homes or buildings, just uninhibited views of the surrounding mountains. Both runs are perfectly suited for canoes, kayaks or small inflatables.

Bear Valley Campground to Poker Meadows Bridge

Basic Stats (Bear Valley Campground to Poker Meadows)

Difficulty: Class I (1.2) Straight stretch of river with no rapids.

Season: Best times are in July and early August when the water is medium-low or low. Avoid the high water period in May and June.

Distance/Time: 3.8 miles / 1-2 hours in medium low water (plan on more time if the wind comes up).

Obstructions: One fence made of belting. A sign is posted upstream from the fence which gives you plenty of time to move close to the shore. Since the fence is made of belting, it can be easily pushed up and out of the way.

Getting to the Take-out. Poker Meadows Bridge. The bridge is located on the road which accesses Boundary Creek, the put-in for float trips on the Middle Fork of the Salmon. To get there, start at Stanley and drive on Idaho 21 towards Lowman (and

Boise) a little over 15 miles. Look for the turn-off to Bruce Meadows, Boundary Creek and Forest Road #579. Turn right and follow the dirt road 9.3 miles to the intersection with the Boundary Creek and Dagger Falls road. Take a right and drive .8 mile farther to the bridge over Bear Valley Creek. The take-out is on river right, upstream of the bridge.

Getting to the Put-in. Bear Valley Campground. From the take-out, drive back out to the Bruce Meadows road. Take a right and drive 1.6 miles to a "Y" in the road. At the "Y", take the right branch and drive another 1.2 miles to Bear Valley Campground and a bridge. You can launch on either the upstream or downstream side of the bridge on river left.

The Trip. This is a laid-back float trip down a wide and straight waterway with a constant gradient and some riffles, but no real rapids. It is removed from roads and other than an occasional plane passing overhead, it is quiet and a perfect trip for wetting a fly or watching for wildlife. You'll encounter one fence, but it's made of belting material and can be lifted up and out of the way as you float by.

Shuttle. 4 miles. Easy bike shuttle.

Craft. Canoes, kayaks (lake kayaks), small inflatables and drift boats (no ramps).

Poker Meadows to Marsh Creek Trail Pack Bridge

Basic Stats (Poker Meadows to Pack Bridge)

Difficulty: Class I+ (1.3).

Distance/Time: 2.9 miles / 1.5-3 hours (longer if it's windy).

Season: Same as Bear Valley Campground Stretch (previous page).

Getting to the Take-out. Marsh Creek Trail Pack Bridge. The turn-off to the Marsh Creek Trail access road is marked with a sign 1.5 miles east (towards Idaho 21) of the Bruce Meadows-Boundary Creek intersection (see description above). Follow the access road .4 mile until it ends at a trailhead parking area. The take-out is downstream of the pack bridge on river right.

Getting to the Put-in. Poker Meadows Bridge. See the directions to the take-out for the Bear Valley Campground stretch on the previous page.

The Trip. Poker Meadows to Pack Bridge. This segment of the stream meanders much more than the previously described stretch. It's a relaxing float with some swift corners, but little danger from overhanging brush or trees—and, it's free of fences. Along the way you'll see places where stream bank restoration work has taken place: logs attached with cables to the stream's banks. The cabling is out of place with the naturalness of the surrounding meadows, but it has helped cut back on silting.

Be sure to take out at the Marsh Creek Trail pack bridge (the only bridge on this stretch). No roads provide access to Bear Valley Creek beyond the campground below the bridge. The river changes considerably downstream with rocky, class III water which is often times obstructed with logs.

Shuttle. 3 miles, good dirt roads. Very easy bike shuttle.

Craft. Canoes, kayaks and small inflatables.

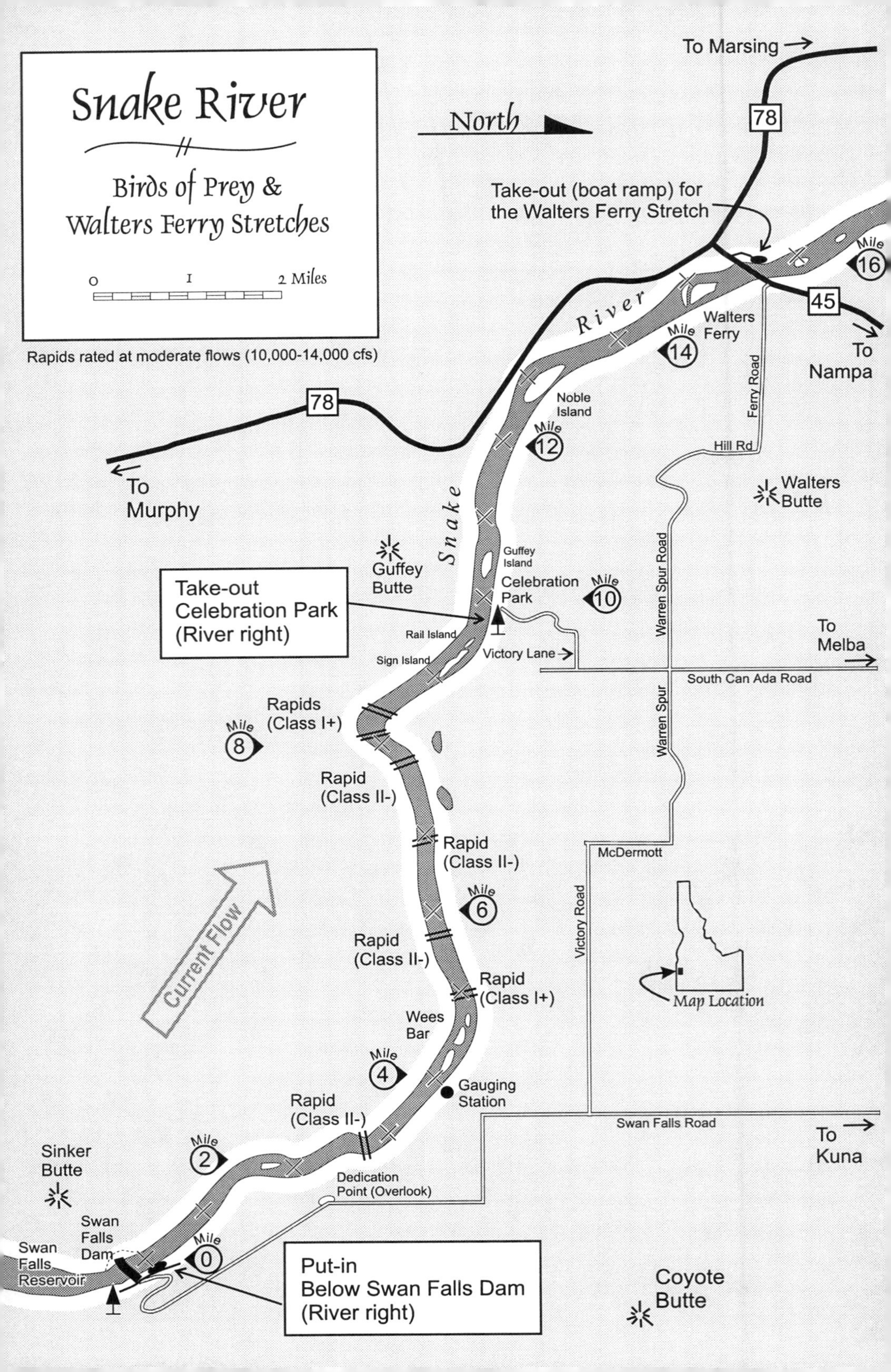
Snake River
Birds of Prey & Walters Ferry Stretches
0
1
2 Miles
Rapids rated at moderate flows (10,000-14,000 cfs)
North
To Marsing
78
Take-out (boat ramp) for the Walters Ferry Stretch
Mile 16
45
Snake River
Walters Ferry
Mile 14
To Nampa
78
Noble Island
Ferry Road
Mile 12
Hill Rd
To Murphy
Walters Butte
Guffey Butte
Guffey Island
Celebration Park
Mile 10
Warren Spur Road
Take-out Celebration Park (River right)
Rail Island
Sign Island
Victory Lane
To Melba
South Can Ada Road
Rapids (Class I+)
Mile 8
Warren Spur
Rapid (Class II-)
Rapid (Class II-)
McDermott
Current Flow
Mile 6
Victory Road
Rapid (Class II-)
Rapid (Class I+)
Map Location
Wees Bar
Mile 4
Gauging Station
Rapid (Class II-)
Swan Falls Road
To Kuna
Sinker Butte
Mile 2
Dedication Point (Overlook)
Swan Falls Dam
Swan Falls Reservoir
Mile 0
Put-in Below Swan Falls Dam (River right)
Coyote Butte

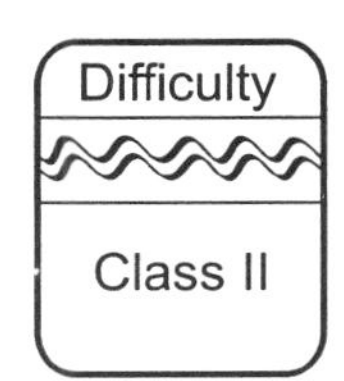

Snake River

Birds of Prey Stretch and Other Nearby Trips

WHETHER YOU ARE LOOKING for an easy whitewater trip or you're hankering to spot some magnificent birds of prey, this is one trip you won't want to miss. Located 35 miles southwest of Boise, this segment of the Snake River starts just below Swan Falls Dam and ends at a boat ramp and beautiful, little museum at Celebration Park. The trip takes you through the northern portion of the 485,000-acre Snake River Birds of Prey National Conservation Area.

In moderate flows, the Birds of Prey stretch is a class II run, suitable for all sorts of river craft: canoes, kayaks, inflatables and drift boats. All sizes of rafts and all types of inflatables can run this stretch. It's a good stretch for kayakers getting started in whitewater, and with some previous experience on smaller rivers, it is a terrific open canoe run.

Basic Stats

Difficulty: Class II in medium flows. Rapids are followed by slow water. No snags or overhanging trees. It is a big river, and it does have some squirrelly water, but with normal precautions it is not dangerous in medium flows.

Levels: Good flows are at the low-medium to medium level, around 10,000-16,000 cfs. The eddies and the river in general becomes more and more turbulent as flows increase. Gauge: Snake River at Murphy.

Distance/Time: 10 miles / 3-4 hours at 10,500 cfs.

Getting to the Take-out. Celebration Park. If you are starting at Swan Falls Dam, drive to the top of the canyon on the Swan Falls Road. At 8 miles from the dam, you come to Victory Road. Take a left. Drive 3 miles and take a right on McDermott. Drive 1 mile and take a left on Warren Spur. Drive 2 miles and take a left on Can Ada. Hang in there, we're getting close. Drive down Can Ada for 1 mile, watch for the turn-off to Celebration Park to the right. (The name of this road is Victory Lane—again.) Turn at the sign, follow the road 2 miles, and finally you're back to the river.

It isn't the easiest place to find, but once there, you'll be delighted. Celebration Park is a beautiful little park with paved parking, a deck, picnic tables, a boat ramp, restrooms, nature trails, and a museum. At this writing there was no charge to use the area. The museum, however, takes donations. Be sure to leave a donation! Donations are a far less intrusive way of raising money to help keep areas like these maintained than required user fees. Even if you can only afford a small amount, show your support.

Getting to the Put-in. Swan Falls Dam. Take the Kuna/ Meridian exit (exit #44) off of Interstate 84 (about 6 miles west of the Boise area). Drive to Kuna and once in Kuna, take Swan Falls Road to the south. Stay on Swan Falls Road. It takes you to the edge of the Snake River Canyon and then down a paved road to the dam. Along the reservoir just behind the dam you'll find a lush green park. Below the dam, Idaho Power has constructed a small ramp where you can launch boats.

The Trip. In moderate flows, four class II- rapids and several class I+ rapids are found on this stretch. All are straightforward with no terrible holes or wrap rocks. This is, of course, a big river with big river hydraulics: eddies here and there that can spin a boat around and an occasional wave that can fill an open canoe (although, the large waves can be avoided).

All in all, however, as long as it is run in medium flows, this is one of those whitewater stretches that you can enjoy without worrying about getting caught in a big, hairy rapid. Everything can be run without scouting, but, if desired, you can stop and take a look. If you fill a canoe or flip over a kayak, the rapids end in slow water where you can stop and get sorted out again.

Besides whitewater, this stretch of the river is known for its birds of prey. It is critical habitat for the prairie falcon which uses the Snake River canyon and nearby cliffs for nesting. Take time while floating the first couple of miles to scan the canyon walls for falcons. You'll see lots of birds along this stretch, but we found that we saw falcons in the early part of the trip rather than later.

Along the way, you can also stop to poke around some old stone houses or visit Indian petroglyphs. Celebration Park, the take-out, has a small museum (Idaho's only archaeological park) where you can learn about early Indian life and take a walk among lava boulders imprinted with petroglyph montages.

World Center for Birds of Prey. The best way of starting a trip on this stretch of river is to first visit the World Center for Birds of Prey. It has exhibits, regularly scheduled programs, and live bird presentations. The center is located at 5666 Flying Hawk Lane on the south edge of Boise. Phone: (208) 362-3716. To get there, take Exit 50 off Interstate 84. Follow Cole Road to the south for about 6 miles and follow the road up the hill to the World Center.

Shuttle. 17 miles, all paved (except .5 mile right before Celebration Park). This makes a pleasant bike shuttle. All the roads are paved secondary roads, but it's open, dry country and it can be hot. Give yourself plenty of time.

Craft. Canoes, kayaks, drift boats and inflatables of all sizes.

Mileage Chart
(Rapids rated for medium flows)

0	Put-in. Base of Swan Falls Dam.
1.7	Island.
2.6	Class II- rapid.
3.8	Gauging station.
4	Island.
4.5	Two islands. Wees Bar Petroglyphs (left).
5	Class I+ rapid.
5.4	Class II- rapid.
6.2	Old stone house, ruins.
6.9	Class II- rapid.
7.7	Drainage enters river on left. Class II- rapid.
8.2	Pumping station (left). Two class I+ wavy areas just above.
8.3	River widens. Class I+ rapid where it narrows on downstream end.
8.5	Petroglyphs (river right). Not visible from the river.
9.1	Upper end of a long island (Sign Island).
9.9	Take-out. Celebration Park. Museum & Petroglyphs (right).

Other Nearby Runs.

Walters Ferry Stretch. Below Celebration Park is a 6-mile, class I (1.1 to 1.2) stretch of river. It isn't as scenic as the Birds of Prey stretch, but it passes three large named islands which are important nesting areas for waterfowl. As long as it is done in medium flows, this is a good stretch if you want to get the feel of a big river. Try to pick a windless day to do it—or get started early in the morning. The current is slow, and if the winds come up, it can turn into a long trip. The take-out is Walters Ferry Bridge. Like the Birds of Prey stretch, you can do a nice bike shuttle all on paved rural roads.

Black Butte to Swan Falls Dam. Upstream of the Swan Falls Dam, a two day canoe—or lake kayak—trip can be made starting at the Black Butte Launch (northwest of Grand View) to the Swan Falls Dam. It's a 20-mile trip through mostly slow, lake-like water. Even though it's slow water, avoid it when the river is high. Be on guard for strong up-canyon winds which can occur at any time, but usually come in the afternoon. You will encounter motorized craft on this stretch. A three-day trip can be done by combining the Black Butte trip with the Birds of Prey stretch. Idaho Power provides a portage trail around the river left side of Swan Falls Dam.

Difficulty

Class I
(1.0)

Boise River

Discovery Park: The Boise River Practice Area

IF YOU'RE LOOKING for a safe, easy place on the Boise River that the whole family can enjoy, then Discovery Park, on the far eastern outskirts of Boise, is the place. Much of the Boise River is swift and is obstructed with overhanging trees and, of course, diversions, but *not* on this short stretch.

The current is slow or not moving at all since it is backed up behind a downstream dam. That enables you to paddle downstream and then back up without the extra hassle of a shuttle. It is an attractive park with grass, picnic tables, restrooms and a beach, a perfect place to practice on the Boise River.

Basic Stats

Difficulty: Class I (1.0). Water is lake-like. One can paddle upstream or downstream. Note that when the river gets low, it has a gentle downstream current, but the water is still very safe with no snags or overhanging trees.

Levels: Any level. All seasons.

Distance: You can make a 3-mile round trip down to the Diversion Dam and then back to the start.

Getting to the Put-in and Take-out. Discovery Park. Discovery Park is reached from downtown Boise by driving out Warm Springs Avenue to its junction with Idaho 21. About 2 miles past the junction on Idaho 21, the park is on the right, marked with a sign. You've gone too far if you come to the Lucky Peak dam. Once you enter the park, take a right and park your vehicle. That will put you close to the beach and launching area. A small fee is required for use of the park.

Difficulty

Class I+
(1.4)

Boise River

Barber Park to Ann Morrison Park

THIS THE FAMOUS SEGMENT of the Boise River which is floated each summer by hundreds of people in inner tubes. But it's not just for tubers. It also makes a pleasant and lively canoe or kayak trip—particularly in the early morning before the tubing crowds arrive.

Normally, you wouldn't think of a river flowing through the state's largest city as very appealing from a floating standpoint. But years of work on the river's greenbelt and efforts by the Fish and Game Department to improve fish habitat have paid off. The Boise River is, indeed, a beautiful trip.

Unfortunately, however, it's not a beginner's trip. Canoeists and kayakers need to have experience on easier rivers before undertaking this one. What is deceptive about the Boise, is all those tubers: many of them are completely and utterly inexperienced with rivers. The catch is that tubing takes no skill—and it's forgiving. Tubers can duck under overhanging trees or gaily bounce over the rocks in diversions (three of which are found in this stretch). If a tuber gets flipped while going over a diversion, he'll laugh, grab his tube, and climb back on.

Not so with a canoe or kayak. It takes skill to keep a canoe away from overhanging trees or to line it up properly to avoid rocks in a diversion. If one flips a canoe, it's no easy task to get the heavy, water-laden craft off the river, particularly if the current is swift and shoreline brushy as it is on the Boise.

But once you've gained some experience on rivers, give this trip a try. It's a wonderful surprise and a terrific way of getting a respite from the stress and noise of a fast-paced city.

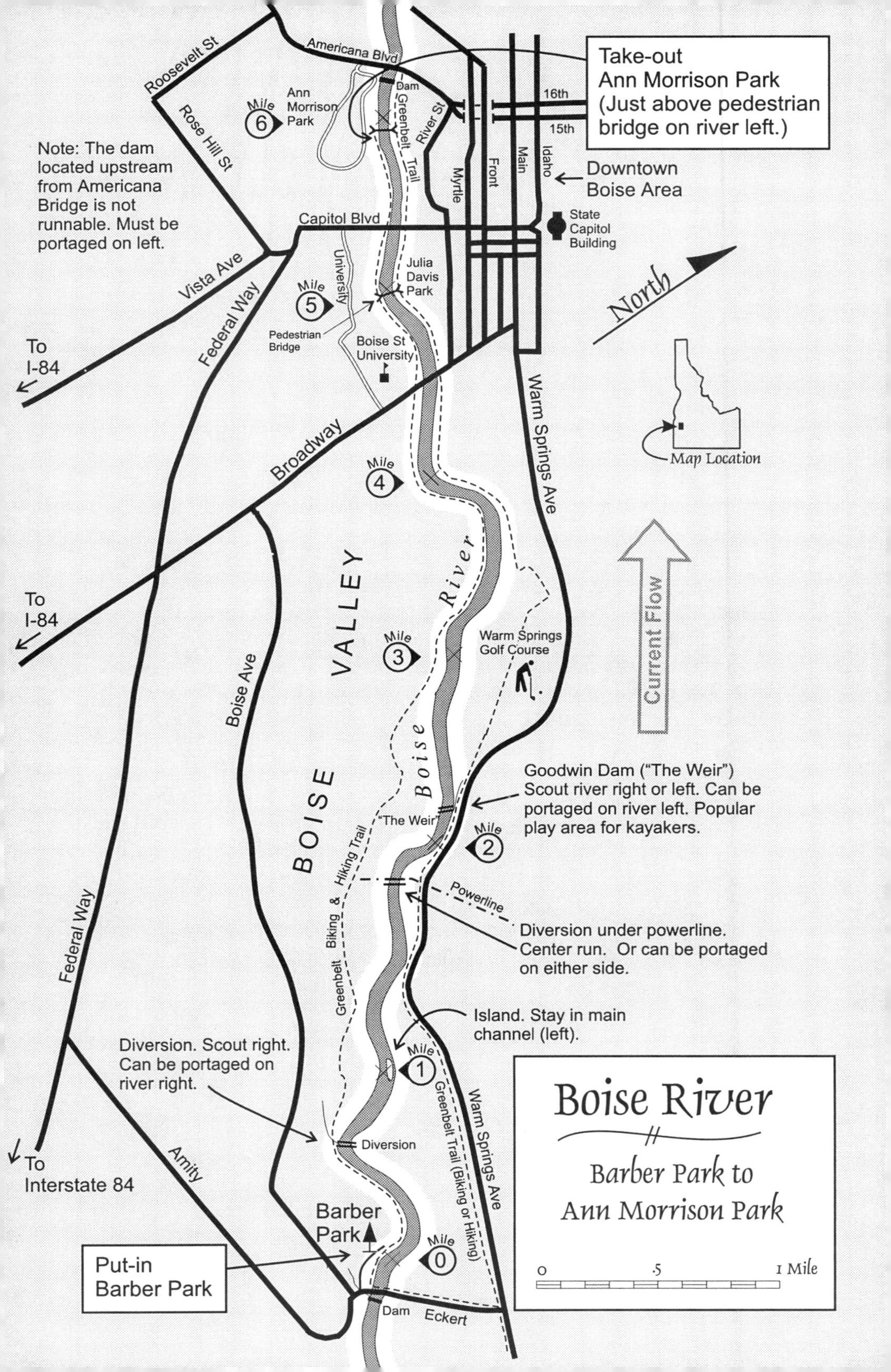
Take-out
Ann Morrison Park
(Just above pedestrian bridge on river left.)
Americana Blvd
Roosevelt St
Rose Hill St
Dam
Greenbelt Trail
River St
16th
15th
Mile 6
Ann Morrison Park
Note: The dam located upstream from Americana Bridge is not runnable. Must be portaged on left.
Myrtle
Front
Main
Idaho
Downtown Boise Area
State Capitol Building
Capitol Blvd
Vista Ave
Federal Way
University
Julia Davis Park
Mile 5
Pedestrian Bridge
Boise St University
North
To I-84
Broadway
Warm Springs Ave
Map Location
Mile 4
Boise River
VALLEY
To I-84
Mile 3
Warm Springs Golf Course
Current Flow
Boise Ave
BOISE
Goodwin Dam ("The Weir")
Scout river right or left. Can be portaged on river left. Popular play area for kayakers.
"The Weir"
Mile 2
Greenbelt Biking & Hiking Trail
Powerline
Diversion under powerline. Center run. Or can be portaged on either side.
Federal Way
Island. Stay in main channel (left).
Diversion. Scout right. Can be portaged on river right.
Mile 1
Greenbelt Trail (Biking or Hiking)
Warm Springs Ave
Diversion
To Interstate 84
Amity
Barber Park
Mile 0
Put-in Barber Park
Dam
Eckert
Boise River
Barber Park to Ann Morrison Park
0
.5
1 Mile

Basic Stats

Difficulty: Class I+ (1.4) if the diversions are portaged. Short class II to II+ if the diversions are run.

Levels: The consensus among Boise boaters, is that you should stay off the river when flows exceed 1,500 cfs (measured at the Glenwood Bridge gauge). High water usually occurs in the spring and early June with flows sometimes exceeding 7,000 cfs. Typical flows in the summer and fall are around 600 to 1,500 cfs, a good level for running the river.

Distance/Time: 6 miles / 2 hours at 700 cfs.

Scouts/Portages: 2 scouts and 2 possible portages around diversions.

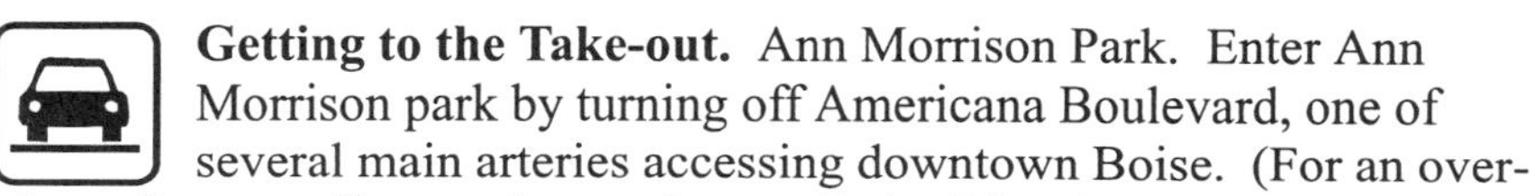

Getting to the Take-out. Ann Morrison Park. Enter Ann Morrison park by turning off Americana Boulevard, one of several main arteries accessing downtown Boise. (For an overview of surrounding roads, see the two Boise River Maps: Barber to Ann Morrison Park and Ann Morrison to Glenwood Bridge). Once you enter the park, drive around the right side of a big fountain, and park near where the pedestrian bridge goes over the river. The take-out is on the upstream side of the pedestrian bridge and involves about a 300-foot carry to the parking lot. Restrooms are available.

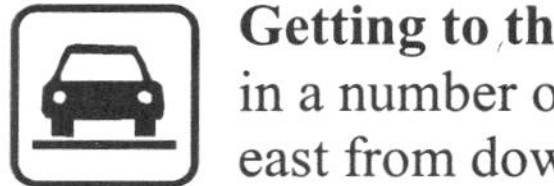

Getting to the Put-in. Barber Park. Barber Park can be reached in a number of ways. One common approach is to drive southeast from downtown Boise on Warm Springs Avenue (heading toward Idaho City). Approximately 5 miles from the downtown area, take a left on North Eckert Road. Continue another .5 mile until reaching the bridge over the Boise River. Just on the other side of the bridge, take a right into the entrance to Barber Park. A small fee is charged for park use. Barber Park closes at sunset, and if you are planning to do an evening trip or will be doing your shuttle on bicycle, you may want to park outside of the park. Some limited parking is available at Eckert bridge. Restrooms and dressing rooms are available.

The Trip. The Boise River is pleasantly surrounded by a band of cottonwoods, willows and maples which isolate it from the busy, surrounding city. You hardly know you're in a city, except when you pass by the backs of commercial and public buildings here and there. The current is swift, and moves along, even in low water levels. Typical of Idaho valley rivers, the Boise has overhanging trees which must be avoided, and maneuvering is required on corners and in the mini-rapids which form where the river slides down gravel bars. The main difficulty on this stretch are three diversions. One is easily passed over, but two should be scouted.

Diversions. The first diversion comes .7 mile from the start. The water slows some here, and you can see what river runners call a horizon line: a line where the river makes a quick drop. In this case the river drops over the rocks and concrete slabs used for the diversion. From above, a horizon line appears as a discontinuity in the river current: a little patch of the river seems to be missing. Pull off on river right and scout.

Diversions can change, but when we ran the river at 700 cfs, the diversion's concrete slabs looked pretty ugly, and we portaged. The portage at that level wasn't difficult. We walked the canoe in the water to the edge of the diversion, pulled it over a couple of the slabs on the right shore and were on our way within 10 minutes. In higher water, you'll need to portage through the trees on the right.

At 1.2 miles from the start, you come to an island. Stay in the main current in the left channel. The right (and smaller) channel is obstructed with concrete blocks on its lower end.

The second diversion is under a powerline which crosses the river, 2 miles from the start. Scouting wasn't necessary. We found no sharp drops here, just some waves, easily run down the middle.

The third diversion (2.3 miles from the start) is called "The Weir," and it's a common place for kayakers to play. It can be scouted on the left or right and, if need be, portaged on the left. We ran it on the right center through some respectably-sized waves.

Just Before the Take-out. Once past the third diversion, the river is much of the same: avoid overhanging trees and stay to the inside of corners. In the University of Boise area (you can see Bronco Stadium from the river) you'll pass under the first pedestrian bridge. The second pedestrian bridge (upstream, river left) is your take-out.

You can run the river below this point (described in the next section), but be aware that you must first portage a dam which is located just before the Americana Boulevard Bridge. Information on the portage is also found in the next section.

Avoiding Crowds. Since this is such a popular inner tube stretch, canoeists and kayakers may want to choose a time when crowds abate some. Early mornings are an excellent time. So is the fall. We ran the river on a beautiful, sunny day in early October. It was Saturday, and believe it or not, other than a couple of fly fishers, we saw no one else on the river!

Shuttle. All paved, 7 miles. In the summer, a shuttle service is available. Check at Barber Park for information. Bike shuttlers have a real treat on this one. The entire shuttle can be done on Greenbelt bike and walking paths.

Craft. Canoe, kayaks, small inflatables. It's a small river and large rafts and drift boats are not recommended.

Mileage Chart

0	Put-in. Barber park. River left.
.7	Diversion. Scout on right. Can be portaged on right.
1.2	Island. Stay in the main (left) channel.
2	Powerline. Small, easy diversion. Most likely a middle run.
2.3	The Weir. Scout on left or right. Can be portaged on left, if need be.
4.5	Broadway bridge.
5.1	Pedestrian bridge.
5.4	Capitol Blvd. bridge.
6	Take-out. Pedestrian bridge at Ann Morrison Park (upstream of bridge on left).
	NOTE: .2 mile past the pedestrian bridge at Ann Morrison Park is a dam which must be portaged on left.

A big brute on the line: Boise River, *circa* 1920.

Idaho State Historical Society

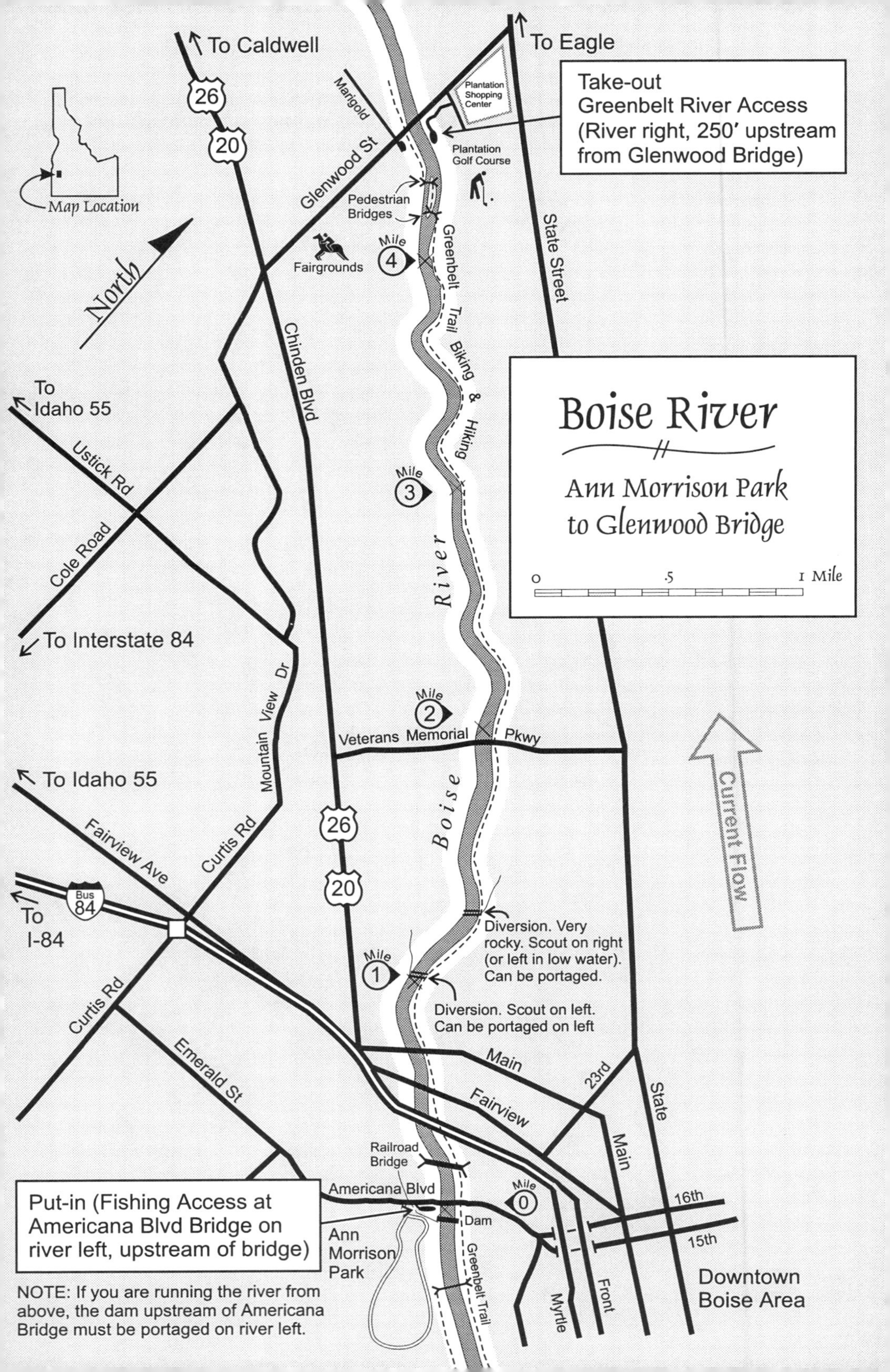
Boise River
Ann Morrison Park to Glenwood Bridge
0 .5 1 Mile
To Caldwell
To Eagle
Take-out
Greenbelt River Access
(River right, 250′ upstream from Glenwood Bridge)
Plantation Shopping Center
Plantation Golf Course
Marigold
Glenwood St
Map Location
North
Pedestrian Bridges
Mile 4
Fairgrounds
Greenbelt Trail Biking & Hiking
State Street
Chinden Blvd
To Idaho 55
Ustick Rd
Cole Road
Mile 3
River
To Interstate 84
Mountain View Dr
Mile 2
Veterans Memorial Pkwy
Current Flow
To Idaho 55
Boise
26
20
Fairview Ave
Curtis Rd
Bus 84
To I-84
Diversion. Very rocky. Scout on right (or left in low water). Can be portaged.
Mile 1
Diversion. Scout on left. Can be portaged on left
Curtis Rd
Emerald St
Main
Fairview
23rd
State
Main
Railroad Bridge
Americana Blvd
Mile 0
16th
15th
Dam
Put-in (Fishing Access at Americana Blvd Bridge on river left, upstream of bridge)
Ann Morrison Park
Greenbelt Trail
Myrtle
Front
Downtown Boise Area
NOTE: If you are running the river from above, the dam upstream of Americana Bridge must be portaged on river left.

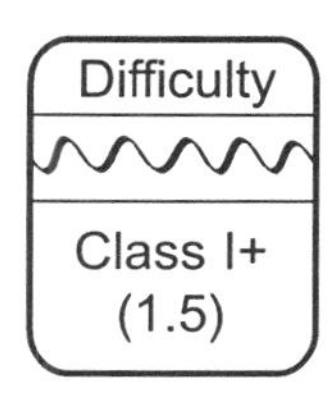

Boise River

Ann Morrison Park to Glenwood Bridge

WHILE MOST PADDLERS focus their attention on the Barber Park stretch (described in the previous section), there's still fine river running on the lower half of the Boise River through the city. Like the upper part, though, you'll want to build up your experience on easier rivers before undertaking this one.

This stretch has two diversions, but both can be portaged. Overall, it is slightly more difficult than the upper stretch. It has swift current and more overhanging trees which require a sureness of one's paddling technique. While it has its visual disappointments here and there, a good part of it, like the upper stretch, is surprisingly natural with a protective buffer of cottonwoods and maples.

Basic Stats

Difficulty: Class I+ (1.5) if the diversion dams are portaged. Short class II to III- if the diversions are run.

Levels: Same comments as the Barber Park stretch. Don't run when levels exceed 1,500 cfs at the Glenwood gauge.

Distance/Time: 5 miles / 2-3 hours.

Scouts/Portages: 2 scouts and 2 possible portages around diversions. Note that if you are running the river from upstream of the suggested put-in, one portage must be made around the dam just above Americana Boulevard Bridge.

Getting to the Take-out. Greenbelt River Access at the Glenwood Bridge. Glenwood Street can be reached in a number of ways, but one way is to begin in downtown Boise and drive out State Street towards Eagle (and Horseshoe Bend). Five miles from the capitol building you'll come to a major intersection with stoplights. Glenwood Street is to the left and Gary Lane is to the right.

Take a left on Glenwood. Drive a couple of blocks and take a left onto a side road just past the Plantation Shopping Center, but before the bridge over the Boise River. Within a block on this side road, take a right on the access road which leads to the Greenbelt parking area. A trail leads from here to the river. The take-out involves about a 150-foot carry from the river's edge to the parking area.

Getting to the Put-in. Americana Boulevard Bridge. You can put in at Ann Morrison Park, but if you do, you'll have to portage a dam. The best place to put in is the Americana Boulevard fishing access (see map for getting to Americana Boulevard). Drive towards downtown Boise on Americana Boulevard. Just after the turn-off to Ann Morrison Park, and immediately before the bridge over the Boise River, you'll find a pull-off. The pull-off is often used for parking by people fishing the river. Park among the anglers and carry your boat (about 80 feet) down to the river.

Note to Boaters Floating from Points Upstream. If you are coming down from Barber Park or other access points higher on the Boise River, you'll need to portage around a sizable dam located just upriver from Americana bridge. At the far edge of Ann Morrison park, pull off on the grass and portage your boat 500 feet around to the fishing access area by the bridge.

When we ran the river at 700 cfs, we found that we were able to paddle our canoe a few feet into the channel leading to the headgate and pull the boat up and over a 5-foot high hump. Then we easily slid the boat down to the river just below the dam. But scout this first! Make absolutely sure there's no current in the diversion channel before attempting it. In higher water or if flows into the diversion channel are swift, this could be dangerous. If you have any doubt, make the longer, but safer portage.

The Trip. Once underway, you'll pass under 5 bridges in a row: Americana, a railroad bridge, Interstate 84 Connector, Fairview, and Main. Beyond Main Street the river slows a little as it approaches the first diversion (1 mile from the start). When you hear the water falling over the diversion and see the horizon line ahead, pull off on the left. This is a colorful and mildly memorable scout. You'll find yourself in the back of a trailer park and you'll have to work your way behind a fence and climb over the concrete diversion channel which leads off on the left side of the river.

We found the waves in this diversion fairly large, and with another diversion almost in sight below, we opted to portage. The normal portage is about 300 to 400 feet. At 700 cfs, we were able to float partway into the diversion channel and pull the boat up out of the channel on the left and then slide it down to the river. But scout it first and do this only when there is no current in the diversion channel. In higher water or when current flows into the diversion, portaging this way would be dangerous. The safest option is to do the longer portage.

The next diversion is .2 mile below the first. In low water, the easiest scout—or portage—is on a rocky shoreline on the left. In higher water, you'll want to scout—and portage—on the right. This is not a quick one drop diversion, but rather it's a rocky rapid that is about 250 feet long. We found a low water run on the far left, but diversions can change and runs vary with water flow, so scout it first. If you decide to portage in low water, drag or carry your boat over the rocky, left-hand shore. In higher water, portage on the right up and over the pedestrian bridge on the Greenbelt path.

That's it for diversions! From here, however, be careful for overhanging trees and brush. There are more sweepers here than the upper stretch. You know that the take-out is nearing when you reach a long island in the river. A pedestrian bridge crosses over the right channel of the island and then at the tail end of the island, another pedestrian bridge crosses over the left channel. At this point you're very close to the Glenwood Bridge. As soon as the bridge comes into view, pull off on the right at the Greenbelt access site.

Shuttle. All paved. 7 miles. Bike shuttling doesn't get any better than this. It's all on the Greenbelt bike and hiking path.

Craft. Canoe, kayaks, small inflatables. Large rafts and drift boats not recommended.

Mileage Chart

0	Put-in. Americana Bridge Fishing Access (river left, upstream from bridge).
1	Diversion. Diverts to left. Pull off on left above diversion channel to scout. Portage may be made on left.
1.2	Diversion. Long, rocky diversion. In low water, may be scouted or portaged on left. In high water, scout and/or portage on right.
2	Veterans Memorial Parkway Bridge
3.8	River splits into two channels around a long island. Pedestrian bridges over left channel at top and over right channel at bottom.
4.5	Glenwood Bridge. Take out just above bridge on right.

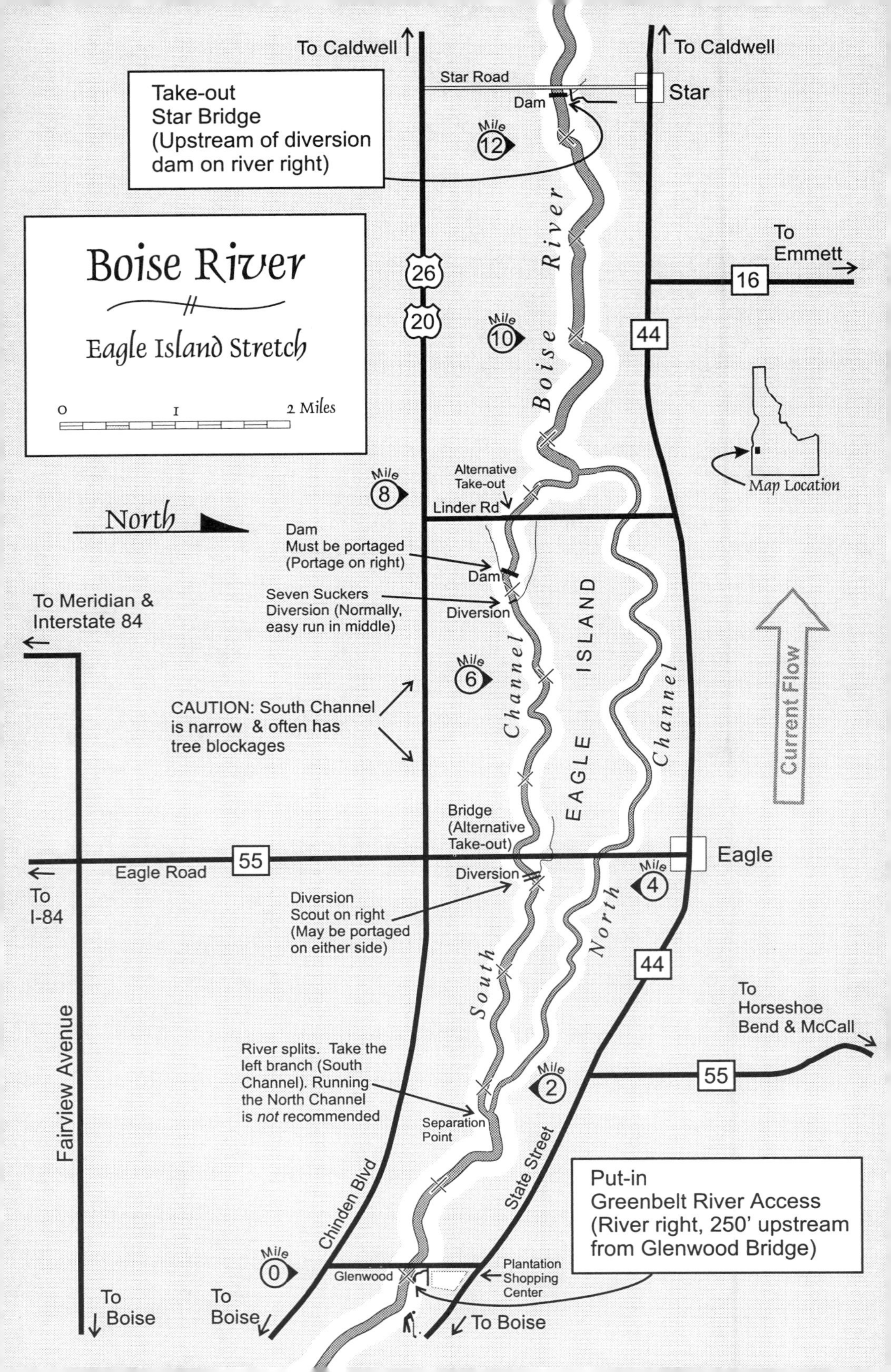

Boise River
Eagle Island Stretch
0
1
2 Miles
To Caldwell
To Caldwell
Star Road
Star
Dam
Take-out
Star Bridge
(Upstream of diversion dam on river right)
Mile 12
Boise River
To Emmett
16
26
20
Mile 10
44
Map Location
Mile 8
Alternative Take-out
Linder Rd
North
Dam
Must be portaged
(Portage on right)
Dam
Seven Suckers Diversion (Normally, easy run in middle)
Diversion
EAGLE ISLAND
To Meridian & Interstate 84
Mile 6
Channel
Channel
Current Flow
CAUTION: South Channel is narrow & often has tree blockages
Bridge
(Alternative Take-out)
55
Eagle Road
Eagle
To I-84
Diversion
Mile 4
Diversion
Scout on right
(May be portaged on either side)
North
South
44
To Horseshoe Bend & McCall
Fairview Avenue
River splits. Take the left branch (South Channel). Running the North Channel is not recommended
Mile 2
55
Separation Point
State Street
Chinden Blvd
Put-in
Greenbelt River Access
(River right, 250' upstream from Glenwood Bridge)
Mile 0
Glenwood
Plantation Shopping Center
To Boise
To Boise
To Boise

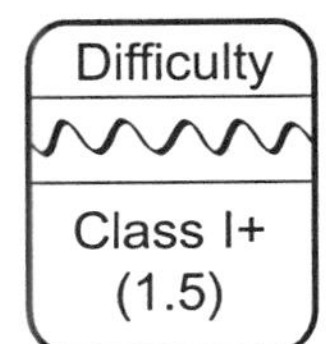

Boise River

Eagle Island Stretch (Glenwood Bridge to Star Road)

FROM GLENWOOD BRIDGE, the Boise River flows away from the urbanized area near Boise and around the south edge of a large island known as Eagle Island. As the Boise metropolitan area has expanded, development has occurred in this area, but the considerable cottonwood forest along the river blocks most outward signs of that growth. The river, here, has a more rural and natural feel than the previous two city stretches.

It isn't any easier here, however. In fact, on this stretch, you'll probably encounter more portages than any other segment of the Boise River. The reason is the size of the south channel. It's smaller than the main Boise River channel, and trees which have fallen into the river can easily block it from one side to the other. Be prepared to stop and portage at any time. When we paddled this segment, we portaged four times around tree blockages.

That all adds up to having experience before undertaking this trip. First, make sure you're comfortable with your boating skills and that you've run the upper two stretches of the Boise first. And secondly, do this stretch when the water is low, below 1,000 cfs. When the water is high, you have far less time to react and eddy-out.

It's because of the portages, however, that you'll find less people on this stretch. With its abundant bird life and natural river scenery this is a very pleasing river trip, indeed.

Basic Stats

Difficulty: Class I+ (1.5) if you portage the diversions. Class II- if the diversions are run.

Levels: Because of the high probability of trees blocking the river, do this in late summer when flows are below 1,000 cfs at Glenwood gauge.

Distance / Time: 13 miles / 4-5 hours at 700 cfs. Alternative take-outs are available at Eagle Bridge (4 river miles) and Linder Road Bridge (7 river miles).

Scouts & Portages: One diversion should be scouted (can be portaged). One dam must be portaged. Expect to find fallen trees blocking the river which will also need to be portaged.

Getting to the Take-out. Star Bridge. Drive to Star which is 14 miles west of Boise on Idaho 44. In the middle of Star, turn south on Star Road and continue for .7 mile. Just before the bridge over the Boise River take a left on Main Street. Drive a couple of hundred feet and park in the pull-off used by anglers. The take-out is just above a diversion dam on river right. It involves carrying your boat about 400 feet.

Alternative take-outs are available at Eagle Road Bridge (river right, upstream of bridge) and Linder Road Bridge (river right, upstream of the bridge). Note that both Eagle Road and Linder Road pass over two bridges: one over the North Channel and the other over the South Channel of the river. You must make sure that you leave your shuttle vehicle at the bridge going over the *southern most* channel of the river.

Getting to the Put-in. Glenwood Bridge Greenbelt river access. The directions to the Glenwood river access point are found in the previous section (Ann Morrison to Glenwood Bridge).

The Trip. It is helpful to understand a little of the character of the Boise River on this stretch. About 1.6 miles from Glenwood Bridge, the westward trending Boise River separates into two channels: the North Channel and the South Channel. Between the two channels is a six-mile long island, called Eagle Island. Experienced Boise river runners highly recommend running the South Channel. While runnable, the North Channel has less water, more downed trees and more obstructions.

It is crucial that you get in the South Channel and not end up in the North Channel. To assure that you do, once underway from the Glenwood Bridge, always take the left channel until you are sure that you are correctly in the South Channel. The actual split of the river occurs 1.6 miles from the start.

The southern channel, is, of course, smaller than the main river channel, and you can expect to find trees which have fallen all the way across the river. Use caution: don't go around blind corners without knowing what's in front of you. At low water (700 cfs), we found the current reasonably easy for stopping. When spotting and approaching downed trees, the water was slow enough to pull off the river at a comfortable distance. It would not be comfortable or reasonable in high water, however, and we strongly recommend that you do this stretch when flows are less than 1,000 cfs.

The first diversion is 4 miles from the start. The water is diverted to the right. You'll be able to see the concrete head gate on the right side of the river as you approach it. Stop and scout on the right. The diversion can be portaged on either side of the river, if desired. At the time we ran it, the run was through moderately-sized waves in the right-center.

The river passes under the Eagle bridge, 4.3 miles from the start. At 6.7 miles is another diversion with the memorable name: Seven Suckers. Despite its name, Seven Suckers was an easy run down the middle through some riffles.

At 7.3 miles, you'll reach the base of a cliff on the left and the backwaters of a dam. It can't be missed. The water slows and from upstream you'll see the decking which has been laid over the top of the dam.

The dam must be portaged. Paddle over to the grassy right shore. We found it easy to drag our canoe 40 feet around on the grass and put in below the dam. Since the dam diverts even more water out of the Boise River, the channel below is even smaller yet—and it's likely you'll find more downed logs or trees in this area. We had one portage around a tree in this section. At this point, however, you're nearly finished with the South Channel.

The Linder Road Bridge comes at 7.6 miles into the trip or .3 mile below the dam. Then finally, 8.4 miles from the start, the North and South Channels come back together.

The river is suddenly wider, the vegetation seems to pull back and everything seems a little brighter. You still need to plan on dodging overhanging trees, but it's unlikely on this stretch that you'll have to deal with any more tree blockages. The take-out is signaled by the Star Bridge and a dam just above the bridge. The dam is obvious. It's an ugly affair with metal bars sticking up out of the river, but you won't have to get close to it. On the right, above the dam, is a concrete head gate. Your take-out is on river right just above the head gate.

Shuttle. 13 miles, all paved. Bicycle shuttle possible, but be aware that the highways are heavily traveled.

Craft. Canoes and kayaks. Because of portaging and narrow channels, rafts and drift boats are not recommended.

Mileage Chart

0	Put-in. Glenwood Bridge (upstream of bridge on river right).
1.6	Separation Point. River separates into South and North Channels. Take the left (South) channel.
4.0	Diversion. Diverts to right. Scout on right. May be portaged right or left.
4.3	Eagle Bridge (alternative take-out or put-in).
6.7	The Seven Suckers Diversion. Diverts to right. Easy run in middle.
7.3	Dam. Diverts to left. Portage on right.
7.6	Linder Road Bridge (alternative take-out or put-in).
8.4	North and South channels come back together.
12.4	Take-out. Just above dam and Star Bridge on river right.

The narrow, tree-lined channel around Eagle Island.

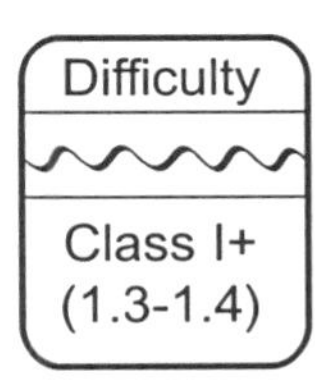

Boise River

Caldwell to Notus and Notus to Wilder Bridge

STARTING AT CALDWELL, the Boise River winds its way through cottonwood lowlands towards its confluence with the Snake. Significant portions of this segment resemble something of what the Boise River was like before Idaho was settled in the mid and late 1800s. Of all of our trips on the river, it was on this segment that we saw the greatest diversity of bird life—and an extravagant great blue heron rookery which literally knocked our socks off. Best of all, there are *no* diversions on this stretch.

Running this portion of the river is a tad easier than all of the upper segments. You still need to develop basic river skills before undertaking this trip, but once comfortable with boating techniques, this a good first trip on a free-flowing portion of the river—and a good one to return to again and again when you need to escape and enjoy some of the best that the Boise River has to offer.

Basic Stats

Difficulty: Much of this stretch is class I (1.2). However, there are also some class I+ (1.3 to 1.4). You need basic maneuvering skills to handle corners and stay away from overhanging trees and brush. The river is wider here than upper portions and tree blockages (except for smaller side channels) are far less likely. No diversions.

Levels: The best levels are in the low to moderate range. Moderate levels are around 1,500 cfs at the Parma gauge. Don't run it too much higher than 1,500 cfs.

Distance/Time: 14 miles / 5-7 hours. Alternative take-out available at Notus Bridge (8 miles) which cuts the trip almost in half.

Getting to the Take-out. Wilder Bridge on US 95. From Interstate 84, take the Notus/Parma Exit (Exit #26) near Caldwell, 25 miles west of Boise. Drive to the west on Highway 20 & 26 for 12 miles until coming to the US 95 junction. Head south on US 95 towards Wilder. At 1.5 miles from the junction, you'll cross a bridge over the Boise River. The banks here are a little steep, and there's no ideal place to take out, but we found that just downstream of the bridge

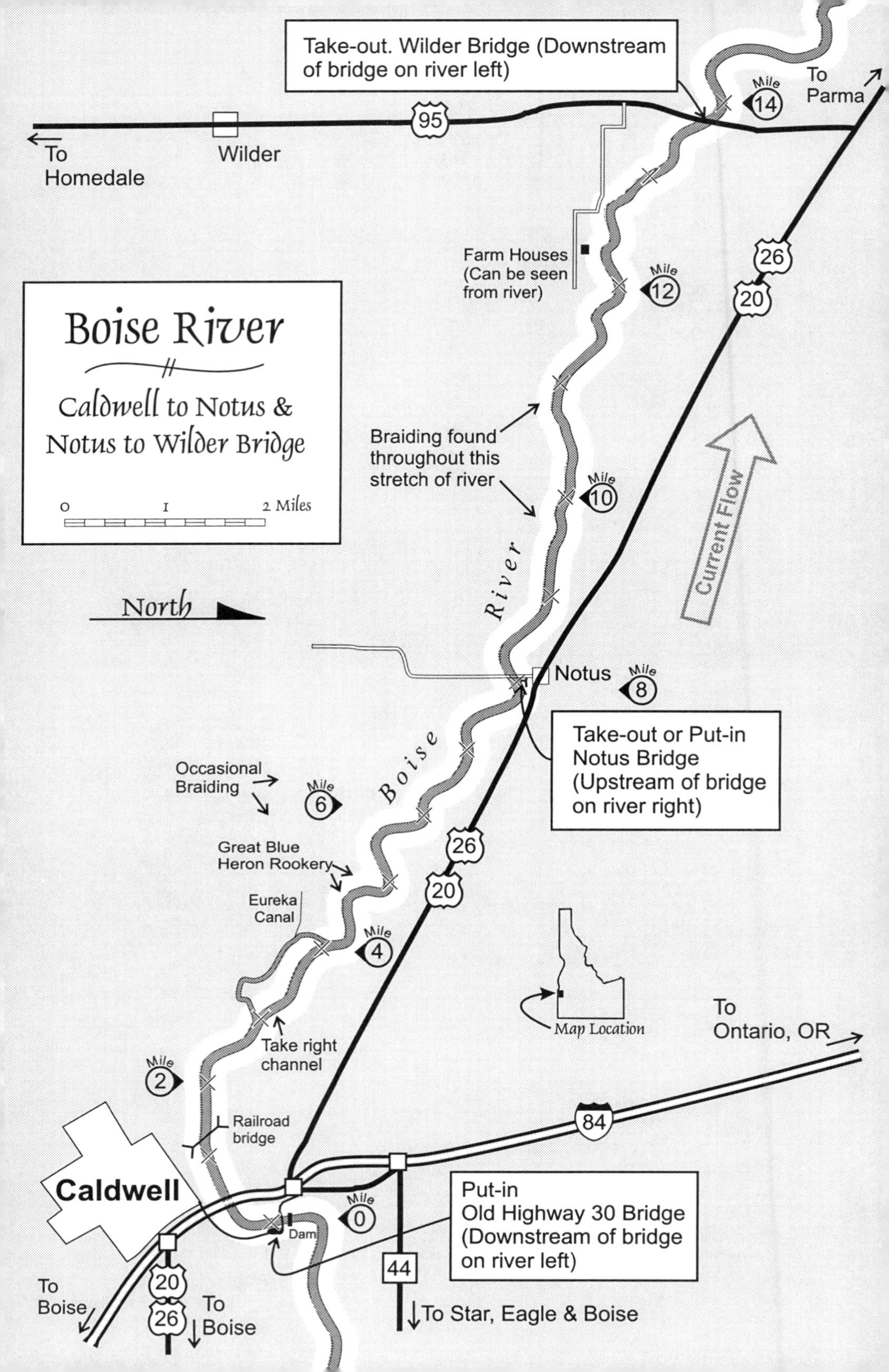
Boise River
Caldwell to Notus & Notus to Wilder Bridge
0
1
2 Miles
North
Take-out. Wilder Bridge (Downstream of bridge on river left)
To Homedale
Wilder
95
Mile 14
To Parma
Farm Houses (Can be seen from river)
Mile 12
26
20
Braiding found throughout this stretch of river
Mile 10
Current Flow
River
Notus
Mile 8
Take-out or Put-in Notus Bridge (Upstream of bridge on river right)
Boise
Occasional Braiding
Mile 6
Great Blue Heron Rookery
Eureka Canal
Mile 4
Take right channel
Mile 2
Railroad bridge
Map Location
To Ontario, OR
84
Caldwell
Mile 0
Dam
Put-in Old Highway 30 Bridge (Downstream of bridge on river left)
44
To Boise
20
26
To Boise
To Star, Eagle & Boise

on river left was an adequate spot for getting our canoe up and out of the water. Small pull-offs are available on either side of the bridge for parking.

Alternative Take-out. Notus Bridge. An alternative take-out which works well if you are limited in time is the Notus bridge. Notus is 6 miles from Interstate 84 on Highway 20 & 26. In Notus, turn left (south) on Notus Road. As soon as you turn, watch for Yourdon Lane and take a left. A few feet down Yourdon, a dirt road, accessing the river, heads towards the river at the base of the bridge.

Getting to the Put-in. Old Highway 30 bridge in Caldwell. From Interstate 84, take the Notus/Parma Exit (Exit #26). When you get off the interstate, head in the opposite direction from Notus and Parma. Within .1 mile you'll come to a "T" in the road which is Old Highway 30. Take a right. The old highway drops down a hill and crosses over the Boise River. Just on the other side of the bridge (river left, downstream of the bridge) is a parking area and a place to launch boats.

The Trip. From the launching point in Caldwell, the river is swift. You'll need to stay in the main current and not allow your boat to drift close to the shore which is overhung by trees. By the end of the first mile, you will have passed under the interstate bridges and will be passing the outskirts of Caldwell.

Three miles from the start, the river begins to braid, which it does throughout the trip. When faced with a choice of channels, stay in the largest of channels, the one carrying the most water. At the first main braid where it is difficult to tell which is larger, stay in the right channel which will eventually pick up more water.

At 4.5 miles from the start, you'll come upon a sprawling great blue heron rookery which occupies a good number of dead cottonwood trees on both sides of the river. It was at this point and extending for several miles downstream that we saw a remarkable diversity of birds. Among others, we saw kingfishers, red tail hawks, a golden eagle, a snowy egret, mergansers, and a green heron. Adding to an already booked entertainment schedule were the theatrics of a great blue heron and an osprey in a tiff over a favored fishing hole.

Near the town of Notus, the river swings close to the railroad tracks and some buildings, but then the river curves away, and you're back in the trees. In the next segment, from Notus to the US 95 bridge, you'll encounter more braiding and a couple of sharp bends. But the bends shouldn't cause any trouble as long as you use the accepted river running technique of entering on the inside of the bend where the current is less forceful. Many gravel bars and even some sandy beaches are found throughout this segment—all of which make nice lunch stops. The end is signaled by the highway bridge.

Shuttle. 15 miles. Bike shuttle possible. Traffic, however, is heavy for a rural area. Highway shoulders are medium width.

Craft. Canoes, kayaks and inflatables (small or large). Although there are no boat ramps, a drift boat can be slipped in the water at Caldwell and without too much effort taken out at the Notus bridge.

Mileage Chart

0	Put-in. Old Highway 30 bridge at Caldwell (downstream of bridge on river left).
.7	Highway and interstate bridges.
1.4	Railroad bridge.
1.8	Gravel pit and slurry line crosses river.
3	Braiding begins. Take right channel at first main braid.
4.5	Large great blue heron rookery.
8	Notus bridge. Alternative take-out. River right.
13.8	Take-out. Wilder bridge on US 95 (downstream of bridge on river left).

A good part of the Boise River below Caldwell resembles something of what the river was like before Idaho was settled in the mid and late 1800s.

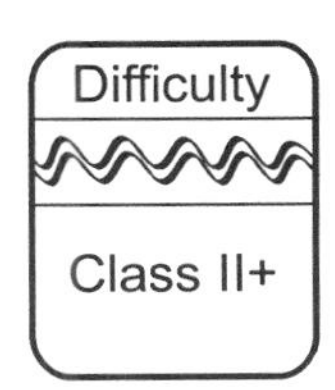

South Fork Boise River

Dam to Danskin Stretch &
Village to Indian Rock

JUST BELOW ANDERSON RANCH DAM (northeast of Mountain Home), is a class I and II segment of the South Fork of the Boise. It's an elegant run on a deep blue river flowing through a canyon with big grassy hillsides and broken lava outcroppings. Boaters have two options. One is to run the entire segment from the dam to the Danskin bridge, a class II+ stretch of water. The other option is to do a short piece of the full run. A mostly class I run with one class II- rapid (which can be sneaked) can be made between two access points (Village and Indian Point).

The South Fork is well known for its fishing. You'll see a lot of fly fishers along the river, and as you can imagine it has ramps for drift boats. Besides drift boats, fisherfolk are out in force in mini-cats, but it is also a great stretch of river for canoeing, kayaking and rafting. The river is wide enough that if you are not fishing, you can give anglers plenty of room as you pass by.

Dam to Danskin Stretch

Basic Stats (Dam to Danskin)

Difficulty: Class II+ at 1600 cfs. Some rocky rapids, particularly toward the end and a few spots where trees overhang.

Levels: Best levels are in the low to medium range (flows under 1600 cfs). Gauge: South Fork Boise below Anderson Ranch Dam.

Distance/Time: 9.7 miles / 3.5 to 4 hours at 1600 cfs.

Getting to the Take-out. Danskin Bridge Access. The Danskin Bridge Access is located about 11 miles downriver from the Anderson Ranch Dam. Drive to the west, following the dirt road which parallels the river. Continue .2 mile past the turn-off to Prairie to the take-out, well-marked with a sign. (Danskin bridge is just below the parking area.) Danskin has a ramp and an outhouse. At the time of this writing no fees were charged for any of the access points along the river—and we hope it stays that way!

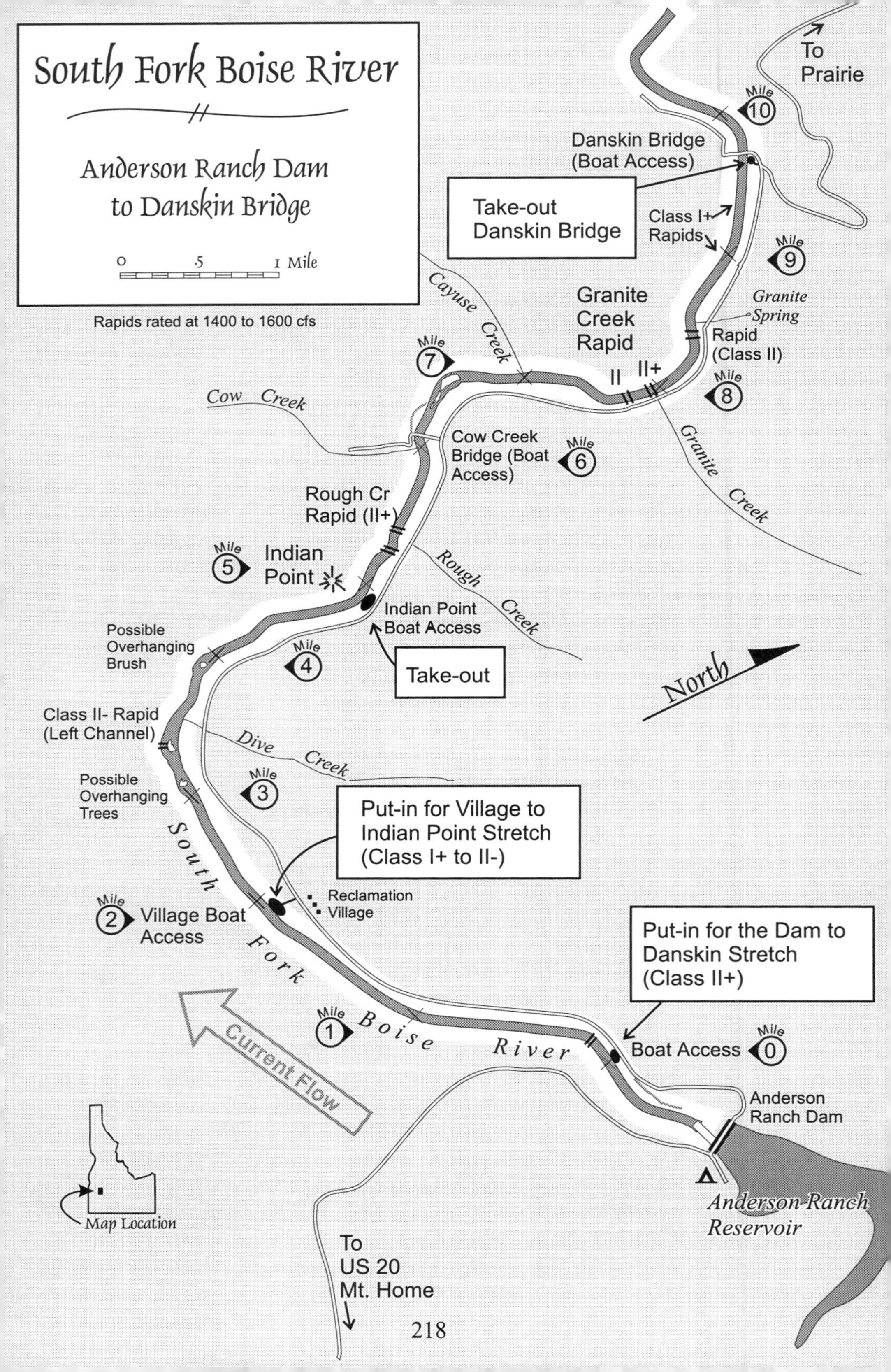
South Fork Boise River
Anderson Ranch Dam
to Danskin Bridge
0
.5
1 Mile
Rapids rated at 1400 to 1600 cfs
To
Prairie
Mile
10
Danskin Bridge
(Boat Access)
Take-out
Danskin Bridge
Class I+
Rapids
Mile
9
Cayuse
Creek
Granite
Creek
Rapid
Granite
Spring
Rapid
(Class II)
Mile
7
II
II+
Mile
8
Cow Creek
Cow Creek
Bridge (Boat
Access)
Mile
6
Granite
Creek
Rough Cr
Rapid (II+)
Mile
5
Indian
Point
Rough
Creek
Indian Point
Boat Access
Possible
Overhanging
Brush
Mile
4
Take-out
North
Class II- Rapid
(Left Channel)
Dive
Creek
Possible
Overhanging
Trees
Mile
3
Put-in for Village to
Indian Point Stretch
(Class I+ to II-)
South
Reclamation
Village
Mile
2
Village Boat
Access
Fork
Put-in for the Dam to
Danskin Stretch
(Class II+)
Mile
1
Boise
River
Boat Access
Mile
0
Current Flow
Anderson
Ranch Dam
Anderson Ranch
Reservoir
Map Location
To
US 20
Mt. Home

Getting to the Put-in. First access point below dam. At the base of Anderson Ranch Dam is a service road which is used by workers to do maintenance work on the dam. Check your odometer there. Drive .5 mile downriver to a small pull-off along the road with a rough, dirt ramp to the river. This is the put-in.

The Trip. *Dam to Danskin Stretch.* (Rapids rated at 1600 cfs.) We thoroughly enjoyed the South Fork and its lavish, wide open canyon and vivacious water. At the beginning of the float, you'll run through a couple of small rapids and then pass by a cliff rising up from the water's edge. Not much happens in the way of rapids after this.

From the 3-mile point onward, you will encounter places along the river with overhanging cottonwood trees that need to be avoided. At 3.8 miles from the put-in, the river divides into two channels. The left channel with the most water has a class II- rapid, but the rapid can be avoided if you stay on the right side of the channel.

A good place to get your bearings is at Indian Rock, a prominent rock outcropping on the left and rocky bar on the right, 4.8 miles from the start. From Indian Rock, it's .4 miles more to Rough Creek which enters the river on the right followed by a rocky class II+ rapid.

The longest stretch of whitewater occurs 7.9 miles from the start with a class II rapid leading down to the mouth of Granite Creek and finishing with a boney, class II+ drop. One more class II rapid follows at the 8.3-mile point. Then it's some class I+ water to the take-out just above Danskin Bridge.

Shuttle. 10 miles. Good dirt road, makes a nice mountain bike shuttle.

Craft. Canoes, kayaks, inflatables, and drift boats, of course. Because the fishing is so good, this is drift boat and mini-cat country.

Mileage Chart
Dam to Danskin

0	Put-in. Upper access site. Rough boat ramp. River right.
.2	Small class I+ rapids before cliff on left.
1	Gauging station.
1.8	Village Boat Ramp.
3.8	Two channels. Stay on the right side of the left channel to avoid rocks (class II-).
4.7	Indian Point (cliff) on left. Rocky bar on right. Alternative take-out or put-in.
4.9	Two class I+ rapids.
5.3	Rough Creek enters on right. Rapid above and class II+ rapid below.
6.2	Cow Creek Bridge. Alternative take-out or put-in.
8	Granite Creek. Class II rapid above and class II+ drop at the mouth of Granite Creek.
8.3	Left-hand bend. Granite Springs area. Class II rapid.
9-9.3	Several class I+ rapids.
9.6	Take-out. Ramp above Danskin bridge. River right.

Note About the Segment of River Below Danskin Bridge. Below Danskin Bridge is the 16-mile Canyon Run, a popular class III whitewater stretch. It is well covered by Idaho whitewater guides (see "References").

Village to Indian Point

Basic Stats (Village to Indian Point)

Difficulty: All class I water, except for one class II- rapid which can be easily sneaked on right.

Levels: Same as the Dam to Danskin stretch.

Distance/Time: 3 miles / 1 to 1.5 hours at moderate flows.

Getting to the Take-out. Indian Point. Indian Point is about midway between the Anderson Ranch Dam and Danskin Bridge. If you start at Danskin Access, Indian Point is 4.9 miles towards the dam. Indian Point is a primitive take-out. You'll have to carry your boat up to parking along the road.

Getting to the Put-in. Village Boat Ramp. The Village ramp is marked with a sign, 3.6 miles towards the dam (to the east) from Indian Point.

The Trip. *Village to Indian Point.* This is a short, but fairly easy alternative to the class II+ stretch described previously. You'll need to watch out for an occasional, but rare, overhanging tree. One rapid is encountered 2 miles from the start where the river divides into two channels.

If the right channel is deep enough, take it. If not, stay to the far right as you go down the left channel and you'll be able to avoid the rocks forming the rapid at the bottom. Even if you get too far to the left, the rapid is not terribly difficult, and it's followed by plenty of easy, flat water below.

The take-out is signaled by Indian Point, a cliff rising up out of the water on the left and a rocky bar on the right.

Shuttle. 4 miles. Good dirt road. Easy mountain bike shuttle.

Craft. Canoes, kayaks, inflatables, and drift boats. Drift boats and mini-cats are common.

Mileage Chart
Village to Indian Point

0	Put-in. Village Boat Ramp (river right).
2	Two channels. Class II- rapid in left channel. Take right channel if deep enough. Otherwise stay on the right side of the left channel to avoid the rapid.
2.9	Take-out. Indian Point (cliff on left). Pull boat out on rocky bar on river right.

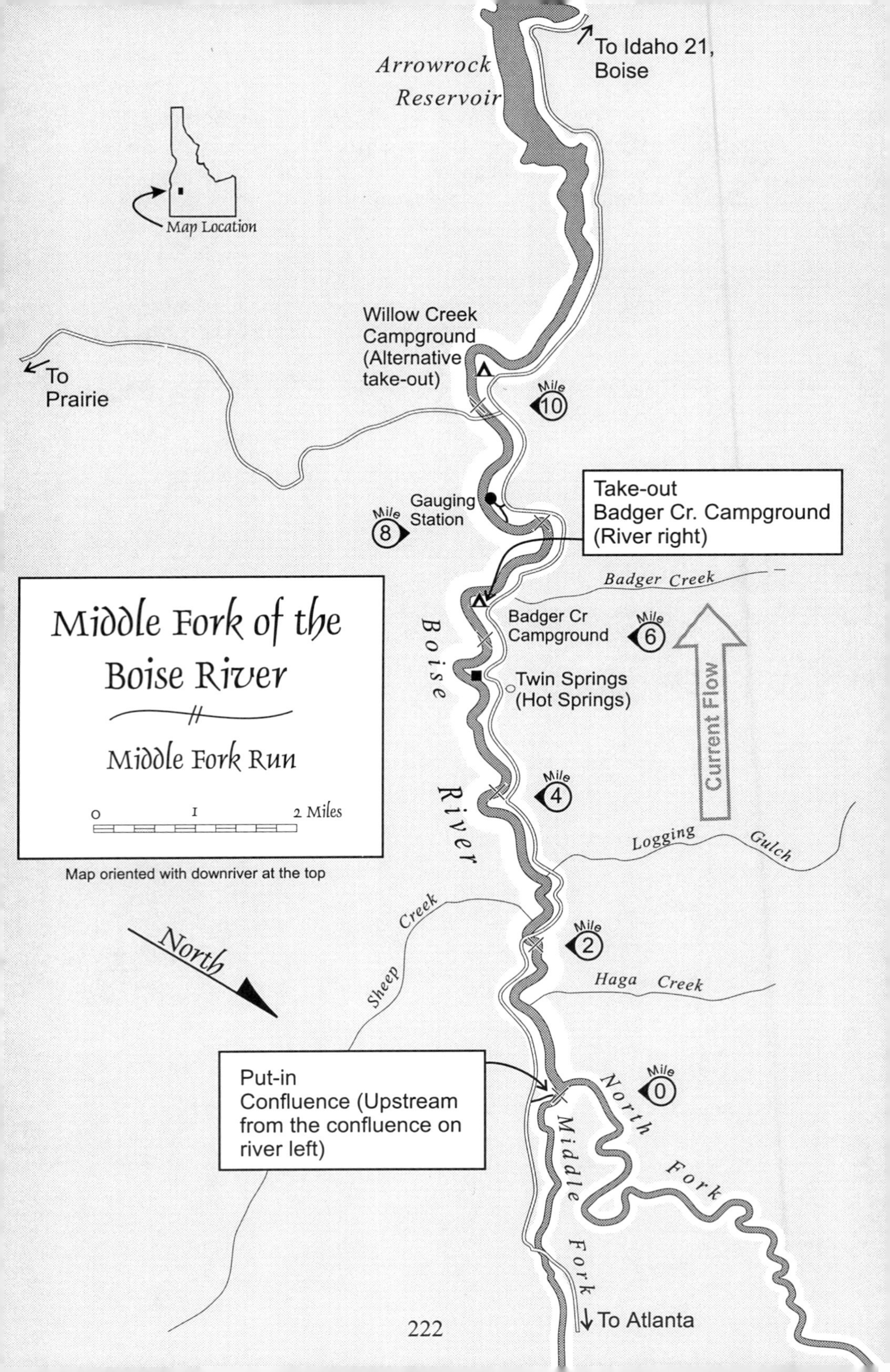

Arrowrock Reservoir
To Idaho 21, Boise
Map Location
Willow Creek Campground (Alternative take-out)
To Prairie
Mile 10
Gauging Station
Mile 8
Take-out Badger Cr. Campground (River right)
Badger Creek
Badger Cr Campground
Mile 6
Twin Springs (Hot Springs)
Boise River
Current Flow
Mile 4
Middle Fork of the Boise River
Middle Fork Run
0 1 2 Miles
Map oriented with downriver at the top
Logging Gulch
Sheep Creek
North
Mile 2
Haga Creek
Put-in Confluence (Upstream from the confluence on river left)
Mile 0
North Fork
Middle Fork
To Atlanta

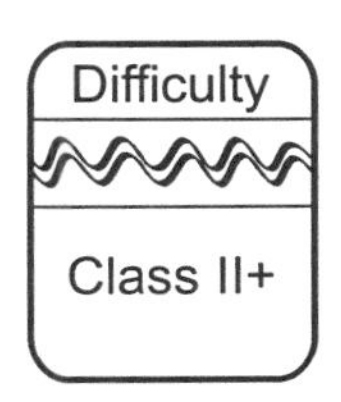

Middle Fork Boise River

Middle Fork Run

THE MIDDLE FORK OF THE BOISE is enormously fun. It gets our vote for one of the best open canoe whitewater runs in the Boise Area. It's also a marvelous stretch for an easy run in a kayak, inflatable or drift boat. The river is sprinkled with class II to II+ rapids and there are no downed trees or blind corners.

It has a little bit of everything: clear water, good fishing, pine forested banks, a small canyon with rocky cliffs coming down to the river and a combination of developed and primitive camping. If you're looking for a whitewater run but don't want to get in over your head, the Middle Fork is a great place to go.

Basic Stats

Difficulty: Class II+ (in medium or low flows).

Levels: Avoid the high water period in May and June. Safe flows are under 1,300 cfs. The river can be run quite low. We had an enjoyable run at 400 cfs in the fall. Gauge: Boise River near Twin Springs.

Distance/Time: 7 miles / 2-3 hours at low flows.

Getting to the Take-out. Badger Creek Campground. From Boise, drive out Idaho 21 towards Idaho City. About 7 miles past Discovery Park at the base of Lucky Peak Dam, watch for the turn-off to Atlanta and Arrowrock Dam. Take a right and stay on the main road. It is a long, narrow, curving dirt road which passes by Arrowrock Dam and Reservoir. At about 20 miles from Idaho 21, you'll come to Willow Creek Campground. From Willow Creek, it's 3.8 miles to Badger Creek Campground. There's no ramp here. Boats are carried from the river up the small hill to the campground.

Alternative take-outs. Alternative take-outs are available in a number of different locations. Willow Creek, mentioned above, is one possible take-out which allows for a longer trip. Slightly upstream from the gauging station, 2.2 miles east of Willow Creek is a pull-out on the road and a take-out. It would involve a short carry, but with some work could be used for a drift boat. A good eddy in the river and another road pull-off is found 3.2 miles upstream from Willow Creek.

Getting to the Put-in. Confluence of the Middle and North Forks of the Boise. From Badger Creek, continue driving up the Middle Fork Road another 6.6 miles until coming to the confluence of the two forks of the river. Just beyond the confluence is a grassy flat, a pull-off, and a place to launch a boat. There's no ramp, but you can get fairly close in your vehicle to the edge of the river.

The Trip. This stretch is commonly called the Middle Fork of the Boise, but technically it's the main Boise River which begins where the North and Middle Forks come together. Nonetheless, since it's known to most people as the Middle Fork, we're following suit. Small rapids ranging from class I+ to II+ are sprinkled throughout this stretch. Even though the rapids can be seen from your boat and don't require scouting, don't be afraid to jump out of your boat and take a quick look if you're a little uncomfortable with something ahead.

There's a little bit of everything in the rapids: rock dodging, ferrying, eddy hopping. Rapids are alternated with some flat water, riffles and inclines down gravel bars. The river moves along without much pause, but you can get off to the side easily—*as long as you run it in medium or low water.*

This a terrific run in an open canoe and a great learning stretch for kayakers, inflatable kayakers, mini-cat boaters and rafters. The fishing, particularly the fly fishing, is very good along this stretch.

Shuttle. 7 miles. Dirt road. Bike shuttle possible, but this road is well traveled in the summer. Be prepared for dust.

Craft. Canoes, kayaks, small inflatables. Drift boats can be taken down, but there are no ramps for loading and you'll have to carry the boat in and out of the water.

Mileage Chart

0	Put-in. Confluence of Middle and North Forks of the Boise.
1	Mouth of Haga Creek (right).
2	Sheep Creek Bridge.
2.2	Mouth of Sheep Creek (left).
5.3	Twin Springs Hot Springs pouring off cliff (right).
5.6	Twin Springs area: car bodies (yuk!) used as rip rap on right.
6.8	Take-out. Badger Creek Campground (right).
	(If you continue downstream, other mileages are: 8.8 river miles to the gauging station, 9.8 miles to the Prairie Bridge, and 11 miles to Willow Creek Campground)

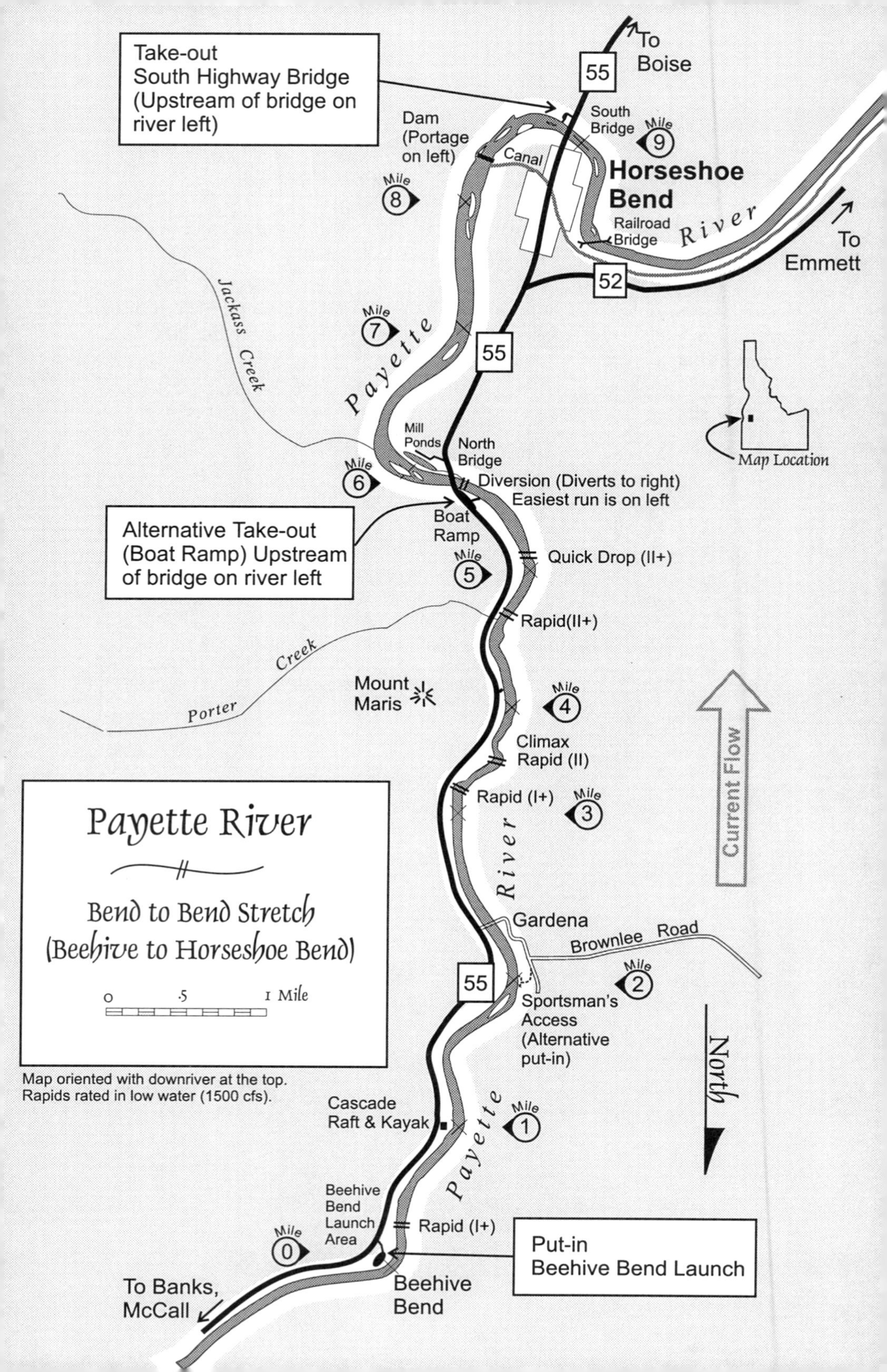

Take-out
South Highway Bridge
(Upstream of bridge on
river left)
55
To
Boise
Dam
(Portage
on left)
South
Bridge
Mile
9
Canal
Horseshoe
Bend
Mile
8
Railroad
Bridge
River
To
Emmett
52
Jackass
Creek
Mile
7
55
Payette
Mill
Ponds
North
Bridge
Map Location
Mile
6
Diversion (Diverts to right)
Easiest run is on left
Alternative Take-out
(Boat Ramp) Upstream
of bridge on river left
Boat
Ramp
Mile
5
Quick Drop (II+)
Rapid(II+)
Creek
Porter
Mount
Maris
Mile
4
Climax
Rapid (II)
Current Flow
Rapid (I+)
Mile
3
Payette River
Bend to Bend Stretch
(Beehive to Horseshoe Bend)
0
.5
1 Mile
River
Gardena
Brownlee Road
Mile
2
55
Sportsman's
Access
(Alternative
put-in)
North
Map oriented with downriver at the top.
Rapids rated in low water (1500 cfs).
Cascade
Raft & Kayak
Payette
Mile
1
Beehive
Bend
Launch
Area
Rapid (I+)
Mile
0
Put-in
Beehive Bend Launch
To Banks,
McCall
Beehive
Bend

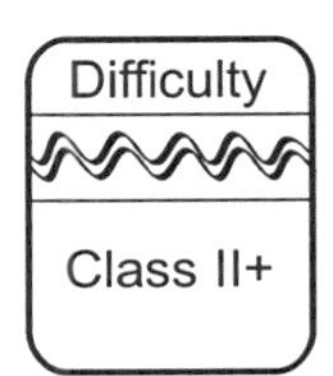

Payette River

Bend to Bend Stretch
(Beehive Bend to Horseshoe Bend)

THE MAIN PAYETTE, north and west of Horseshoe Bend, has several easy whitewater stretches that are suitable for open canoes—or as warm-up runs for kayakers or inflatable boaters. The easiest whitewater is the segment below Horseshoe Bend—described in the next section—rated as class II. This section of river from Beehive Bend to Horseshoe Bend is the next step up in difficulty and is rated as class II+ to III-. (A third whitewater run on the Main Payette is the popular and often crowded class III run which begins at Banks and ends at Beehive Bend, the put-in for this run. The Banks to Beehive Bend run is well covered in other books so we aren't including it here.)

If you're in the mood to do a little whitewater, but don't want to get in too deep, Beehive to Horseshoe Bend is a nice run. Before doing this, however, be sure to practice your skills on an easier stretch (like the Horseshoe Bend to Montour segment) and build up to it. What's so appealing about this segment is that in low flows, rapids are followed by slow water. If you fill up your canoe or flip a boat, the river gives you plenty of time to pull off and get sorted out before continuing.

Basic Stats

Difficulty: Class II+ to III- in low water. In low water, rapids are followed by pools or slow stretches.

Levels: A safe level is on the low end of medium flows, around 3,000 cfs or lower, generally occurring mid summer into the fall. Gauge: Horseshoe Bend.

Distance/Time: 9 miles / 3-4 hours at 1,500 cfs. It is a 6 mile trip to the alternative take-out at the north Horseshoe Bend bridge.

Portages/Scouts: All of the rapids can be scouted if desired. Generally scouting is not necessary, except for one place: a dam, 8.1 miles from the start. A channel which by-passes the dam may be run—or it may be easily portaged on river left.

Getting to the Take-out. Horseshoe Bend (south bridge). Horseshoe Bend is located 30 miles north of Boise on Idaho 55. As you drive into town, you'll come to a bridge over the Payette. Just before the bridge on the right is a parking area and a place to launch or take-out boats (river left, upstream of the bridge).

Alternative take-out. Horseshoe Bend (north bridge). An alternative take-out is the north Horseshoe Bend bridge, which is about a mile farther north of town on Idaho 55 from the south bridge. On the far (north) side of the bridge, you find a large pull-off. At the north end of the pull-off, a road leads to the river and a concrete ramp.

Getting to the Put-in. Beehive Bend Launch Area. Beehive Bend is located on Idaho 55, 6.7 miles north of the Idaho 55 and 52 junction in the town of Horseshoe Bend. It is well marked with a sign. It has restrooms, dressing rooms and paved parking. It does not have a ramp, but a wide trail leads to the launching area at the river. Beehive is a fee area.

Alternative Put-in. Gardena. If you'd like to get away from the crowds and paying fees, we have a spot for you. There is a hard-to-find, weedy launch site, 2 river miles below Beehive. It's an Idaho Fish and Game access site, located near Gardena.

The Gardena bridge is 2.2 miles south of Beehive Bend. Drive over the bridge to the west. At .2 mile from the highway the main road (Brownlee Road) curves to the left. When you reach the curve keep going straight on Watson Lane. At .1 mile down Watson Lane, turn off on a faint road to the right. You'll have to open and close a couple of gates near where the road crosses the railroad tracks. Once across the railroad tracks, the road leads out across a field. The best put-in is on a faint road which leads downriver for 300 feet. You won't be able to get all the way to the iver, but it allows you to get close enough to launch boats. It's a little ork finding this place, but we guarantee you won't find any crowds.

The Trip. We ran the river at a low level (about 1,500 cfs at Horseshoe Bend) and the ratings of the rapids are based on our observations at that water flow. It was a good flow for an open canoe. If you run the river at higher levels, some of the rapids and one, in particular, Climax Rapid becomes more difficult.

Just around the corner from the put-in at Beehive, is an easily runnable class I+ rapid. At 1 mile from the start, you'll pass the Cascade Raft and Kayak headquarters which provides lessons and guided trips on the river. Just before the 2-mile point, the river flows around an island with the left channel being the deepest. Beyond the island on river right is the free Sportsman's access put-in that we described on the previous page, just before the Gardena bridge.

At the 3-mile point, you'll have a good view of Mount Maris, the steep hill rising above the river on the left. As you begin to curve around the base of Mount Maris, on a right hand bend, you'll encounter another class I+ rapid.

Climax Rapid comes next, 3.5 miles from the start. At 1,500 cfs, we rated Climax as a class II, and ran it by paddling from the left to the right. (Stephen Stuebner in his book P*addling the Payette* rates it a class III in higher flows). The water quiets down after Climax, and if you've filled your boat, you'll have plenty of time to bail.

The next stretch is a pretty part of the run with some sandy beaches and big granite boulders. At 4.6 miles from the start, just below the mouth of Porter Creek on river left, is a class II+ rapid. We ran a left-middle run on it.

Five miles from the start you'll pass by a gauging station on the left and immediately below is a quick drop (class II+ to III-). It has a couple of good sized waves, and afterwards, we had to stop to bail out our canoe. At 5.5 miles you come to the north Horseshoe Bridge. Just before the bridge is a take-out on the left, and many people end their trip here.

Beyond here, things slow down for a while until reaching a dam at mile 8 (from the start). You'll know it's coming. The water backs up and slows down, and warning signs are posted above the dam. As you get close to the dam, paddle to the left side. Just below an irrigation pump on the left, a road comes down to the river to a small concrete boat ramp. Pull your boat off here.

On the left side of the river, alongside of the dam is a man-made channel. The water flowing through this by-pass channel develops a series of sizable waves which are runnable. We didn't feel comfortable running it in our open canoe and opted to do the portage. The road around the dam makes the portage very easy, and it only took us about 15 minutes. At the bottom of the by-pass channel, you'll have do a little rock dodging to get back out in the main current, but once in the main current, it's smooth sailing around the big bend (for which Horseshoe Bend is named) to the bridge and take-out on river left.

Shuttle. 8 miles, all paved. Bike shuttle possible, but Idaho 55 is a very busy highway with a medium-width shoulder.

Craft. Kayaks, inflatables and canoes. This is a splendid whitewater canoe run.

River Mileages (Rapids rated at 1,500 cfs)	
0	Put-in. Beehive Bend Launch Area (left).
.2	Class I+ rapid.
1	Cascade Raft and Kayak headquarters.
1.7	Island. Left channel deepest.
2	Gardena Sportsman's Access (right). Alternative put-in.
2.4	Gardena bridge.
3.2	Right bend, rapid (class I+ to II-).
3.4	Climax Rapid (class II in low water, III in higher flows).
4.3	Cliff diving rocks (left).
4.6	Porter Creek (left) followed by a rapid (class II+).
5	Gauging station (left).
5.1	Quick drop (class II+ to III-).
5.6	North Horseshoe Bend bridge (concrete ramp on left just before bridge).
8.1	Dam. Pull off on left. Portage on left or run by-pass channel on left.
8.8	South Horseshoe Bend bridge (take out on river left, just upstream of bridge).

Before bridges: ferry (and row boat) used to cross the Payette River near Horseshoe Bend.

Idaho State Historical Society

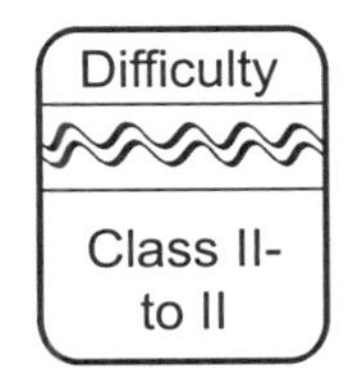

Payette River

Horseshoe Bend to Montour Bridge

LOCATED TO THE WEST of Horseshoe Bend, this is the easiest whitewater stretch on the Main Payette. You'll find fewer people here. It's even less crowded than the segment of river just above Horseshoe Bend. Much of the water is unhurried, but there are places here and there where you need to stay on your toes. It's a great place to start learning about rapids, with some rocks to avoid and waves to run. It is very suitable for an open canoe, but kayakers and inflatable boaters looking for easy runs will also enjoy it.

The Payette River is going through a transition zone on this segment. It's the tail end of ponderosa pine territory and the beginning of the cottonwood and willow ecosystem which will be with it for the remainder of its journey to the Snake.

Basic Stats

Difficulty: Some class II- to II rapids, but it has a lot of class I.

Levels: Best levels are in the low to low-moderate range, under 3,000 cfs (Horseshoe Bend gauge). Stay off it in high water.

Distance/Time: 9.5 miles / 4-5 hours at 1,500 cfs.

Getting to the Take-out. Montour Bridge. From Horseshoe Bend, drive west on Idaho 52. About 9 miles from Horseshoe Bend, take a left on Montour Road. Drive 1 mile to the bridge over the river. Continue a little farther, about .1 mile, to a dirt road which takes off to the right and parallels the paved road back to the bridge. We took out here, immediately on the downstream side of the bridge on river left, but you can also take out in a sandy area about 60 feet farther downstream.

Getting to the Put-in. Idaho 55 bridge at Horseshoe Bend. See directions for the take-out in the previous section (Beehive to Horseshoe Bend).

The Trip. (Rapid ratings are based on a flow of 1,500 cfs. Ratings will change in higher flows.) The first rapid of consequence on this stretch comes .7 mile from the starting

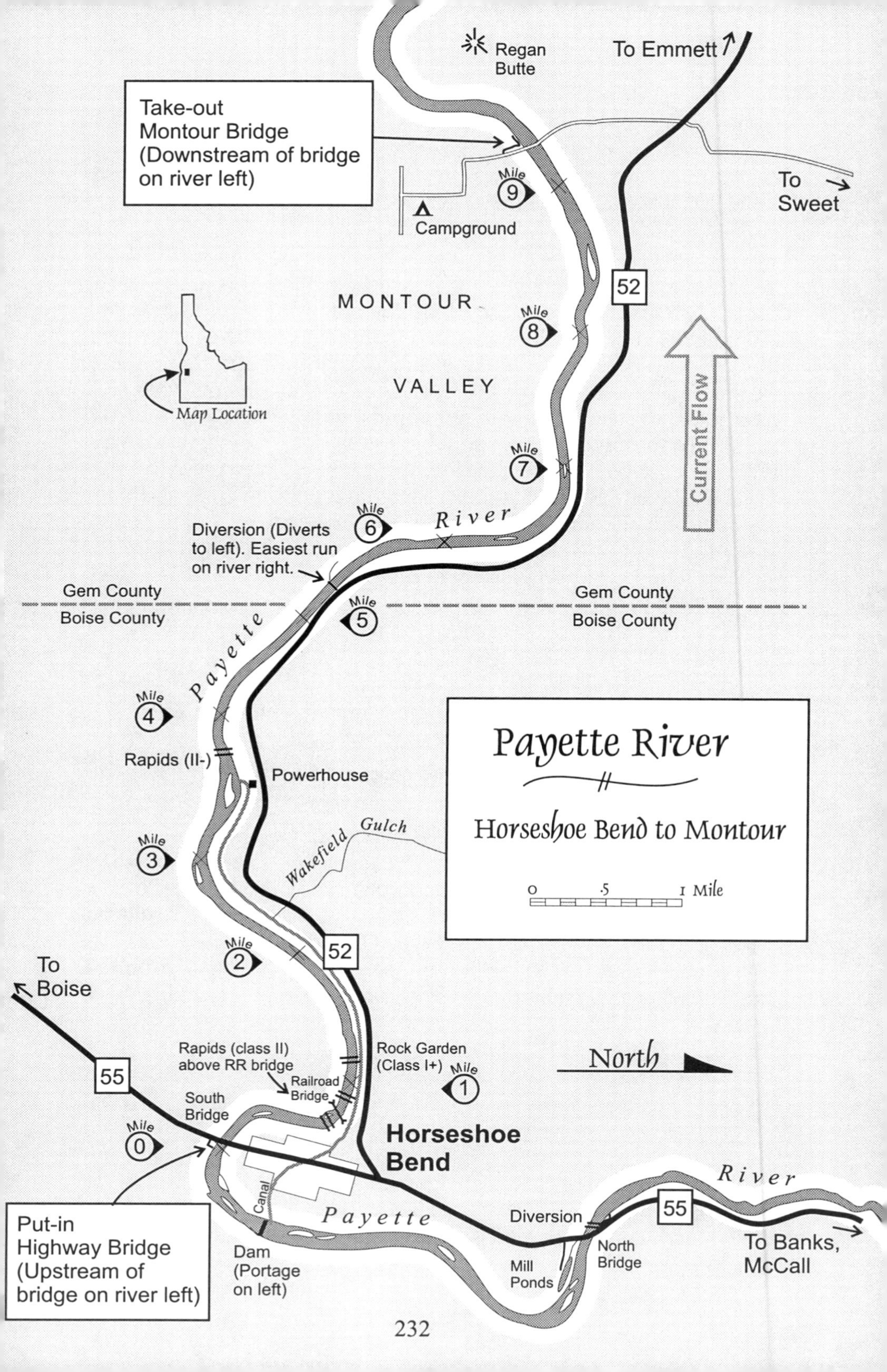

Regan Butte
To Emmett
Take-out
Montour Bridge
(Downstream of bridge on river left)
To Sweet
Campground
Mile 9
52
MONTOUR
Mile 8
VALLEY
Map Location
Current Flow
Mile 7
Mile 6
River
Diversion (Diverts to left). Easiest run on river right.
Gem County
Boise County
Mile 5
Gem County
Boise County
Payette
Mile 4
Rapids (II-)
Powerhouse
Payette River
Horseshoe Bend to Montour
0 .5 1 Mile
Wakefield Gulch
Mile 3
Mile 2
52
To Boise
Rapids (class II) above RR bridge
Rock Garden (Class I+)
Mile 1
North
55
Railroad Bridge
South Bridge
Mile 0
Horseshoe Bend
River
Canal
Payette
Diversion
55
Put-in
Highway Bridge
(Upstream of bridge on river left)
Dam
(Portage on left)
Mill Ponds
North Bridge
To Banks, McCall

point at the Horseshoe Bend bridge. The rapid (rated class II) is upstream of a railroad bridge over the river. Just after the railroad bridge is another, but easy class I+ rapid. This is followed, at 1.1 miles, by an easy (class I+) rock garden—a place in the river where boulders stick above the surface of the river. Weave your way through the boulders. Afterwards the river calms down for a while.

For the next couple of miles, on river right, is a canal. The canal is actually a welcomed feature along the river, since it blocks out the highway noise and makes floating on this part of the river peaceful. At 3.7 miles from the start, you'll see a powerhouse on the right shore which uses the water from the canal you've been floating along to generate power. Just past the powerhouse is a long drop (class II-) across a gravel bar with some avoidable waves at the bottom. Now you can cruise for a while.

You'll pass through a couple of easy class I+ rapids and then at mile 5.1, you'll reach the county line. The highway is right next to the river at this point. You may be able to see the sign along the highway which indicates the line between Gem and Boise counties. That's a good land-mark to spot, for just below the county line is a diversion. The diversion draws water out of the far left side of the river. If you stay on the right side of the river, there's barely a ripple.

If you haven't seen a diversion before, this will give you a chance to see what one looks like. In this case, large boulders have been pushed out into the river so that some water is forced from the left side of the river into a canal.

At 6.5 miles from the start, the river divides into two channels. The right channel is shallow, but clean. When we ran the river, the left channel had a good-sized boulder and sweeper on the far left at the bottom. We found that both were easily avoided, but you should be prepared to move away if you run the left channel.

That's it for any rapid water. From here it's an easy paddle (class I, 1.2) all the way to Montour Bridge.

Shuttle. 11 miles, all paved. Bicycle shuttlers expect moderate to moder-ately high traffic on Idaho 52. Unfortunately, Highway 52 has a narrow shoulder.

Craft. Canoes, kayaks, inflatables of all sizes. No ramps, but with a bit of work drift boats can get in and out at the access points.

Mileage Chart
(Rapids rated at 1,500 cfs)

0	Put-in. Horseshoe Bend Bridge (upstream of bridge, river left).
.7	Class II rapid.
.75	Railroad bridge.
.8	Class I+ (1.3) rapid.
1.1	Rock garden rapid, class I+ (1.3).
3.7	Powerhouse (right).
3.9	Rapid (class II-).
5.1	River very close to highway. County Line.
5.3	Diversion (Diverts water to left). Very easy run on river right.
6.5	River divides. Left channel is class II-. May have an overhanging tree.
9.5	Take-out. Montour Bridge (river left, downstream of bridge).

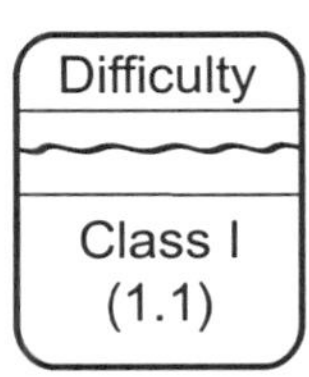

Payette River

Montour Wildlife Refuge Paddle

THIS IS A BEAUTIFUL, relaxing trip on the main Payette river, 10 miles to the west of Horseshoe Bend. It's a great trip for families, bird lovers, or for anyone who wants to get away for a day.

The river in this segment passes through the Montour Valley and the Montour Wildlife Refuge into the backwaters of Black Canyon Reservoir. For the majority of the trip, the highway is out of sight and out of mind, behind Regan Butte which makes it the most peaceful and quiet stretch on the Payette.

Basic Stats

Difficulty: Class I (1.0 to 1.1). There's a little current at the beginning and then the river slows into lake-like water.

Season: Spring through fall.

Distance/Time: 4.6 miles / 2-4 hours (much longer in wind).

Getting to the Take-out. Upper Black Canyon Reservoir Boat Access. This small boat access site on the upper end of Black Canyon Reservoir is located 7.1 miles east of Wild Rose Park at Black Canyon Dam or 2.7 miles west of the Idaho 52 and Montour Road junction.

Getting to the Put-in. Montour Bridge. For directions on how to get to Montour Bridge, see the description of the take-out for the previous river segment (Horseshoe Bend to Montour).

The Trip. You'll have a little current at the beginning of the trip, but the river gradually slows as you get into the backwaters of Black Canyon Reservoir. During the first half of the trip, the Payette River makes a huge horseshoe-shaped bend around Regan Butte, the predominate cone-shaped butte on river right.

Slightly less than a mile from the put-in, you'll come to the start of expansive sand bars lying just beneath the surface of the water which have formed as the river has slowed and released sediments. The sand bars create an interesting problem for canoeists and kayakers: how to find the

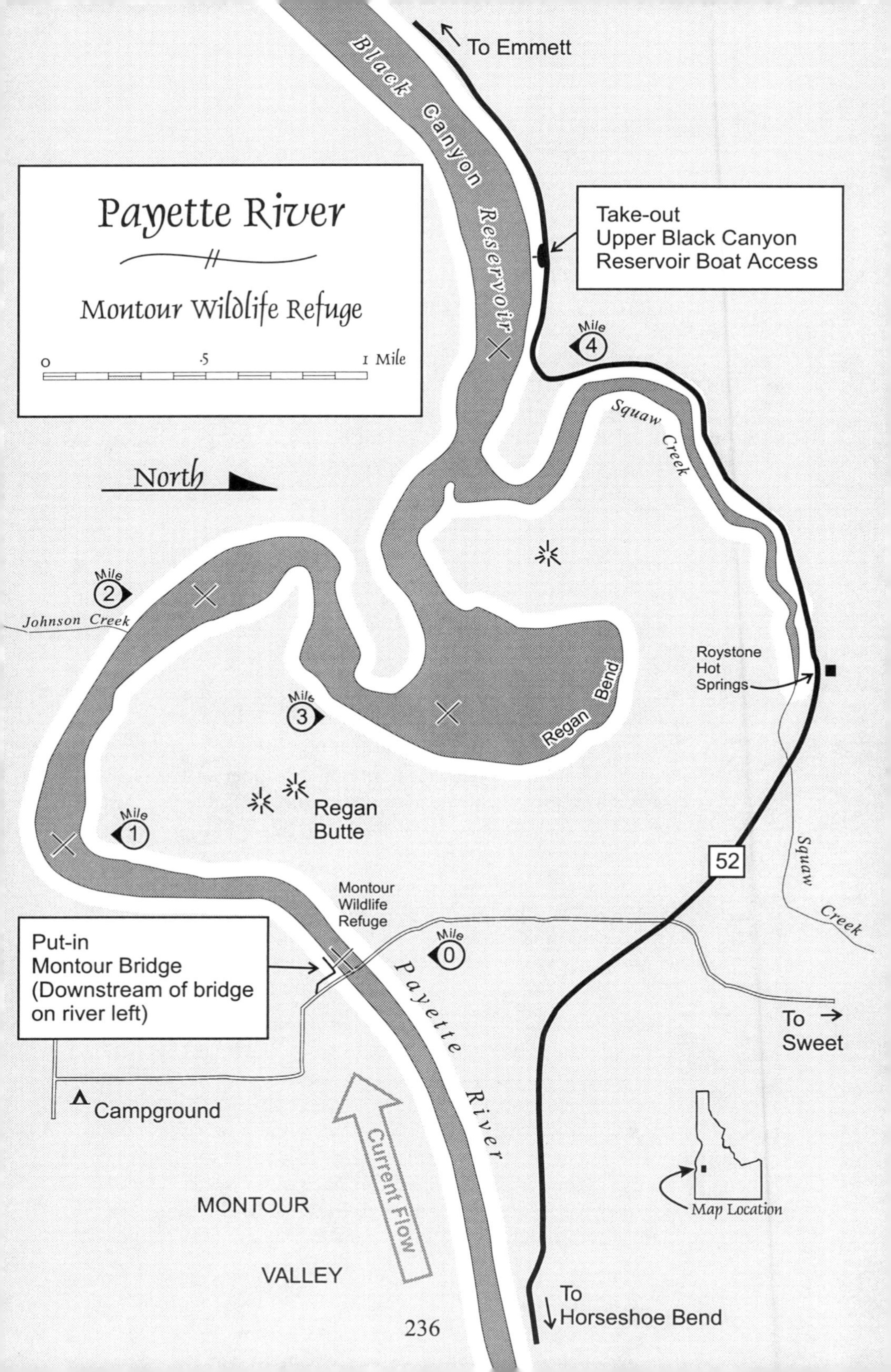
Payette River
Montour Wildlife Refuge
0
.5
1 Mile
North
To Emmett
Black Canyon Reservoir
Take-out
Upper Black Canyon
Reservoir Boat Access
Mile
4
Squaw Creek
Mile
2
Johnson Creek
Mile
3
Regan Bend
Roystone
Hot
Springs
Regan
Butte
Mile
1
52
Squaw Creek
Montour
Wildlife
Refuge
Mile
0
Put-in
Montour Bridge
(Downstream of bridge
on river left)
Payette River
To
Sweet
Campground
Current Flow
Map Location
MONTOUR
VALLEY
To
Horseshoe Bend

deepest pathway. We started on the left and worked our way right as the river curved around Regan Butte, but it is a six-of-one-half-dozen-of-another problem. We did have to jump out two or three times to drag the boat over shallows to deeper water.

Despite the shallows, we found this a lovely area. Through the clear water, you can see the sand textured with riffles like those you can see on the North Fork of the Payette in lower Long Valley.

On river left is a rail line, but it's infrequently used. You may or may not see a train on your trip. Otherwise, with the highway tucked behind Regan Butte, during windless days, this is a tranquil and reflective place to paddle.

After making the huge horseshoe—it almost seems like you're going around in a circle—the river, now the wide arm of the reservoir, makes a shorter U-shaped bend (called Regan Bend) followed by Squaw Creek which enters from the right. After passing Squaw Creek, move close to the right shore. Even though the reservoir is narrow, you'll want to be near land in the event the wind comes up. If the waves get too big, you're in a good position to move to shore and get off quickly.

Follow the shoreline around the side of the reservoir until you reach the take-out, 4.6 miles from the put-in.

This trip is not advised on windy days. It can be very difficult to make progress in the shallow backwaters of the reservoir, and it can be dangerous in deep portions if the waves are large. On good days, start early. Generally winds will come up as the day heats up, and you can usually avoid them by simply getting an early start.

Shuttle. 4 miles, all paved. A bike shuttle is possible but expect moderate to heavy traffic and a narrow shoulder.

Craft. Canoes and kayaks are ideal for this stretch. Since there's no current, inflatables are not recommended.

Mileage Chart

0	Put-in. Montour Bridge (downstream of the bridge on river left.)
1.7	Mouth of Johnson Creek (left).
2.4	Sharp right-hand bend.
2.8	Regan Bend, a long, left-hand bend starting at the 2.8-mile point and finally finishing .5 mile later.
3.8	Squaw Creek Arm of Black Canyon Reservoir on right.
4.6	Take-out (right). Upper Black Canyon Reservoir boat launch site.

The take-out for the Montour Wildlife Refuge paddle.
Regan Butte is the prominent point in the background.

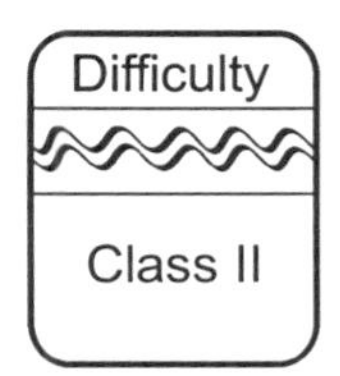

South Fork Payette River

Garden Valley Stretch

THE GARDEN VALLEY SEGMENT of the South Fork of the Payette is located about 25 miles north of Horseshoe Bend. This is one of those river segments that has often been underrated. Some boaters call this a beginner's stretch, an easy ride in an inner tube. It is not. It is class II water complicated with overhanging trees. In fact, because the river has obstructions and swift water flowing through sweepers, it's a very poor candidate for an inner tube run. This is a stretch for a canoe, kayak or inflatable boat which can be maneuvered away from trees and other obstructions.

Although it is not a beginner's stretch, it is an enjoyable piece of water once you've built up your skills and feel comfortable maneuvering your boat. The tree problems are mostly at the beginning of the run while the more difficult (class II) rapids lie near the end.

Basic Stats

Difficulty: Class II. Watch for downed trees and sweepers in the first half, and rocky rapids in the second half.

Levels: Good levels, particularly for canoeists, are in the moderately low to low range, below 1,200 cfs. Gauge: South Fork at Lowman.

Distance/Time: 6.3 miles /1.5 to 2.5 hours at 600 cfs. (4 miles to the alternative take-out at the confluence of the South Fork and Middle Fork).

Permits: Parking permits are required at launch sites along the South Fork. They may be picked up at convenience stores in Banks or Garden Valley.

Getting to the Take-out. Deer Creek Access Site. Deer Creek is one of a number of developed river access sites along the South Fork of the Payette. From Banks, about 15 miles north of Horseshoe Bend, drive to the east, 4.8 miles on the Banks-Lowman Highway. Watch for the Deer Creek parking area on the right (south) side of the highway. If you're coming from the other direction, Deer Creek is located 3.4 miles from the Crouch turn-off.

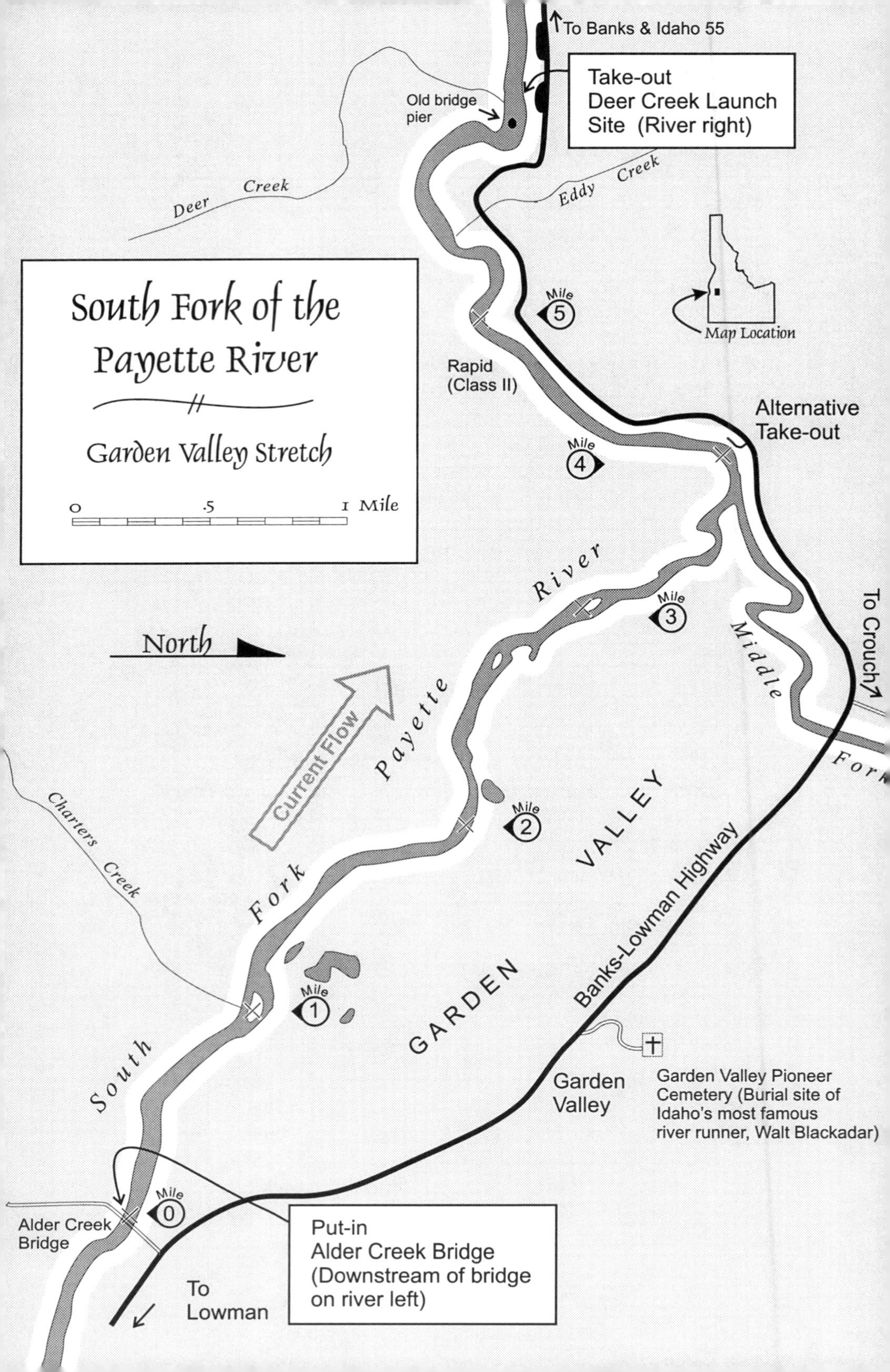
South Fork of the Payette River
Garden Valley Stretch
0
.5
1 Mile
North
Current Flow
To Banks & Idaho 55
Take-out
Deer Creek Launch Site (River right)
Old bridge pier
Deer Creek
Eddy Creek
Map Location
Mile 5
Rapid (Class II)
Alternative Take-out
Mile 4
River
Mile 3
Middle Fork
To Crouch
Payette
Mile 2
VALLEY
Banks-Lowman Highway
Charters Creek
Fork
Mile 1
GARDEN
South
Garden Valley
Garden Valley Pioneer Cemetery (Burial site of Idaho's most famous river runner, Walt Blackadar)
Mile 0
Alder Creek Bridge
Put-in
Alder Creek Bridge (Downstream of bridge on river left)
To Lowman

There isn't much room at the Deer Creek access site and the Boise County Sheriff asks boaters to park in the parking area about 500 feet downriver. The access area, itself, is used only for loading or unloading. A fee is required for the use of Deer Creek.

Alternative Take-out. Confluence of the Middle Fork and the South Fork. You can avoid the rocky rapids at the end of this run by taking out just past the confluence with the Middle Fork, midway through this segment. From Deer Creek, drive 2.2 miles toward Garden Valley. Watch for Milepost 7 on a curve in the road and pull off to the right (south) side of the road. There's a small place to park and a trail to the river.

Getting to the Put-in. Alder Creek Bridge. Start at the Garden Valley Store, located 2 miles to the east of the turn-off to Crouch on the Banks-Lowman Highway. Drive 1.3 miles to the east and take a right on Alder Creek Road. Follow the road a short distance to the bridge over the South Fork. The put-in is on the far side of the bridge (downstream of the bridge on river left).

The Trip. The first half of the segment down to the confluence with the Middle Fork of the Payette (4 miles from the start) has a number of small class I+ rapids. The main task in this section is watching for and avoiding overhanging trees and snags in the river. The water is clear and the banks of the river are a mix of stately ponderosa and cottonwood. It's not a primitive stretch. You will see houses, particularly on a thin strip of land between the South Fork and its confluence with the Middle Fork.

The river narrows after the Middle Fork comes in and it's midway through this next stretch that you'll encounter a lengthy class II rapid which entails some rock maneuvering. The take-out is signaled by the concrete piers of an old bridge that have been removed from the river. About 200 yards beyond the piers, pull off on the right at the take-out.

The take-out has a wooden ramp which may be used to hoist boats up and out of the river—or a path to carry boats. Be prepared: Deer Creek can be crowded since it's the put-in for the whitewater run on the lower stretch of the South Fork.

Historical Note. While in the Garden Valley area, you might want to take a side trip to visit Walt Blackadar's grave in the Pioneer Cemetery (the location is marked on the map). Walt Blackadar, who was a doctor from Salmon, Idaho, is the world's most famous river runner. He died in a kayaking accident upstream from Garden Valley on the South Fork of the Payette. To learn more about Blackadar and his remarkable life, pick up a copy of Ron Watters' biography, *Never Turn Back.*

Shuttle. 7 miles, all paved. Bike shuttle possible: highway is busy and the shoulder is narrow.

Craft. Canoes, kayaks, inflatables.

Mileage Chart

0	Alder Creek Bridge (downstream of bridge on river left).
3.8	Confluence with Middle Fork (right).
4.0	Alternative take-out (right).
5	Class II rapid.
6.2	Old bridge pier in river.
6.3	Take-out. Deer Creek Access Site (right).

Here's one way to amuse yourself while waiting for the shuttle: Alder Creek Bridge, the put-in for the Garden Valley Stretch.

Difficulty

Class I+
(1.3)

Middle Fork Payette River

Lower Middle Fork (Near Crouch)

IF THE WORD "QUAINT" could be used to describe a river, the Middle Fork of the Payette is the one river in Idaho that deserves it. Located 25 miles northeast of Horseshoe Bend, this quaint (couldn't resist) river is a delight to run.

Flowing out of the Boise National Forest, the water is clear and crystalline. For a short distance at the beginning of this trip, the river is shaded by a ponderosa pine and Doug fir forest, but as the land unfolds, the Middle Fork flows into pasture land, and the pines are replaced by a fringe of willows. Even though you'll see quite a few homes and cabins along the first half of the trip, they don't seem to detract too much from the scenery.

This is a great river to float when you are ready to make that next step from a flat stream to one with a touch of whitewater. It has a few mini-rapids, barely over a class I rating (1.3), and a few boulders to avoid. But at mid or low levels, the current is friendly, not forceful. In most places, you can stand up and walk off the river if you wanted. Moreover, in low flows, it's highly unlikely that you'll have any problem with overhanging trees or snags. In other words, if you want a lot of fun, but a high degree of safety, this is the place to go.

Basic Stats

Difficulty: Class I+ (1.3). A great transition river from flat water to minor whitewater.

Levels: Stay off the river during the high water period in May and June. By July it should be fine. We found it very relaxed at a flow of 1,100 cfs (at Lowman gauge). It can be a little higher—or lower. Boaters were still running it several weeks later at lower flows. (The gauge used to judge flows on the Middle Fork is on the South Fork of the Payette at Lowman.)

Distance/Time: 9 miles / 4-5 hours at 1,100 cfs.

Getting to the Take-out. Crouch. Crouch is just .8 mile off the Banks-Lowman Highway. To get to the highway, drive from Horseshoe Bend (30 miles north of Boise) to the north. About 15 miles from Horseshoe Bend on Idaho 55, you'll come to Banks. Just past

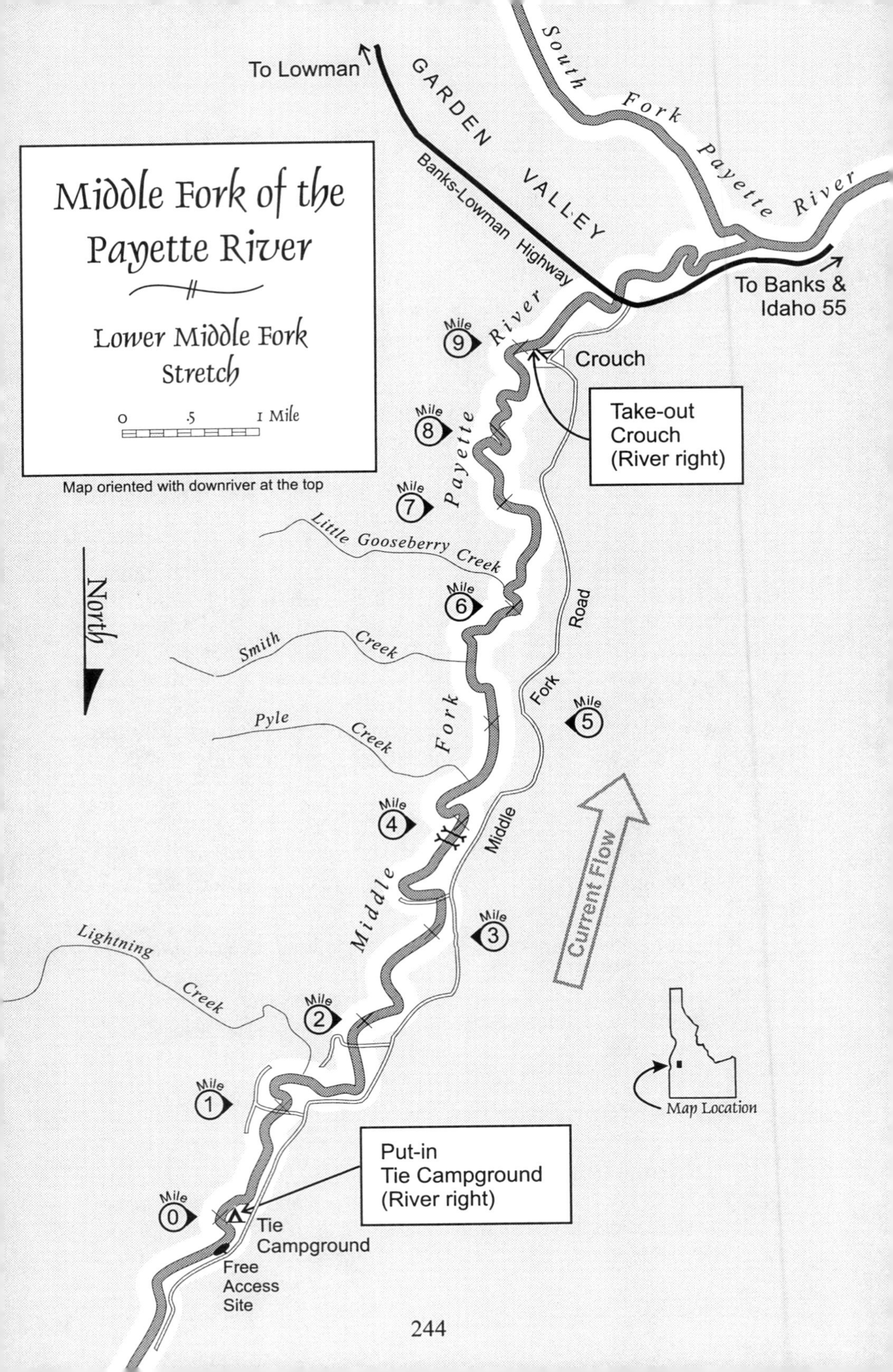
Middle Fork of the Payette River
Lower Middle Fork Stretch
0
.5
1 Mile
Map oriented with downriver at the top
North
To Lowman
GARDEN VALLEY
Banks-Lowman Highway
South Fork Payette River
To Banks & Idaho 55
River
Payette
Crouch
Take-out Crouch (River right)
Little Gooseberry Creek
Smith Creek
Pyle Creek
Fork
Middle
Middle Fork Road
Current Flow
Lightning Creek
Map Location
Put-in Tie Campground (River right)
Tie Campground
Free Access Site
Mile 0
Mile 1
Mile 2
Mile 3
Mile 4
Mile 5
Mile 6
Mile 7
Mile 8
Mile 9

Banks is a sign indicating the Banks-Lowman highway. Take a right and drive about 8 miles, until reaching the turn-off to Crouch, marked with a sign. Turn left and drive .8 mile into the small, but sprightly town crouched (sorry, we couldn't resist this one, either) alongside the Middle Fork .

Look for the Crouch Merc. As you face the Merc, the river is a stone's throw to the left. Near the river is a place to park and a small cut in the bank where boats can be taken out.

Getting to the Put-in. Tie Campground. Tie Campground is located 8 miles north of Crouch on Middle Fork Road. Middle Fork Road is paved until the Forest Boundary at which point it turns into gravel, .2 mile before the campground. There's no ramp here. Rather, boats are carried down a short stairway to the river. The stairway must have been constructed by Paul Bunyan, since the steps are really big. You'll have to pay the campground picnic fee to use the area.

Alternative Put-in. If you're wary of public land fees, there is a free put-in just upriver—and a better place if you plan to launch a drift boat. Drive up Middle Fork Road to the north (away from Crouch) another .2 mile from the campground. Here, you'll find a small road going down to the river and places for several vehicles to park.

The Trip. No rapids of consequence are found on this stretch, just fun riffles and a few boulders and eddies to play in. We had a delightful time in a canoe, but it is also a fun trip for kayaks, drift boats, small rafts, and other inflatables. Short parts of it are even nice for inner tubing. Every so often, you'll come across sandy beaches and—hold on to your hat—sensually sculpted granite boulders. Bridges conveniently cross the river here and there, and with them you can pretty much keep track of your location.

Besides its attractiveness, it's a good trip for bird watching. On the day we floated, we spotted an exposed snag with a disheveled mop of twigs and small branches on top: an osprey nest. With no intervening trees to get in the way, it was a perfect location from which to spy fish. Yet, exposed as it was, the nest was like an oven that mid summer day. We watched, fascinated, as the female osprey remained perched on the side of the nest and kept her wings spread to provide shade for the fledgling. Expect to find many more treats like this on the way down.

Shuttle. 8 miles on a paved secondary road with a slight bit of gravel when you cross the National Forest boundary. It's a great road for a bike shuttle.

Craft. Canoes, kayaks, inflatables and drift boats. Drift boats can be launched at the free access point above Tie Campground and taken out at Crouch. Neither access point has developed boat ramps, but the rutted roads to the water's edge suffice.

Mileage Chart

0	Put-in. Tie Campground (river right).
1	Lightning Creek Bridge.
1.4	Mouth of Lightning Creek (left).
3.3	Elk Springs Road Bridge.
3.6	Twin Bridges. The first bridge is followed by the second a short distance below.
4.9	Smith Creek Bridge.
6.8	Rib of pine trees comes down to the river on the right.
9	Take-out. Crouch (river right).

Difficulty

Class I
(1.0)

North Fork Payette River

Upper North Fork Meanders

WHAT A PRICELESS STRETCH of water, the North Fork of the Payette just above Payette Lake in McCall. It's so clear and flat that on calm days its surface becomes a mirror which reflects the pines standing along its sides. Called the North Fork Meanders, or simply "The Meanders," it is rated a solid class I (1.0), the easiest water there is. Anybody can paddle this part of the North Fork: small children and grandma—and even great aunt Maude.

You can start this trip in one of several places. Because the river is flat, with no current, paddling may be done downstream or upstream—which is what most people do. At the north end of Payette Lake is a small park called North Beach. Launch your boat there and paddle a short distance (about .1 mile) to the mouth of the North Fork and then start your trip up the river. If you don't have a boat, don't worry. You can rent canoes and kayaks at North Beach.

Go as far as you want up the river. When you're ready, turn around and head back to the start. It is a premier family stretch and one you won't want to miss when you're in the McCall area.

Basic Stats

Difficulty: Class I (1.0). Flat, lake-like water.

Season: This a flatwater trip and can be done anytime.

Distance/Time: Variable. The most common trip is to paddle up the river from North Beach. You can paddle about 3 river miles upstream before the current becomes too swift to continue. A typical outing is 5 to 6 miles round trip, but you can adjust the length to your comfort.

Getting to the Put-in and Take-out. The most common starting place is North Beach. To get there from McCall, follow Idaho 55 towards New Meadows. On the western edge of McCall, look for Warren Wagon Road. Take a right onto Warren Wagon Road and follow it around the west side of Payette Lake. At the lake's northern end (approximately 6.5 miles from Idaho 55) you'll come to North Beach. It has a boat ramp, restrooms, and a place to rent kayaks and canoes.

Alternative Put-in. Eastside Bridge. To get to Eastside Bridge, continue driving past North Beach 1 mile and take a right on Eastside

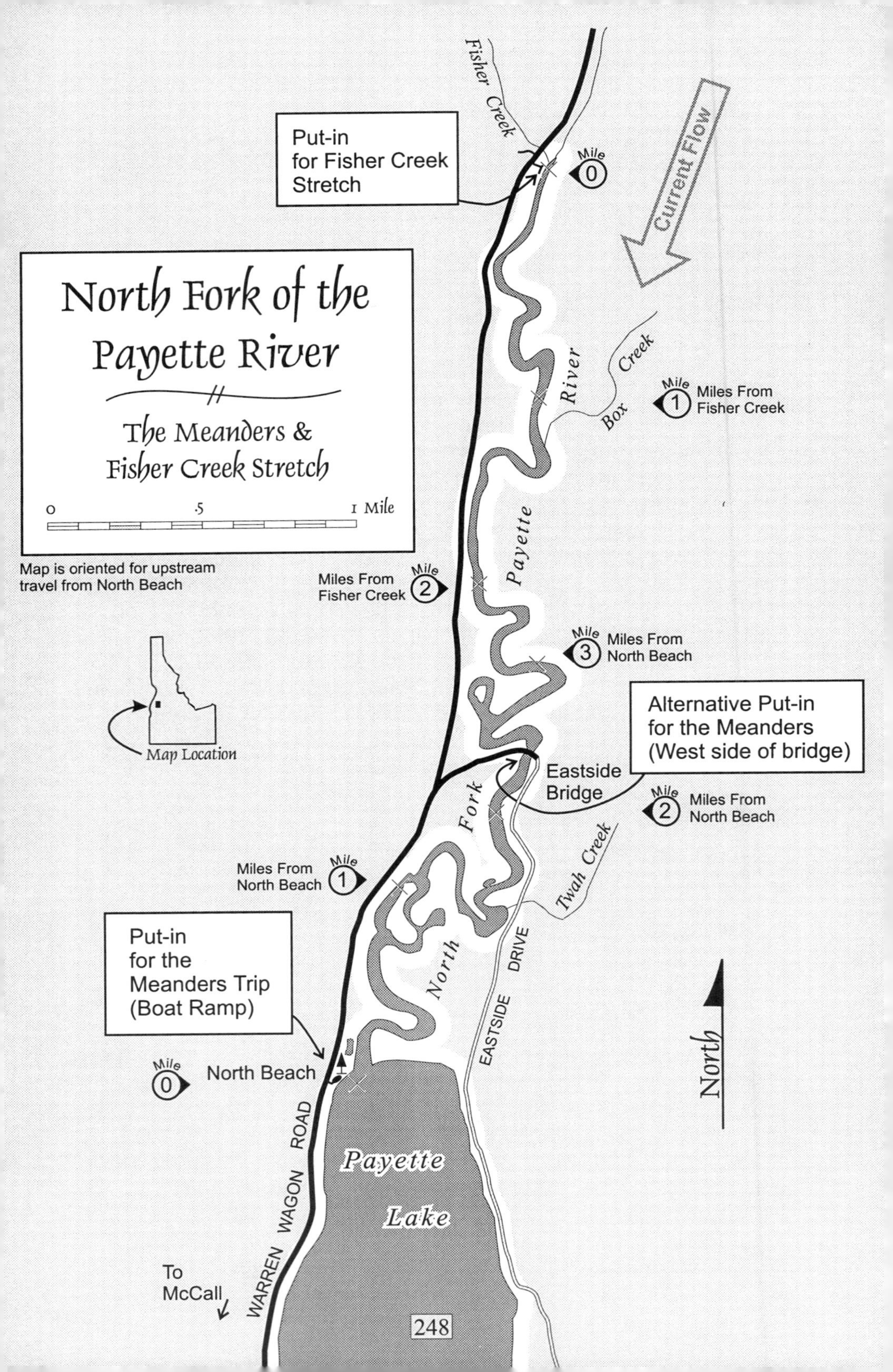

North Fork of the Payette River
The Meanders & Fisher Creek Stretch
0
.5
1 Mile
Map is oriented for upstream travel from North Beach
Put-in for Fisher Creek Stretch
Fisher Creek
Current Flow
Mile 0
Box Creek
River
Mile 1 Miles From Fisher Creek
Payette
Miles From Fisher Creek Mile 2
Mile 3 Miles From North Beach
Alternative Put-in for the Meanders (West side of bridge)
Eastside Bridge
Mile 2 Miles From North Beach
Fork
Twah Creek
Miles From North Beach Mile 1
Map Location
Put-in for the Meanders Trip (Boat Ramp)
North
EASTSIDE DRIVE
North
Mile 0
North Beach
WARREN WAGON ROAD
Payette Lake
To McCall

Drive. Drive .3 mile to a bridge across the North Fork. Boats may be launched on the west side of the bridge. There's no ramp, just a well-worn incline to the water. A good sized pull-off for parking is found on the east side of the bridge. In addition to the Eastside Bridge, other launch sites used for this trip are a state park campground and two or three dirt roads that come to the water's edge.

The Trip. The usual trip on the North Fork Meanders is to start from North Beach or the Eastside Bridge and paddle up the North Fork (away from Payette Lake) until the water gets too swift to continue any farther (about 3 river miles from North Beach). The Meanders stretch is the same level as the lake and the water is flat and the paddling very easy.

You should be aware that a log jam blocks one channel of the North Fork. It's not a dangerous log jam by any means since the river has no current. You can paddle up to it, look it over, and paddle away. But if you want to avoid it, the general rule that North Fork paddlers use is that when faced with a choice of channels, stay to river right. Remember that river right is as you look downstream. So if you're paddling upstream, you would want stay in the channel on your left. Then, when you paddle back downstream, take the channel on your right.

The river bends back and forth through a cool conifer forest with a few cottonwoods mixed in for variety. Along the way are gravel and sand bars which make nice places for lunch stops or a swim. Rising up on either side of the river valley are green forested mountains with scattered rocky outcrops. The chances of seeing wildlife are good. On our trip we watched a deer come out of the forest for a drink and saw a fair number of mallards and mergansers. It is, altogether, a magical place to paddle.

Motorized Use. The only downside of this trip is that motorized vehicles are allowed here, and worst of all, jet skis. Why jet skis should be allowed on this beautiful, quiet stretch is beyond us. We encourage you to write the McCall Chamber of Commerce and the Idaho State Parks Department. Tell them what a great asset they have in the North Fork and that they can do much to keep this area pristine and attractive to visitors by making it a non-motorized area.

Even though motorized craft use this area, it is possible to avoid the noise by going early in morning. Motorized activity usually doesn't start occurring until things warm-up later in the day. Moreover, early mornings are a wonderful time to visit the Meanders. It's quiet, the water is calm, and you are much more likely to see wildlife.

Shuttle. Not necessary. Up and back trip.

Craft. Everything goes here: canoes, kayaks, lake kayaks or other types of hard-shelled craft. Inflatables will work, but they will be sluggish in the lake-like water.

Mileage Chart

(Mileages start at North Beach and work upstream)

0	Put-in. North Beach on Lake Payette, north of McCall.
.1	Mouth of North Fork of the Payette River.
.3	River is close to road (river right).
2.3	Eastside Bridge. Alternative take-out or put-in.

The still and reflective waters of the North Fork Meanders.

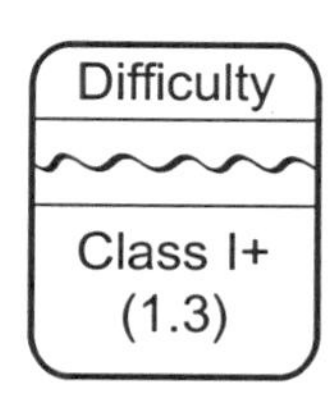

North Fork Payette River

Fisher Creek Stretch
(Map on page 248)

THE MEANDERS STRETCH of the North Fork of the Payette covered in the previous section is a mellow, class I stretch that you can paddle up or downriver. But upstream from the Meanders is a short and easy whitewater stretch (class I+, 1.3) that can be added to liven things up.

It begins at Fisher Creek and has mini-rapids for about a mile until coming to flat water. Like the Meanders, it's a pretty stretch: a crystal-clear river surrounded by a wonderfully aromatic pine and fir forest.

Basic Stats

Difficulty: Class I+ (1.3) in medium or low water.

Season: The window of opportunity is narrow on this short segment. You'll want to wait until after the high water period passes in May and early June, though once high water has passed, the river drops quickly. By mid July, it is getting very low and eventually becomes too low to run. Getting flow information is difficult. Your best bet is to look at the river. If the river is full and swollen, do the Meanders stretch. If the river is not lapping up to the edge of the trees and a rocky bar shows at the put-in—and the river is deep enough to float a boat—you're in luck.

Distance/Time: 5.4 miles (Fisher Creek to North Beach) / 3 hours.

Getting to the Take-out. North Beach on Payette Lake. See description in previous section (Upper North Fork Meanders). An alternative take-out is the bridge on Eastside Road, also described in the previous section.

Getting to the Put-in. Fisher Creek. Start at North Beach, the take-out, and drive upriver 3.1 miles. Fisher Creek may not be signed, so you'll want to check your odometer at North Beach. Just before the Fisher Creek bridge, pull off to your right and follow a dirt road to the river. Often people camp here. There are no ramps, and you'll need to carry your boat down to water's edge.

The Trip. This section of river bends here and there and has small, playful rapids. It does a little braiding before it reaches the Meanders, but, all in all, running it is not all that difficult—as long as you run it in medium or low water. Avoid it when the water is high. When you reach the flat water of the Meanders, it's time to kick back, relax, and enjoy the scenery.

Shuttle. 3 miles, all paved. Warren Wagon Road is a paved, secondary road and makes a nice bike shuttle. It does get a fair amount of traffic, but bike riding on it is common.

Craft. Since this stretch includes paddling out through the slow North Fork Meanders stretch, hard-shelled craft such as canoes and kayaks are recommended.

Mileage Chart

(Mileages start at Fisher Creek and work downstream)

0	Put-in Fisher Creek and North Fork confluence (right).
.3	River is close to road (right).
1.7	River is again close to road (right).
3.1	Eastside Bridge. Alternative take-out.
5.4	North Beach on Lake Payette, north of McCall.

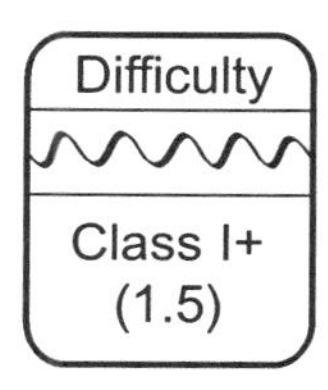

North Fork Payette River

Upper Long Valley
(Sheep Bridge to Hartzel Bridge)

THIS TRIP NEAR THE RESORT TOWN of McCall is one of Idaho's classic overnight canoe runs—and if you are a canoeist, it is one trip that you must do sometime in your lifetime. In this segment of river, the North Fork of the Payette flows from Payette Lake in McCall in a devilish, twisting path across upper Long Valley towards Cascade Reservoir. Lining the banks are ponderosa and lodgepole pine, Doug fir, cottonwoods and aspen. Above its forested banks is Red Ridge to the west, and across the valley to the east is the outer edge of the Salmon River Mountains.

Stately ponderosas lining the banks of the North Fork of the Payette below McCall.

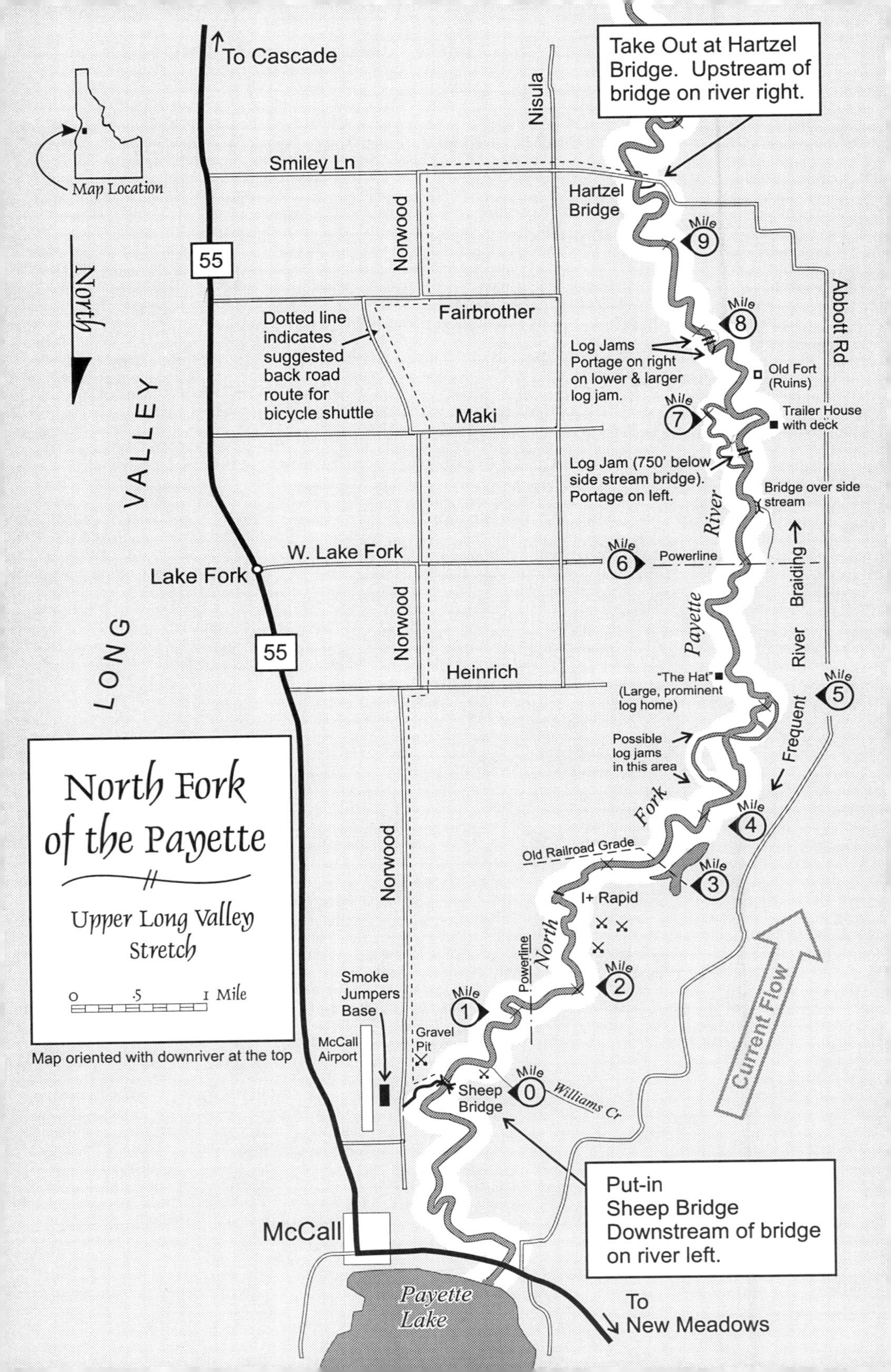

To Cascade
Take Out at Hartzel Bridge. Upstream of bridge on river right.
Nisula
Smiley Ln
Map Location
Hartzel Bridge
Norwood
55
Mile 9
North
Abbott Rd
Dotted line indicates suggested back road route for bicycle shuttle
Fairbrother
Mile 8
Log Jams Portage on right on lower & larger log jam.
Old Fort (Ruins)
VALLEY
Maki
Mile 7
Trailer House with deck
Log Jam (750' below side stream bridge). Portage on left.
Bridge over side stream
River
W. Lake Fork
Mile 6
Powerline
Lake Fork
Braiding
Payette
Norwood
55
LONG
River
Heinrich
"The Hat" (Large, prominent log home)
Mile 5
Frequent
Possible log jams in this area
Fork
Mile 4
North Fork of the Payette
Upper Long Valley Stretch
0 .5 1 Mile
Old Railroad Grade
Mile 3
Norwood
I+ Rapid
North
Powerline
Mile 2
Current Flow
Smoke Jumpers Base
Mile 1
Gravel Pit
McCall Airport
Sheep Bridge
Mile 0
Williams Cr
Map oriented with downriver at the top
Put-in Sheep Bridge Downstream of bridge on river left.
McCall
Payette Lake
To New Meadows

The North Fork here is home to one of Idaho's greatest concentrations of osprey, but you'll also see bald eagles, great blue herons and other birds. As we passed around an island late the day we ran the river, a four-point buck ambled into the water and stood watching us for the longest time before finally dashing off into the woods.

Yet, like any worthwhile endeavor, you have to be prepared for some work. The river is blocked by two log jams which must be portaged. You'll probably encounter one or two other places with log blockages that will also require lining or portaging.

Nothing on the river is harder than a class I+ and it's all very canoeable. Hard-shelled boats such as canoes and kayaks are the craft of choice. Canoes are the best since you'll have plenty of room to carry overnight gear. Before undertaking the trip, build up your river skills. You'll want to feel comfortable on sharp corners, be able to avoid overhanging trees, and run through small rapids around gravel bars.

It can be done in one day, but it's a long day. As an overnight trip, on the other hand, it is sublime. While it has much private land along it, you can camp on beaches, gravel bars or islands, and some BLM land is found in the area of the first major log jam.

Basic Stats

Difficulty: Class I+ (1.5) in low water (100 cfs). The difficulty of the river itself is only around 1.4, but when the portages are added, 1.5 is more appropriate.

Distance/Time: 10 miles / 8 hours at 90 cfs. Makes an enjoyable overnight trip.

Levels: Don't run the North Fork during the high water period in May and early June. Things usually start slowing down by mid June. Good flows are around the 100 or 200 cfs range. Gauge: North Fork of the Payette at McCall.

Portages: Two log jams must be portaged, and it's likely that one or two additional places may require short portages.

Getting to the Take-out. Hartzel Bridge. To get to Hartzel bridge, drive north on Idaho 55 from Donnelly (located south of McCall). About 3.9 miles out of Donnelly, take a left on Smylie Lane. Drive 3.1 miles to the Hartzel Bridge. About 500 feet past the bridge is a road turning off to the right and leading to a sandy beach alongside the river (river right, upstream of bridge). Park in this area.

Getting to the Put-in. Sheep Bridge. If you are driving to McCall from Cascade, take a left on Dienhard Street on the south edge of McCall near the airport. Continue until you reach a "T" in the road and take a left. After a couple of blocks, you'll come to the Smoke Jumper base on your left. To the right, one or two roads lead down to a bridge (Sheep Bridge) over the river. The put-in is on river left, downstream of the bridge.

The Trip. Portages always keep the crowds down, and that certainly is the case on the North Fork. Moreover, it's a very long trip to try to do in one day. When you look at the North Fork of the Payette on a map, it's obvious that it flows any which way but straight. All those twists and turns combined with very little water volume take time, lots of time. But by making it into an overnight trip, and spreading it out into two days, it will be much more enjoyable. When preparing for the trip, remember to take along large packs that you can use to carry your equipment around on the portages.

The North Fork is a very typical Idaho valley river. One minor, but easily run, rapid is found at the 2.4-mile point, but the river otherwise involves negotiating corners, handling some swift water and paddling through riffles along gravel bars. The reason this trip should be done in low water is because of logs which, in several places, block the entire channel. In low water when the current is sluggish, it's easy to stop. We found the water slow enough that in most cases we could edge the canoe right to the log, and in one case, even pulled the canoe over the log. In high water, however, you'd have precious little time to stop. So wait until the water comes down before you run it.

You'll see a few houses along the way. Yet the river, overall, is still natural and undeveloped. We really hope that sensible land-use policies are adopted in Long Valley which will keep homes far back from this beautiful and critical riparian zone.

Portages. We were surprised how difficult it was to keep track of where we were on the river. The river channels have changed since the latest 7.5 minute maps have been published. You'll find the mileage chart on page 259 helpful, but you may even want to take along a GPS as well. The two log jams found on this stretch are historic fixtures on the North Fork. They've been there for years. Buster McBride, whose family has lived in upper Long Valley for generations, recalls his father portaging the two log jams some 60 years ago.

Above the two major jams, you'll probably come across other small log blockages, most likely around the mile 4 or 5 point. (We encountered two: one we dispatched by sliding the boat around the log on a gravel bar and the other by pulling our canoe up and over the log.)

One of the easy portages along the North Fork.

The landmark which signals that you are getting close to the first major log jam is 6 miles from the start. Here, a powerline crosses the river. Once past the powerline, keep watching off to the right for a side stream. The side stream has a small falls over a slab of concrete with a bridge directly over it. The log jam is located 750 feet downstream from here. (We know it's 750 feet since we paced it).

When we ran the river at 90 cfs, the current was very slow and you could float up next to the log jam if you wanted. A faint portage trail, however, is located on river left, about 40 feet above the log jam. Pull out here and take a walk downstream. In addition to the main part of the log jam, other logs block the river below. Take a look and decide how you want to do the portage. We portaged part way, then pulled our boat down a shallow channel and portaged once again around the lower logs. Overall, you're probably portaging around 250 feet.

The portaging occurs in an area that has some BLM land around the river, and after doing the portage, you may decide to camp. There are other places, of course, if this area doesn't suit you.

The second major log jam comes 7.8 miles from the start. It's about .4 mile below the old fort ruins (see mileage chart). Take a walk downstream when you reach the jam. This area also has a couple of spots where the river is blocked. We tried hoisting our boat over the lower and largest blockage—which, in retrospect, ended up taking a lot more work than a simple carry around the faint portage trail on the right. The portage around the second log jam is longer than the first, probably about 400 feet in all, but on parts of it, you can drag your boat through shallow water.

Camping. The river is surrounded by private lands, but in Idaho you are not trespassing as long as you choose a place to camp below the high water mark. You'll want to pick an area well out of sight of the few houses along the river. That's not much of a problem on this stretch. In low water, you'll find lots of lovely camping spots on sand and gravel bars, well-screened from the rest of the valley by the band of trees along the river.

Idaho State Historical Society

Spencer Tracy starred in *Northwest Passage,* a major motion picture made in the McCall area in 1939. The North Fork of the Payette River served as one of the locations for the film.

Historical Information. The old fort ruins at the 7.4-mile point are all that remain of a movie set that was built for *Northwest Passage,* a Metro-Goldwyn-Mayer (MGM) movie that was filmed in the McCall area in the summer of 1939. The movie also included elaborate sets built on the west and east sides of Payette Lake. Stars of the movie included Spencer Tracy, Robert Young, and Walter Brennan. The movie is about a daring raid staged by an intrepid group of American Colonists known as Rogers' Rangers during the French Indian war in the 1750s.

The set along the North Fork of the Payette served as the movie's Fort Wentworth, a place where the Rangers hoped to find help during their long and daring escape. Upon arriving, they found it abandoned. You'll have to see the video to learn what happened to the Rangers.

The *Idaho Mountain Record* reported in a November 1979 article on the film that MGM assured the public in the 1940s that Fort Wentworth would be preserved as a tourist attraction. But for better or worse, it was a promise never kept.

Shuttle. 9 miles, all paved. For a bike shuttle use the secondary back roads on the east side of the river (the route is shown with a dotted line on the river map). Bike shuttle roads are paved, except for 2 miles of gravel.

Craft. This is a traditional and honored Idaho canoe run, but it is also suitable for kayaks. Inflatables and drift boats not recommended.

Mileage Chart

0	Put-in. Sheep Bridge (river left, downstream of bridge).
.5	Mouth of Williams Creek (right).
2.4	River widens followed by I+ rapid (1.4).
3.1	Old railroad crossing.
4-5	Lots of braiding. Trees across river are likely.
5.4	"The Hat." Large, prominent log home on river left.
6	Powerline crossing.
6.4	Stream comes in from right. Small bridge over stream.
6.6	(750 feet below stream) Major log jam. Portage on left.
7	Trailer house with deck near river (right).
7.4	Cement slab on river right. Old fort ruins on right (not visible from the river). Remains of Fort Wentworth, a set used for the MGM movie *Northwest Passage*.
7.8	Log jam. The lower and major part of the log jam is portaged on right.
9.4	Take-out. Hartzel Bridge (upstream of bridge on river right).

Idaho State Historical Society

One of the elaborate forts constructed for *Northwest Passage*. Hanging on the pole in the foreground are some of the 700 scalps that festooned the film's sets. The scalps were made of human hair held together by a rubber compound.

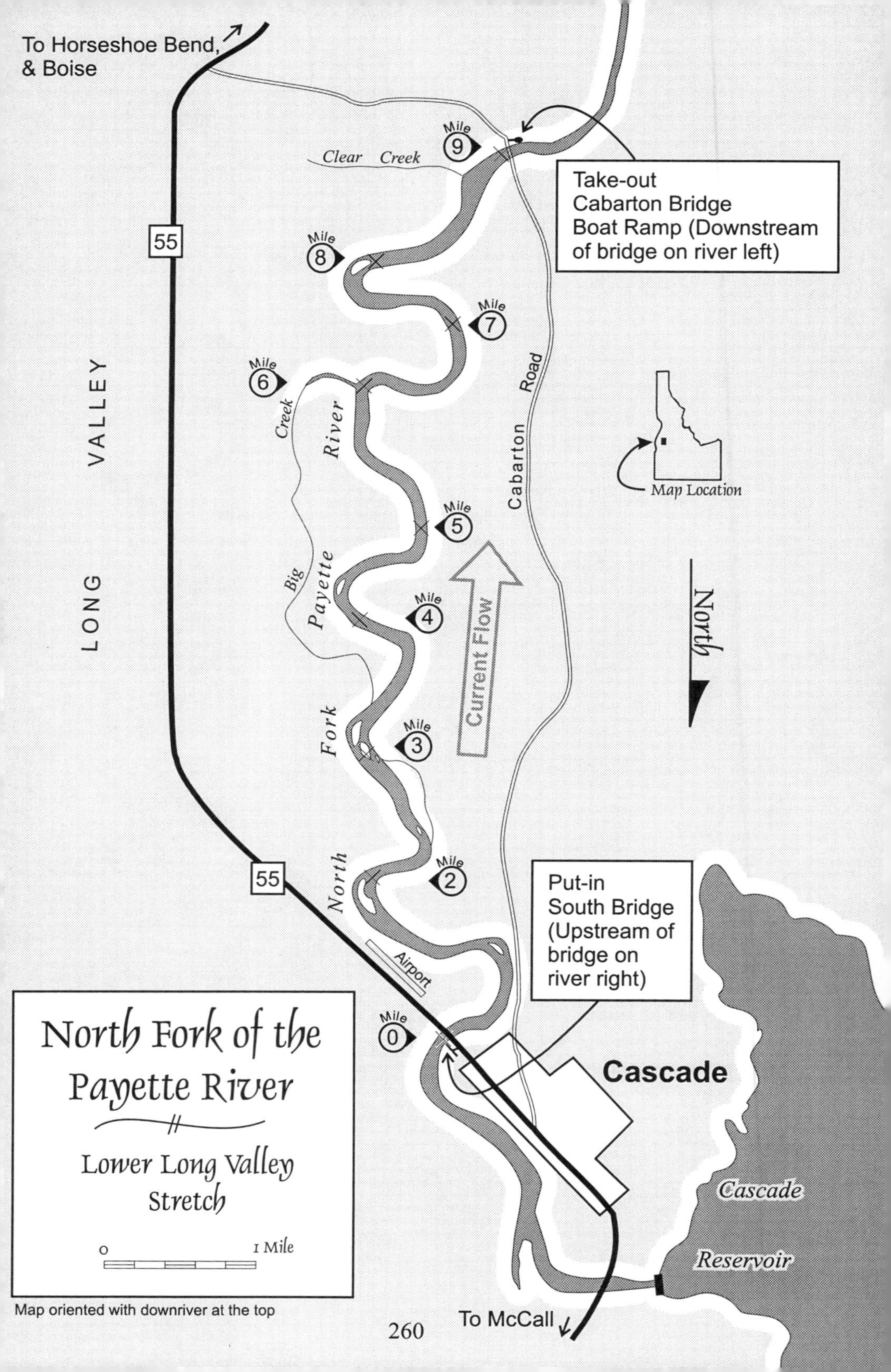
To Horseshoe Bend, & Boise
Mile 9
Clear Creek
Take-out
Cabarton Bridge
Boat Ramp (Downstream of bridge on river left)
55
Mile 8
Mile 7
Mile 6
Creek
River
Cabarton Road
VALLEY
Map Location
Mile 5
Big
Payette
Mile 4
Current Flow
North
LONG
Fork
Mile 3
North
Mile 2
55
Put-in
South Bridge
(Upstream of bridge on river right)
Airport
Mile 0
Cascade
North Fork of the Payette River
Lower Long Valley Stretch
0
1 Mile
Cascade
Reservoir
Map oriented with downriver at the top
To McCall

Difficulty
Class I (1.1)

North Fork Payette River

Lower Long Valley
Cascade to Cabarton

THE NORTH FORK OF THE PAYETTE, south of the town of Cascade, is wide and shallow and serenely flows through lower Long Valley. It's a lazy stretch of river (class I, 1.1) that can be enjoyed by the whole family.

You'll have nice views of Snowdrift Mountain to the west, and it's likely you'll see osprey, eagles, and a variety of ducks and other bird life. On our trip, we even saw a falcon deftly flying in and out of a flock of crows, keeping them on edge and thoroughly riled up.

Basic Stats

Difficulty: Class I (1.1). River is wide and shallow and the water is slow.

Levels: Below 2,000 cfs. It's rare for the river to go above 2,000 cfs. Usually, the water level is much lower, but occasionally in early to mid June, it will have a spike of high water and during those times, we recommend avoiding it. Gauge: North Fork of the Payette at Cascade.

Distance/Time: 9 miles / 3 hours at 1,400 cfs (if you paddle). It will take longer if you just float—or if the wind comes up.

Getting to the Take-out. Cabarton Bridge. Cabarton Road is about 9 miles north of Smith's Ferry or 7 miles south of Cascade on Idaho 55. Look for the Clear Creek Inn and Restaurant which is close to the Cabarton Road intersection on Idaho 55. Turn west on Cabarton Road and drive 1.7 miles to the bridge. Just before the bridge on the left is a small parking area and river access site. (You'll probably see a number of people putting in here. They are running the class III whitewater stretch below.)

Getting to the Put-in. South Bridge & Cascade Sports Park. As you drive into Cascade from the Boise area, you'll cross the first bridge (south bridge) over the North Fork (there's a second bridge over the North Fork on the north side of town). Just past the first bridge to the right, a road leads to Cascade Sports Park. Follow the road to the river, and near the bridge, you'll find a place to park and launch your boat. (Upstream of the bridge on river right).

Alternative Put-in. North Bridge. An alternative put-in is the second (north) bridge. This stretch is runnable, but a bit more difficult because of two diversions. No diversions are located below the first (south) bridge, and it's the better put-in for families.

The Trip. The North Fork below the south bridge in Cascade is a broad and flat river with no rapids. In a couple of locations, you'll encounter some overhanging trees and snags, but the water moves slowly and they pose little problem. The water is clear as glass, and you can see the river's sandy bottom textured with the riffle marks of the unhurried current.

Along the banks are scattered ponderosa pine and open vistas across pasture land. On the right is Snowdrift Mountain which gradually appears closer as you progress down the river.

Since the water is slow moving, this can turn into a very long trip if the wind comes up. You're more likely to have less wind in the morning which is a good time for families and bird aficionados to float it .

Shuttle. 9 miles, all paved. A pleasant bike shuttle may be made by following Cabarton Road beyond the take-out point back to Cascade. It's about the same distance as taking the highway and a lot quieter. Cabarton Road comes into the north end of Cascade, and it is necessary to turn to the right on Idaho 55 to get back to the south bridge, the put-in site. You'll want a mountain bike for the shuttle since it involves 3 miles of gravel.

Craft. Canoes, kayaks, and drift boats. Inflatables can do it, but they will be slow in the flat water.

Mileage Chart

0	Put-in. Cascade Sports Park at South Bridge over the North Fork (river right, upstream of bridge).
1.8	Island in river and end of Cascade airstrip on left.
3	Islands.
3.3	Big Creek channel (left).
6	Big Creek channel return (left).
9	Take-out. Cabarton Bridge. River left, downstream of bridge.

Difficulty
Class I+ (1.2-1.3)

Little Salmon River

Meadows Valley Stretch

THE LITTLE SALMON flows through a lovely agrarian valley north of New Meadows. Although changing, the Meadows Valley is still far less crowded and developed than the area around McCall just to the south. It has a downhome Idaho, rural feel to it. One attraction of running this stretch is Zim's Hot Springs located near the put-in. After a trip down the river, you can stop and catch a soak or a refreshing shower. They also have a campground for overnight stays.

The Little Salmon is . . . well, it's little. In most places on this shoestring of a river, you can easily wade across it. It meanders through lush green meadows and pasture land inhabited by inquisitive cows which pause long enough from the business of eating to watch a rare boat go by. The open fields allow unhindered views of the peaks to the northeast and northwest.

For bird watching, the Little Salmon through the Meadows Valley is outstanding. We saw a greater diversity of birds here than in any other stretch in the McCall area, including the bird-rich runs on the North Fork of the Payette.

Basic Stats

Difficulty: Class I (1.2-1.3) in low water (700 cfs). It has some riffles and mini-rapids. Most of it is a very relaxed class I. It does, however, have some fences, and you'll need to get out and slide your boat under.

Levels: Avoid the high water period in May and June. Suggested levels are from 500 to 1000 cfs. Gauge: Little Salmon River at Riggins.

Distance/Time: 9 miles / 4 hours at 650 cfs.

Portages/Obstructions: This stretch has fences which cross the river. In low flows, less than 1,000 cfs, the water is slow enough that you have plenty of time to pull off. (On our trip, we came across 4 fences. All of them were located in slow water and didn't pose any hazards. On three of them, we were able to float under. For one we got out and floated the boat under.)

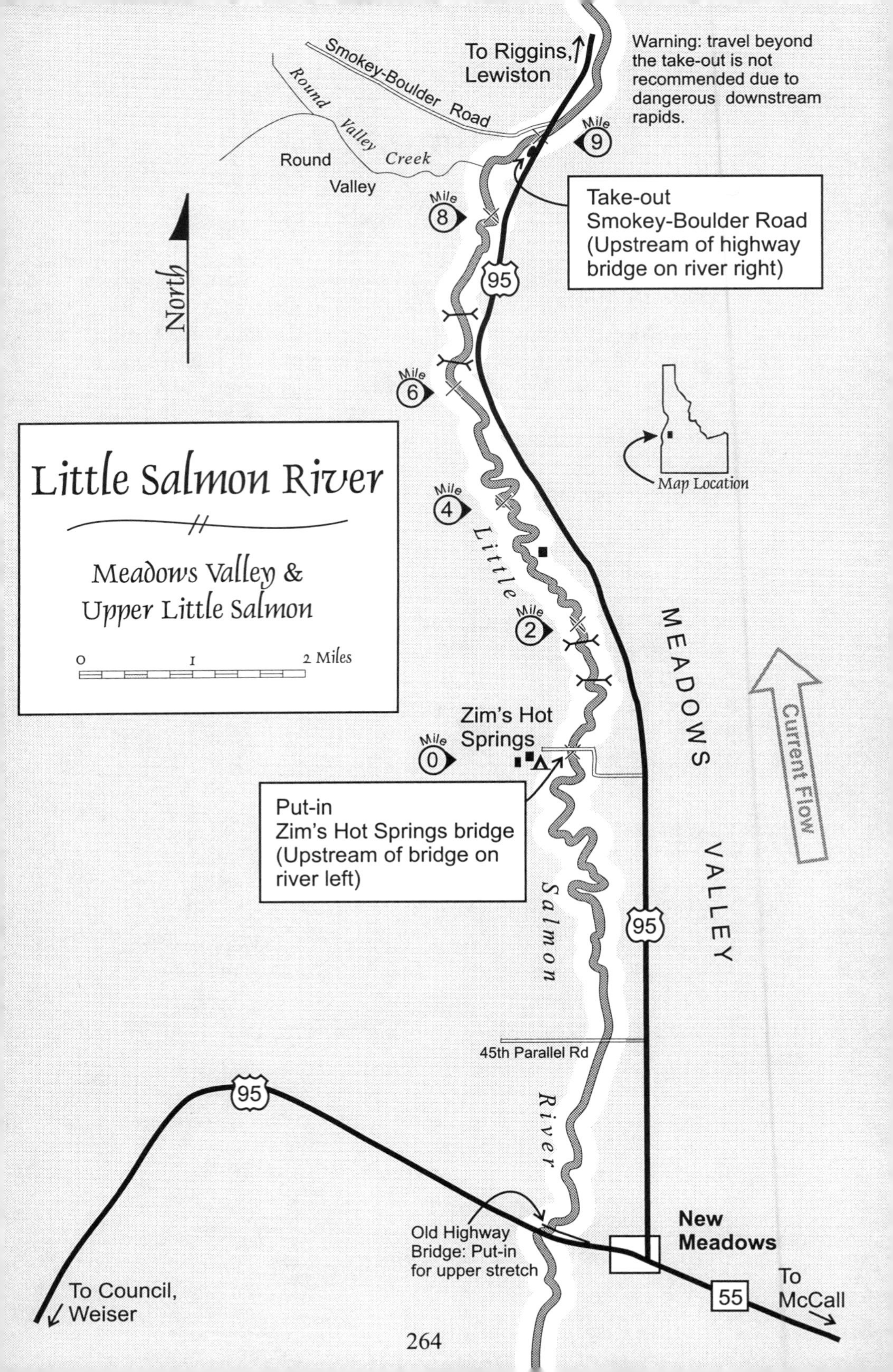
Little Salmon River
Meadows Valley & Upper Little Salmon
0 1 2 Miles
North
To Riggins, Lewiston
Warning: travel beyond the take-out is not recommended due to dangerous downstream rapids.
Smokey-Boulder Road
Round Valley Creek
Round Valley
Mile 9
Mile 8
Mile 6
Mile 4
Mile 2
Mile 0
Take-out
Smokey-Boulder Road
(Upstream of highway bridge on river right)
95
Map Location
Little Salmon River
MEADOWS VALLEY
Current Flow
Zim's Hot Springs
Put-in
Zim's Hot Springs bridge
(Upstream of bridge on river left)
45th Parallel Rd
Old Highway Bridge: Put-in for upper stretch
New Meadows
55
To McCall
To Council, Weiser

Getting to the Take-out. Smokey-Boulder Road. From New Meadows, drive 10.7 miles to the north on US 95. You'll see a large pull-off on the left just before Highway 95 crosses the Little Salmon and Smokey-Boulder Road leading off to the left. Park in the large pull-off. There's no ramp here. The take-out involves carrying your boat up a 15-foot high grassy bank. Note that *you don't want to float below the bridge* since there's some very serious whitewater below. You'll have no problem taking out. It's quiet water with very little current.

Getting to the Put-in. Zim's Hot Springs bridge. From the highway junction in New Meadows, the turn-off to Zim's Hot Springs is 4.3 miles to the north on US 95. From the take-out near Smokey-Boulder Road, the turn-off is 6.4 miles to the south. Turn to the west and drive .6 mile to the bridge over the Little Salmon. The bridge is located just before the hot springs complex.

This put-in requires one or two gymnastic moves. We found that the best place to get the boat in was on river left, upstream of the bridge. You'll need to slide your craft down a short (15 feet), but steep embankment to river level. It can be done without too much of a fuss, but you'll need to watch your footing while sliding the boat. There's no parking at the bridge. A small place to park is on river right, 50 feet to the east, where a road enters from a farmer's field. Be sure not to park in front of the farmer's gate. You can also park at the Zim's Hot Springs parking lot, which is close to the bridge, but if you do, be sure that you patronize them.

The Trip. Give yourself some time on this trip. The Little Salmon is a small river with lots of twists and turns. The openness of the country makes it more deceiving. A landmark that you can see a short distance downstream takes forever to reach on the curvy and petulant Little Salmon.

Keep an eye out for fence posts which lead down to the river, your visual clue that a fence might cross, and be prepared to pull-off. We found that we could float under most of the fences, but on one, we got out and slipped the boat under before continuing. (We suggest having a thick pair of leather gloves along. It makes pushing barbed wire fences up and out of the way much easier on the hands.)

Most of the trip is through open pasture, but there's a short, pretty section with ponderosa pine shading the river in late afternoon. It's located just before the two bridges, around 5 river miles from the start. Canoeists take short paddles if you have them. It's a shallow river and a short shaft makes paddling easier.

Shuttle. 7 miles, mostly paved. A little gravel near the Zim's Hot Springs bridge. Bike shuttle: US 95 is a very busy highway, but it does have a wide paved shoulder.

Craft. Canoes, kayaks and small inflatables. Hard-shelled boaters will find this stretch more appealing than those in inflatables since the current is sluggish and you need to do quite a bit of paddling.

Mileage Chart

Mile	
0	Put-in. Zim's Hot Springs bridge (upstream of the bridge on river left).
1.1	Bridge.
1.7	Bridge with "Union Pacific" printed on the upriver side. (A short distance later on a bend we encountered a fence.)
2.8	House near the river. (A short distance later was a fence.)
6.4	Bridge.
6.7	Bridge.
8.4	Mouth of Round Valley Creek (left).
9	Take-out. Just above Highway 95 bridge on right. Note: don't paddle below this point. Serious whitewater is found downstream of the bridge.

Upper Little Salmon (Above Zim's Hot Springs). You can also run from the town of New Meadows to the 45th Parallel Road (class I, 1.2-1.3), or from the 45th Parallel Road to Zim's Hot Springs (class I, 1.2-1.3). We found the stretch from New Meadows the least desirable since at 650 cfs, we had to drag our canoe now and then—and it passes by the New Meadows Sewage ponds. But after the first mile, the scenery gets better and the bird viewing is excellent.

The put-in for the New Meadows segment is the bridge on the "Old Highway Road" .5 mile to the west of town, just off of US 95. You'll have to slide the boat down a short embankment and under a fence.

The 45th Parallel Road is located 2.3 miles north of New Meadows on US 95. Turn left (west) here, and .1 mile from the highway is a steel bridge spanning the Little Salmon. No parking is available at the bridge, and you'll have to park your vehicle back a distance from the bridge. There's no easy put-in here. It entails sliding the boat down a 10-foot embankment to the river. The river makes a couple of sharp corners class I+ (1.3) just below the bridge, but otherwise it's a slow, relaxed current, class I (1.2), to Zim's Hot Springs.

On either of these stretches, you'll encounter fences which cross the river. We found that in low water (650 cfs) the river was slow enough that the fences posed no danger, and they were more annoying than anything.

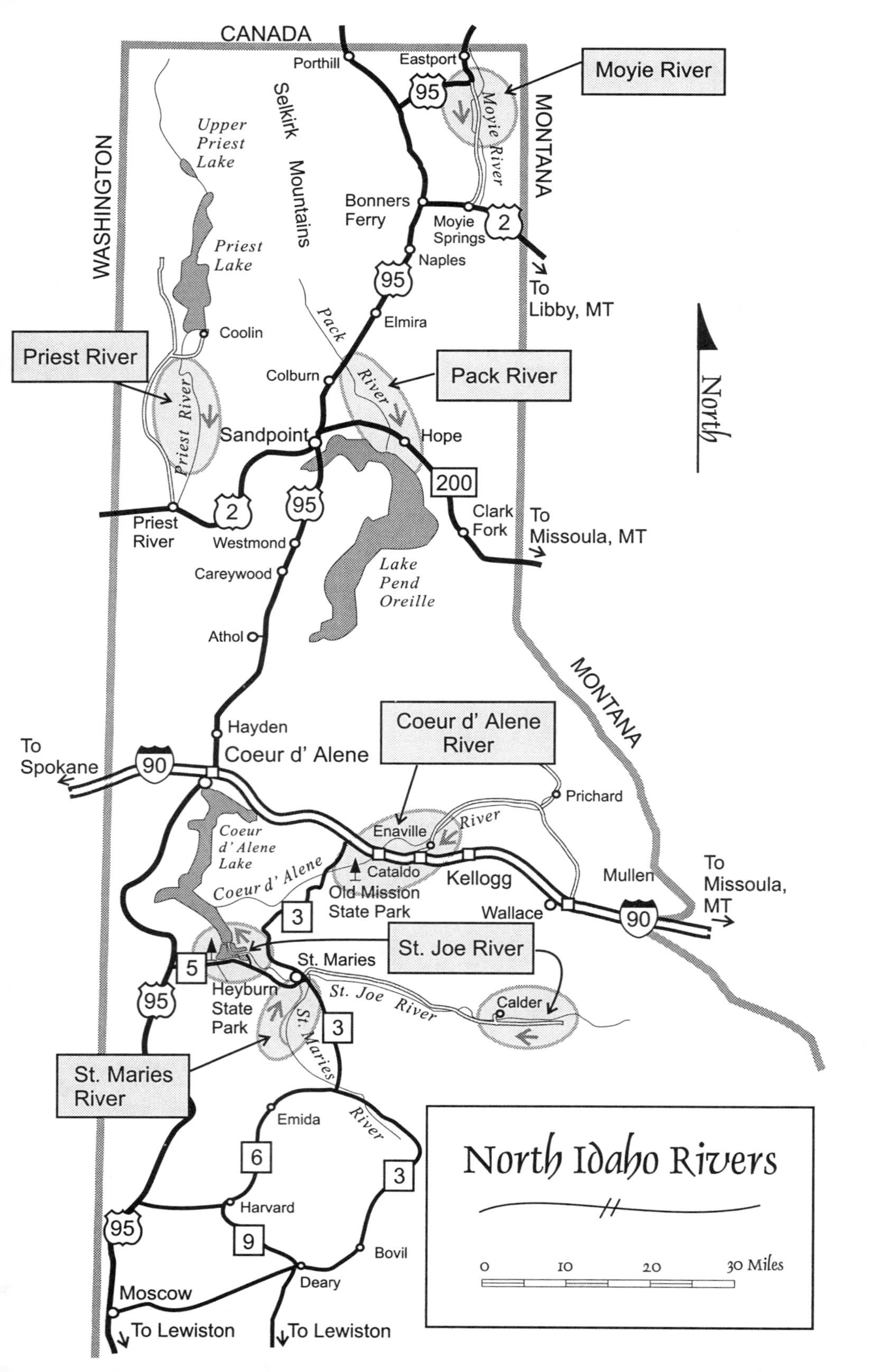
CANADA
Porthill
Eastport
95
Moyie River
Selkirk Mountains
Upper Priest Lake
Moyie River
MONTANA
WASHINGTON
Priest Lake
Bonners Ferry
Moyie Springs
2
Naples
95
To Libby, MT
Pack
Elmira
Coolin
Priest River
Colburn
River
Pack River
North
Priest River
Sandpoint
Hope
200
2
95
Clark Fork
To Missoula, MT
Priest River
Westmond
Careywood
Lake Pend Oreille
Athol
MONTANA
Coeur d' Alene River
Hayden
To Spokane
90
Coeur d' Alene
Prichard
Coeur d' Alene Lake
Enaville
River
Cataldo
Kellogg
Coeur d' Alene
Old Mission State Park
Mullen
To Missoula, MT
3
Wallace
90
St. Joe River
5
St. Maries
St. Joe River
Heyburn State Park
Calder
95
St. Maries
3
St. Maries River
River
Emida
6
3
North Idaho Rivers
Harvard
95
9
Bovil
0
10
20
30 Miles
Moscow
Deary
To Lewiston
To Lewiston

North Idaho Paddling Trips

St. Maries River, St. Joe River, Coeur d' Alene River, Pack River, Moyie River, and Priest River

NORTH IDAHO IS A WORLD APART from the southern part of the state—and so is the paddling. While there is a transition zone, most canoe and kayak trips in the north travel down rivers wrapped in lush green growth and hidden within aromatic forests of cedar, fir, white pine and larch.

Some excellent outside resources are available on the paddling opportunities in North Idaho. In fact, as we were working on the research for this project, a new guidebook appeared entitled *Paddle Routes of the Inland Northwest*. The book is by Rich Landers and Dan Hansen. Both are experienced boaters, excellent writers and care deeply about rivers and wild lands. Rather than repeat something they have already done so well, we'll summarize paddling opportunities in the north country.

If you're planning to do some northern paddling, you'll want to have their book which, in addition to Idaho, covers parts of Washington, Oregon, Montana and British Columbia. It's available at book and outdoor stores or directly from their publisher: The Mountaineers, 1001 SW Klickitat Way, Seattle, WA 98134. Phone: 800-553-4453. Web: www.mbooks@mountaineers.org.

Starting from the south and working north, the following are outstanding North Idaho trips:

St. Maries River
(Class I)

The bottom 7 or 8 miles on the St. Maries is a sweet and easy run for families. The put-in for the lower run is about 6 miles from St. Maries on the St. Maries River Road (watch for a road that goes over the railroad tracks to the river) and the take-out is at the Sportsman's Access on Idaho 3 just south of town.

Just upstream from the family stretch is a 20-mile mostly class II run with one class III rapid. The put-in is near the bridge at Mashburn and the take-out is the same as the put-in for the lower St. Maries trip. You'll have to catch it early in the year when the water is up, but kayakers, rafters and whitewater canoeists will enjoy the rousing water and the canyon scenery.

St. Joe River
(Class I)

The St. Joe has many different floating options. It has everything from highly technical whitewater on its upper reaches to lake-like water lower down. One short class I sampler on the St. Joe starts at Huckleberry Campground, just to the east of Calder on Forest Road 50. It ends at a primitive boat ramp in Calder.

A marvelous canoe or flatwater kayak trip is within Heyburn State Park, accessed from US 95 between Moscow and Coeur d' Alene. Here the lower St. Joe flows between three lakes, but the banks of the river are high enough that the tree-lined channel of the river remains, even though it is surrounded by lake water. Like the trip to the base of Shoshone Falls, it's one of those Idaho paddle trips that you should make a point of doing.

A river surrounded by lakes: the remarkable paddle trip on the lower St. Joe River through Heyburn State Park.

Ross Hall / Idaho State Historical Society

Coeur d' Alene River
(Class I to I+)

A popular 10-mile trip on the picturesque Coeur d' Alene River starts north of Enaville, about 30 miles to the east of Coeur d' Alene. The take-out is at the Mission Flats boat ramp at Old Mission State Park. It has some riffles, bends and lots of gravel bars. It's runnable most of the year, but like any river, stay off of it during periods of high water. Upper portions of the Coeur d' Alene can be run, including stretches from Senator Creek Campground to Prichard (class II-III) and Prichard to Enaville (class I+).

Pack River
(Class I)

This laid-back trip through pasture lands, meadows and scattered wealds is a fine one for families. In addition to fun bird watching, there's a chance you'll see larger wildlife including deer and moose. The put-in is the US 95 bridge over Pack River about 10 miles north of Sandpoint. Take-outs are available at bridges at the Colburn-Culver Road, Lightening Creek Road and Idaho 200. Although slow moving, be watchful for downed trees.

Moyie River
(Upper stretch is class I+ in low flows)

Ron was first attracted to the Moyie's beauty in the 1970s when he was working on *Winter Tales and Trails*, a book on ski and snowshoe trails in Idaho. It's a lovely, clear-stream river flowing through heavily forested country. The put-in for the upper canoe run is at Copper Creek Campground, just south of the Canadian border. The campground is located north of Bonner's Ferry on a side road off US 95. The take-out is the bridge on Meadow Creek road, accessed from US 95 farther to the south. The trip is 12-13 miles long. It has a short season, and you'll want to catch it early in the year in June or early July.

Two other runs are available on the Moyie. Below Meadow Creek Bridge to the Meadow Creek Campground is a 7-mile class II+ stretch for more experienced canoeists and kayakers. The most difficult stretch on the river is below Meadow Creek Campground. It is a class III to IV stretch of whitewater with one gnarly rapid at an old dam which can be very dangerous in high flows.

Priest River
(Class I with one class II rapid)

The Priest is another river that Ron first saw on a pair of cross-country skis. That's when he got his first look at Chipmunk Rapids, a class II stretch of water. Although it's pretty in the winter, wait until summer or fall to run it (as if we had to tell you that).

The put-in for the Priest River run is at Dickensheet Campground. From Priest River, take Idaho 57 to its junction with Coolin Road. The campground is off Coolin Road, a mile past the junction. The take-out for an 18-mile trip suggested by Landers and Hansen is Big Hole, located off Forest Road 334 north of Priest River. Lower portions of the river can also be run. It's mostly class I except for two rapids: McAbee Falls (class II) and Eightmile Rapid (class III).

An occasion to dress up: canoeing on Lake Coeur d'Alene in the 1890s.

Idaho State Historical Society

Appendices
References
Index

Ross Hall / Idaho State Historical Society

Appendix A

Public Access to Idaho Rivers: Private Lands and Paddlers' Rights

Many of the rivers described in this book pass through private lands. That brings up a whole series of questions about running them. The most important question is: Can rivers which flow through private land in Idaho be used by paddlers?

If so, additional questions immediately come to mind: Can you stop along the river to have lunch? How about camping? If you come across diversions, do you have the right to portage on private land? And what about those gnarly barbed wire fences that are sometimes strung across rivers? Can landowners really do that?

For years, these questions have been batted around by boaters, fishermen, hunters and river users. Paddlers' rights are becoming more important as we see more and more no trespassing signs going up along our streams.

Since people hold many differing opinions on the topic, we felt that it was important to get some authoritative information on what is proper and what is not. Thus, we contacted the Idaho Attorney General's Office to have some of these questions clarified. Steven Schuster, the Deputy Attorney General, provided us with a considerable amount of material, and we are grateful for his time and work. In the space below, we'll attempt to summarize this information, and answer those nagging river access questions in more detail.

1. Can rivers which flow through private land be used by paddlers?

Yes, if it is navigable. The test for navigability is found in the Idaho State Code, Section 36-1601(a):

> Any stream which, in its natural state, during normal high water, will float cut timber having a diameter of six (6) inches or any other commercial or floatable commodity or is capable of being navigated by oar or motor propelled small craft for pleasure or commercial purposes . . . .

The test of using six-inch logs was actually used in Idaho. In 1968, six fishermen were floating through private land on Silver Creek, one of the rivers covered in this book. They were accused of trespassing by the landowner and ordered off the river. The fishermen went to court over the matter.

To help prove that Silver Creek was navigable, they turned loose 9 logs with diameters in excess of 6 inches at a bridge upstream from the landowner's property. At a bridge downstream from the property, they were able to retrieve 4 of the logs. When the Idaho Supreme Court eventually ruled in the fishermen's favor they cited the log test as establishing the navigability of Silver Creek. Thus, since Silver Creek was navigable, it could be used by the public for fishing and other recreational purposes.

By in large, if you can paddle a river, then it probably meets the legal test for navigability. If you were testing a stream for it's navigability, though, and really wanted to follow the letter of the law, then you would want to use an oar-powered craft—and maybe toss in a few 6-inch logs as well.

2. If a stream is "navigable," what can the public use it for?

Once a stream is considered to be navigable, then the Idaho Code Section 36-1601(b) assures that the public can use it for boating, swimming, fishing, hunting and all other forms of recreation:

> Navigable rivers, sloughs or streams within the meander lines or, when not meandered, between flow lines of ordinary high water thereof, and all rivers, sloughs and streams flowing through any public lands of the state shall be open to public use as a public highway for travel and passage, up or downstream, for business or pleasure, and to exercise the incidents of navigation—boating, swimming, fishing, hunting and all recreational purposes.

It is our opinion—and we have to qualify this and say that we are not lawyers and law is always open to interpretation—that all the rivers within this book meet the navigability test and can be used by the public for boating and recreational purposes.

2. What about stopping along a river that has private land on both sides? Can you pull off and have lunch on the bank? Can you walk down the side of the stream and do some fishing? What about camping?

The answer to all of these questions is yes, if you stay below the high water mark. The high water mark is defined in Idaho Code 58-104(9):

> The term "natural or ordinary high water mark" as herein used shall be defined to be the line which the water impresses on the soil by covering it for sufficient periods to deprive the soil of its vegetation and destroy its value for agricultural purposes.

That means that if you stop and have lunch on a sand or gravel bar which the river normally covers in high water, you're fine. If you climb up on the bank into the trees then you're likely above the high water mark and are trespassing. But like anything, you want to use discretion. You don't want to lay out a picnic and have the kids splashing in the water right below someone's deck overlooking the river.

Likewise, if you're on one of the overnight rivers covered in this book, you don't want to camp on a sandbar in sight of the landowner's house. That only causes unnecessary conflicts which do nothing to advance the public's right to use waterways. We doubt, however, that river users would want to camp in sight of someone's house. It takes all the fun out of it.

For camping, islands are usually a good bet since on a navigable river they would probably belong to the state as a part of the river bed.

3. What about diversions or low bridges? Do boaters have the right to portage the diversion, even though land on either side of the river is private?

Yes. State law is quite clear in this matter. You can portage around obstructions as long as you re-enter the river immediately below the obstruction and as long as you started your trip from a public access area. Idaho Code Section 36-1601(c):

> Nothing herein contained shall authorize the entering on or crossing over private land at any point other than within the high water lines of navigable streams except that where irrigation dams or other obstructions interfere with the navigability of a stream, members of the public may remove themselves and their boats, floats, canoes or other floating crafts from the stream and walk or portage such crafts around said obstruction re-entering the stream immediately below such obstruction at the nearest point where it is safe to do so.

4. Finally, the question about fences. Barbed wire fences are not the most welcome obstruction on rivers and can be dangerous. Are they legal?

When we posed the question to the Attorney General's office, their response was: "Generally, no. If a stream is navigable under the federal test and thus owned by the state, it would be a civil trespass on State land. If a stream is navigable under the federal or the State tests, it might also be considered a public nuisance."

Idaho Code Section 52-101 defines a nuisance as:

> Anything which . . . unlawfully obstructs the free passage of use, in the customary manner, of any navigable lake, or river, stream, canal or basin . . .

Mr. Schuster adds, however, that boaters should work cooperatively to solve fence problems. Lawsuits are expensive for both parties and tend to solidify opposition among private landowners on other recreational access causes. In almost all cases, a friendly and cooperative approach can solve the problem.

"Many or most landowners," wrote Mr. Schuster, "are cooperative and balance their need for fencing for management purposes with the public's right on the stream. We would urge any parties desiring to use a navigable stream blocked by a fence to attempt to work cooperatively with the landowner involved so that public access and private management concerns can both be satisfied."

One of the best ways that we have seen which keeps a rancher's cattle from wandering off the pasture, yet makes the stream paddler-friendly is to string wide belting material across the stream in the place of a wire fence. Belting material is easy to see and can be pushed up and out of the way easily as you pass by in a boat.

Appendix B

List of Rivers and Associated Topographic Maps

All the river segments covered in detail in this book are listed below in alphabetical order. Along with each river are the associated 7.5 minute United States Geological Survey Topographic Maps. All maps are Idaho maps, unless indicated otherwise. If desired, you can obtain special booklets with all the necessary topographic maps assembled in a convenient form for river running directly from the Great Rift Press at 1-800-585-6857.

Bear River (Gentile Valley & Oneida Reservoir)
- Grace Power Plant
- Thatcher
- Thatcher Hill
- Oneida Narrows Reservoir

Bear River (Georgetown to Soda Springs)
- Alexander
- Fossil Canyon
- Georgetown
- Nounan
- Soda Peak
- Soda Springs

Bear River (Oneida Narrows)
- Oneida Narrows Reservoir
- Treasureton
- Riverdale

Bear River (Mink Creek to Utah Border)
- Banida
- Riverton
- Weston

Big Lost River
- Harry Canyon

Blackfoot River (Below Blackfoot Reservoir)
- Dunn Basin
- Grizzly Creek
- Meadow Creek Mtn
- Miner Creek
- Paradise Valley
- Reservoir Mtn

Blackfoot River (Blackfoot Management Area and the Blackfoot Narrows)
- Lower Valley
- Upper Valley

Boise River (Discovery Park to Ann Morrison)
- Lucky Peak
- Boise South

Boise River (Ann Morrison to Glenwood)
- Boise South
- Boise North
- Eagle

Boise River (Eagle Island: Glenwood to Star)
- Eagle
- Star

Boise River (Star to Caldwell)
- Middleton
- Caldwell

Boise River (Caldwell to Wilder)
- Caldwell
- Notus
- Wilder

Boise River, Middle Fork
- Arrowrock NE
- Twin Springs

Boise River, South Fork
- Anderson Ranch Dam
- Cathedral Rocks
- Long Tom Reservoir

Bear Valley and Elk Creek
- Bear Valley Mtn
- Blue Bunch Mtn

Buffalo River
- Island Park
- Island Park Dam

Henrys Fork (Big Springs)
- Big Springs
- Island Park

Henrys Fork (Box Canyon)
- Island Park Dam
- Last Chance

Henrys Fork (Upper & Lower Harriman Park)
- Last Chance

Henrys Fork (Riverside to Hatchery Ford)
- Last Chance
- Lookout Butte

Henrys Fork (Warm River to Ashton Reservoir)
- Warm River
- Ashton

Henrys Fork (Ashton Reservoir to Chester Dam)
- Ashton
- Lemon Lake

Little Salmon
- Bally Mountain
- New Meadows

Marsh Creek
- Arimo
- McCammon

Payette River (Beehive Bend to Horseshoe Bend)
- Dry Buck Valley
- Horseshoe Bend

Payette River (Horseshoe Bend to Montour)
- Horseshoe Bend
- Montour

Payette River (Montour Wildlife Refuge)
- Montour
- Northeast Emmett

Payette River, Middle Fork
- Pyle Creek
- Garden Valley

Payette River, North Fork (Fisher Creek & the Meanders)
- Granite Lake
- McCall

Payette River, North Fork (Upper Long Valley)
- McCall
- Meadows
- No Business Mtn
- Lake Fork

Payette River, North Fork (Lower Long Valley)
- Alpha
- Cascade

Payette River, South Fork (Garden Valley)
- Garden Valley
- Banks

Portneuf River (Upper River to Pebble Bridge)
- Chesterfield
- Bear Camp Gulch
- Haystack Mtn
- Bancroft

Portneuf River (Lava Hot Springs area)
- Lava Hot Springs
- Haystack Mtn.

Portneuf River (City of Pocatello Run)
- Pocatello North
- Pocatello South
- Michaud

Salmon Falls Creek
- Jackpot, Nevada
- Meteor
- Browns Bench South

Salmon River (Redfish Area)
- Stanley

Salmon River (Alturas Lake Cr. & Decker Flat)
- Alturas Lake
- Obsidian
- Casino Lakes
- Stanley

Salmon River (Challis Area)
- Bradbury Flat
- Challis
- Ellis
- Gooseberry Creek

Salmon River (Salmon City to Deadwater)
- Bird Creek
- North Fork
- Salmon
- Ulysses Mtn

Salmon River (Stanley Scenic Float)
- Stanley
- Casino Lake
- East Basin Creek

Silver Creek
- Gannett
- Picabo

Snake River (Birds of Prey)
- Sinker Butte
- Initial Point
- Walters Butte

Snake River (Blackfoot to American Falls)
- Blackfoot
- Moreland
- Rockford
- Pingree
- Springfield

Snake River (Massacre Rocks & American Falls)
- American Falls
- American Falls SW
- Neeley

Snake River (Palisades Dam to Heise)
- Conant Valley
- Heise SE
- Palisades Dam
- Poplar
- Red Ridge
- Swan Valley
- Wheaton Mtn

Snake River (Shoshone Falls Scenic Trip)
- Twin Falls

Teton River
- Bates
- Tetonia

Valley Creek
- Elk Meadow
- Stanley
- Stanley Lake

References & Acknowledgments

References, Acknowledgments and A Closing Note

Selected References on Idaho Paddling

Amaral, Grant. *Idaho—The Whitewater State: a Guidebook.* Garden Valley, Idaho: Watershed Book, 1995. (The most complete guidebook to Idaho *whitewater* rivers.)

Carrey, Johnny and Conley, Cort. *River of No Return.* Cambridge, Idaho: Backeddy Books, 1978. (One of several historical works on Idaho rivers written and published by Cort Conley. Conley, a consummate pocketor of old stories, is one of our favorite Idaho authors.)

Chelstrom, Tom. *Canoeing the Boise River.* Boise: Recreational Equipment, 1997. (This 4-page guide is packed full of useful information.)

Boone, Jim, ed. *Boating the Bear.* Logan, Utah: Bridgerland Audubon Society, 1992. (A wonderfully informative 90-page, spiral-bound guide to the Bear River. Includes information on river running, history, geology, and wildlife.)

Geier, Dick and Graeff, Todd. *A River Runners Guide to Idaho.* Boise, Idaho: Idaho Department of Parks and Recreation. Boise, Idaho, 1980. (No longer in print but available in Idaho libraries, this small booklet was one of the first Idaho guides to include a number of easy paddling rivers along with whitewater trips.)

Landers, Rich and Hansen, Dan. *Paddle Routes of the Inland Northwest* by Rich Landers and Dan Hansen, Seattle: The Mountaineers, 1998. (A well-done, environmentally sensitive guide to North Idaho's easy rivers.)

Moore, Greg and McCaran, Don. *Idaho Whitewater: The Complete River Guide for Canoeists, Rafters and Kayakers*. McCall: Class VI, 1989.

Stuebner, Stephen. *Paddling the Payette.* Boise, Idaho: Boise Front Adventures, 1988. (A comprehensive paddling and historical guide to whitewater and flatwater runs on the Payette River system).

Watters, Ron. *Never Turn Back: The Life of Whitewater Pioneer Walt Blackadar.* Pocatello, Idaho: Great Rift Press, 1994. (The fascinating and gripping story of whitewater kayaker, Walt Blackadar from Salmon, Idaho. Much of the book takes place on Idaho rivers.)

Acknowledgments and A Closing Note

We want to express our deep appreciation to the following individuals for providing information, suggestions and other assistance in the preparation of this book: Jo Cassin, Dana Olson-Elle, Alan Hartman, Roger Rosentreter, Jim Schneider, Steven J. Schuster, and Paul Todd. Thanks to Bill Studebaker for providing details and turning us on to the spectacular Shoshone Falls paddle trip, and to Tom Chelstrom for his excellent work, *Canoeing the Boise River,* which greatly helped in our peregrinations on the river.

We are indebted to the Idaho Historical Society for their kind permission to reprint photographs. A special thanks to Ellie Erickson for her meticulous editing and proofing work. Ron particularly wants to thank his colleagues at Idaho State University, the College of Education and the Department of Student Affairs who have provided a nurturing and supportive environment in which to conduct outside research and writing.

In closing, we send best wishes to our boating family and friends, but also extend a wish to you, kind reader. We hope that someday, someplace, on a river in Idaho, we have the good fortune to meet you. Let's drift a spell together and share a few stories. Until then, happy paddling—and all good things.

Kathy and Ron
Pocatello

Index

About the Authors

Kathy Daly and Ron Watters have been running Idaho rivers together for many years. Kathy's degree in journalism led her to Pocatello where she worked as a news reporter and anchor for KPVI Channel 6. She first met Ron when she interviewed him upon his return from a month-long ski traverse across the River of No Return Wilderness.

They started taking trips together into the Idaho outdoors and later married on the headwaters of the Salmon River. She is presently the owner and editor of the Great Rift Press, a publisher specializing in outdoor and western regional titles.

Ron is the author of six previous books including the *Whitewater River Book* and *Never Turn Back*: *The Life of Whitewater Pioneer Walt Blackadar*. He is the former director of the Idaho State University Outdoor Program, a position he held for over 25 years. Currently, he is a member of the faculty of Idaho State University's Physical Education Department where he teaches outdoor education classes.